HITLER'S THREE STRUGGLES

THE NEO-PAGAN REVENGE

CUTHBERT CARSON MANN

CHICAGO SPECTRUM PRESS
EVANSTON, IL 60201

CHICAGO SPECTRUM PRESS
1571 Sherman Ave., Annex C
Evanston, Illinois 60201
1-800-594-5190

Printed in the U.S.A.

10 9 8 7 6 5 4 3 2 1

Library of Congress catalog card number 95-68749

ISBN: 1-886094-16-0

"The suffering of the Jews is a distinct thing for me. I, for one, believe that not enough has been made of the tragedy of the destruction of six million Jews. Somebody has to cry—even if it's a writer, many years later."

BERNARD MALAMUD

"Europe was renounced not only politically, but culturally and morally. Triumphant National Socialism amounted to a veritable revolt against Western civilization, to its negation."

PIETER GEYL

"Rome against Judea, Judea against Rome—there has hitherto been no greater event than *this* struggle, *this* question, *this* deadly contradiction."

NIETZSCHE

"It's not a bad idea, by the way, that public rumor attributes to us a plan to exterminate the Jews. Terror is a salutary thing."

HITLER

"The fight for equal rights is actually a symptom of a disease."

NIETZSCHE

"The extermination of six million Jews is no more saddening than the extermination of Gypsies, Christians, and millions of others. Yet, the Holocaust takes on a much greater significance by virtue of the seminal role of the Jewish people in revolutionary historical transformation."

CUTHBERT CARSON MANN

To my wife Veronica, and our children:
Damian, Kieran, Hilary, Greer, and Bradford.
Also to Jeff.

TABLE OF CONTENTS

INTRODUCTION

At the end of the Second World War, thousands of rank-and-file American, British, and Allied servicemen saw with their own eyes the myriad dead and dying victims of Nazi extermination, labor, and concentration camps. Among other witnesses were British, French, Russian, and American generals including Dwight D. Eisenhower, the supreme commander of the Allied forces and, later, President of the United States.

From Jerusalem to Alexandria, Virginia; from London to Moscow, and elsewhere, photographs, films, and documents of the Nazi horrors are available, as well as the testimony of perpetrators and victims alike. Yet, fifty years after the war, bedazzled minds can be found insisting the Nazi terror never happened. And while such as these can, and should, be dismissed as crackpots, what can one say about those historians who, while not denying that the Holocaust is a matter of historical record, yet try to sink it in the vast swamp of 20th Century cruelty?

How is it, then, that Adolf Hitler can so rule from the grave that otherwise reputed German historians can present him as the intended savior of Western civilization from the "Asiatic barbarians" of Russia? That same Hitler whose twelve-year rule was marked by genocidal camps, awful medical experiments, forced labor, as well as plans for the roundup and execution of designated victims in Britain, Ireland, Turkey, and wherever German conquest would have led. What kind of Western civilization was Hitler bent on saving that would have had terror and death built permanently into its system with millions of "lesser breeds" taught only to read road signs directing them to starvation-until-death labor?

Fifty years ago, it would have been unimaginable and, one would have thought, unnecessary, that such questions would one day have to be asked. That they must now be asked forces the despairing conclusion that the millions of words written about Hitlerism and the Holocaust have failed to come to grips with their central meaning. Nowhere is this failure more evident than among contemporary German historians who, one had hoped, would have been among the most eager to uncover that meaning instead of covering it up.

Now the 50th anniversary of Hitler's death and the end of the Second World War are producing voluminous accounts of his life and death in which one historian and scholar after another grapples with the meaning of his short and hideous career. And while a mass of new details has been uncovered about the Nazi era, it has done little to answer old questions about Hitlerism. Even among Jews and Christians, the "how?" of Hitlerism has received greater attention than the "why?"

The justification for this work lies not in the accumulation of new facts, although it contains some, but in a fresh interpretation of those already available; an effort to uncover the "why?" What follows, therefore, is submitted as a clue to the long-sought answer to anti-Semitism, and possibly history itself.

As I see it, Hitler was not just a German phenomenon, but a European one. I have, therefore, attempted to redirect the focus on Hitler by placing him in the broad context of Western civilization's cultural-psychology rather than centering it on the solely localized Germanic aspects of his malign mission. By cultural-psychology, I mean that process through which the dominant ideas of one culture become cross-fertilized with another, thereby creating change in the mental outlook of the peoples of both. This is something that has gone on throughout human history, but took a dramatic new turn when three innovative cultures, the Hebraic, Greek, and Roman became mixed in contentious dynamism to produce the world democratic revolution that continues to this day. A pervasive undercurrent of this dynamism has been an anti-Semitism that Hitler displayed in extreme form but, in various expressions, remains at the heart of Western civilization's difficulties with the potential for erupting in yet tragic ways unless its real meaning is squarely faced.

The very persistence of Jew hatred for two thousand years, along with the survival of the Jews despite expulsion, dispersal, pogroms, and Holocaust, is evidence enough that the answer to the problem of anti-Semitism must be sought in the historical significance of the Jews rather than in economic and social conditions that merely aggravate preexisting antagonisms. Hence, liberal and disavowed Jews and Christians, who insist that the Jews are no different than other people, do violence to the historical record of the revolution in secular ideas and values that has emerged from the universal and imperfect dissemination of sacred Hebraic and Judeo-Christian literature. It is this literature, and the teachings based upon it, that leavened the secular world, and inaugurated intentional-prospective rather than retrospective-reactive history.

In a negative way, Hitler paradoxically recognized the historical importance of the Jews that many Jews and gentiles have greatly downplayed, or discarded. I have had to use a wide lens, therefore, to capture a picture of Hitler that includes a background of history, philosophy, literature, and cultural-psychology. This has meant some necessary compression, but it also presents a challenge to intelligent and interested readers, as well as specialists, to pursue the clue to history and anti-Semitism that I have set forth.

An essential key to understanding *Hitler's Three Struggles* is the concept of cultural-psychology that involves the interaction and reaction involved when humans of one culture encounter those of another. At its simplest level this can be seen when a member of a family from one cultural, racial, or religious background marries into a family from a quite different background—a Jew, say, or an Irish Protestant, marrying a Catholic, a Christian marrying a Muslim, or a black marrying a white. Any such unions demand a willingness to make adjustments; to give and take, and this often involves a shake-up in one's cultural-psychological makeup. Other examples can be presented of businessmen, soldiers, missionaries, and diplomats assigned to serve lengthy periods among foreign peoples; immigrants to a new culture, or subject peoples under foreign rule.

History's greatest, longest, and continuing cultural adjustment began when three old cultures: the Hebraic, the Roman, and the Greek, were mixed to form the basis of Western civilization. Hitler's mind offers an opportunity to see, in exaggerated form, the tensions among these three antagonistic constituents in the Western consciousness. For him, the Jewish spirit was evident in all things international such as finance, trade, social democracy, liberalism, communism, etc., and he perceived these to be antithetical to German nationalism and culture. The physical presence of the Jews, therefore, became the embodiment of all these "evils." Thus, he set out to eliminate the Jews.

I have traced what I have called Hitler's neo-pagan revenge, through his *mental*, *political*, and *military* struggles and have shown how this contributes to an understanding of history and anti-Semitism. Although many factors, some of them complex, must be considered, at heart the answer is simple. Hitler saw the advent of Judeo-Christianity as the destroyer of Greco-Roman civilization. In place of the classical world in which power, heroism, and strength of will were highly valued, Christianity taught, even though it did not always (perhaps even rarely) practice it, a new ethic of charity, forgiveness, racial equality, universal and human community. When this ethic belatedly and imperfectly found widespread expression in 19th and 20th Century social democratic politics, it generated fierce reaction that, both overtly and covertly, often contained an anti-Semitic basis. So long as Judaic and Judeo-Christian values were largely confined to ritual and theory and, in the case of the Jews, to ghettos, expressions of anti-Semitism were sporadic and limited. But, once these values were translated into political action, anti-Semitism took on a much more virulent and widespread reaction culminating in Hitler's attempted, and nearly successful, "Final Solution" to the Jewish "problem." Invariably, such reaction assumed the form of chauvinistic nationalism.

The Judaic and Judeo-Christian transvaluation of values, Hitler believed, was part of a Jewish conspiracy inaugurated by Saul (St. Paul), the Hellenized Jew, and Roman citizen, whose triadic cultural-psychological makeup was best equipped to mediate Judeo-Christian beliefs into the Greco-Roman world. To Hitler, these beliefs represented the first Bolshevism that, over the centuries, led to social democracy, parliamentarianism, interracialism, internationalism, and much more. In other words, much of what today is being promoted by Western democracies as universally desirable, and is spelled out in the Universal Declaration of Human Rights. Thus, democracy, in giving political expression to Judeo-Christian ideas, now bears the brunt of fascistic antagonisms that harbor anti-Semitic and anti-Christian hatred in both overt and covert forms.

He saw communism, particularly in its Soviet expression, as the final stage in a Jewish "conspiracy," aimed at world domination, and this triggered in him a sense of frenetic urgency. Either this "conspiracy" must be attacked and defeated, or the world would be lost forever to those forces that represented the democratic "slave revolt" of weak and racially-mixed peoples banded together to rule the strong and "pure" races.

In order to battle these egalitarian forces, Hitler needed power but, since his homeland, Austria, was part of an already "mongrelized" empire and was otherwise unsuitable as a power base, he moved to Germany. But, whatever political aspirations he had then were put on hold while he served in the army in the First World War— an experience that solidified his political ideology.

After the war, he became politically active. But, since Germany's mainline political parties were, in his view, already committed to "Jewish" parliamentary democracy, he joined a small party whose parliamentary form he quickly extinguished. He then shaped the party in accordance with his own ideology as he would later do with the German state and, less successfully, the German army. This ideology, that the world came to know as National Socialism, or Nazism, used many ideas including pseudo-German mythology, xenophobic nationalism, anti-Semitism, and social Darwinism.

But its central inspiration was a hatred of the Jews—the "poison" that Hitler believed had infected the world with Christianity and its many secular offshoots aimed at elevating the masses.

There was little originality in Hitler's ideology. It was derivatively eclectic, drawing from German and Austrian anti-Semitic ideas, the racist writings of Britisher Houston Stewart Chamberlain and Frenchman Arthur Gobineau, as well as Darwin and others. And while there is not enough known about his reading habits, it could be posited that he was one end-product of the kind of vitriolic, antireligious thought associated with Voltaire and other Enlightenment boosters of the classical world. His main themes, however, were clearly borrowed from Nietzsche. But where Nietzsche, like Hitler, looked to the classical world for inspiration, he was not anti-Semitic. And although Nietzsche declared the Judeo-Christian God dead, Hitler would, in effect, attempt to kill all belief in God as well as to exterminate all those he considered to be God's earthly agents. In this respect, he differed from Nietzsche and all those who had influenced him. They were mere thinkers; he believed in action. He became committed, therefore, to eradicating the Jews as the original carriers of the "poison" that gave rise to Christianity and, what he perceived to be its most advanced secular avatar, communism. He launched, in effect, a neo-pagan counterattack against all that Judeo-Christianity had inspired through its teachings which he believed, not without substance, had been displaced, even if unacknowledged, into secular political movements aimed at achieving freedom, justice, racial equality, human rights, and common humanity.

Precisely because these aims were being advanced in such countries as England, France, America, and in the Weimar Republic itself, they gave rise to racist, fascist, and antidemocratic reactions throughout Europe. And it is significant that, with the recent influx of foreign workers into Germany, as well as the movement toward European unity, the revival of Nazism in Germany has erupted in racial and anti-Semitic hatred. Even Japan, despite the absence of a Jewish population, has shown signs of an otherwise inexplicable anti-Semitism, as global trade, politics, and communications, have exposed this very homogeneous nation to Western moral and egalitarian political influences. There are also indications that these Western-inspired influences are being increasingly resisted, most notably in the Muslim world.

While it is not currently fashionable in our predominantly secular world, to acknowledge the historical imperatives of religion, it is unnecessary to believe in the ultimate validity of Judaic and Christian beliefs to see how they have revolutionized the fundamental concept of what it is to be free and human. Yet, the question remains unanswered: if Judaism and Christianity gave rise to a revolutionary outlook on human purpose and meaning, why was that so? Indeed, many of the world's current problems, in lands least touched by Western culture, can be traced to the need, on the one hand, to embrace Western technology and economic and social improvements while, on the other hand, resisting the politics of democracy, justice, religious, racial, and human rights that are part of the imperfect moral legacy derived from Judaism and Christianity. Consequently, politics around the world frequently display aspects of reaction familiar to Europe with anti-Semitism sometimes directed at Israel. Yet, even nations opposed to the West are often self-servingly inspired by Western ideologies, as well as the right to self-determination.

Hitler's Nazism went far beyond mere resistance to this legacy, but initiated his neo-pagan revenge in an attempt to put an end to the Judeo-Christian episode in history. Hence, the Jews (in Hitler's mind the original carriers of this spiritual "poison") became his priority victims. Where Judeo-Christianity had brought a transvaluation of values to the pagan world, Hitler sought to reverse this development by achieving a neo-pagan transvaluation of Judeo-Christianity. In so doing, he exhibited in extreme form an anti-Semitic, anti-Christian, and antidemocratic animosity that still pervades the West in varying degrees of intensity depending upon economic and political circumstances. The resurgence of nationalism and anti-Semitism in Russia in the aftermath of the fall of the Soviet Union, and in reunified Germany, are among the more obvious examples. The breakup of Yugoslavia, with the long-suffering strife in Bosnia-Herzegovina, has also tragically demonstrated the fierce resistance of ethnic nationalism to the democratic spirit of unity with diversity.

How Hitler developed his Nazi ideology and translated it into political and military action is the subject of this book. As with all Europeans, Hitler shared a mentality that was cultivated through religion (in this case, Roman Catholicism), education, tradition, and other influences. Although the German, Celtic, and other cultures have contributed to the rise of Western civilization, and the development of its consciousness, historians have long recognized that the major formative influences in the West have come from the Hebraic, Roman, and Hellenic cultures. And, just as in ancient times, individual Jews, Romans, and Greeks would find it difficult to agree on life's fundamental issues, so these three cultural types are perpetually at odds within the Western psychological makeup.

It is easy enough to recognize these three elements as symbolically found in architecture, as we do in the innumerable public and church buildings throughout the world, some of which have Christian spires (one expression of the Judaic spirit) superimposed, sometimes extraneously it seems, on Greco-Roman substructures. But it is much more difficult to discern them in our minds, since they do not always operate in their own separate ways, but in a confused and dynamic interplay. They are part of what Marx called the "world-historical necromancy" that brings us all into involuntary involvement in history. Or, to quote Isaiah Berlin, we all inherit from our ancestors "ancient spectacles through which we are still looking." For Hitler, as for all Europeans, these psychological spectacles were Jewish, Greek, and Roman trifocals, though he would have preferred them to be Greco-Roman bifocals tinted with Germanic myth.

Hitler's mind offers an opportunity to see, in exaggerated form, the tensions among these psychological constituents. Paradoxically, it is the attempt to work out these tensions through politics, war, and revolution, that has produced Western civilization's unique, yet often tragic, dynamism that is now affecting the entire world. The refinement of reason and estheticism that is the major Greek contribution to civilization; the pragmatic jurisprudence and organizational skills of the Romans, and the prophetic inspiration and honing of conscience of Judaism and Christianity provide the strange spiritual alchemy that is now convulsing the world.

Hitler's self-confessed "mental struggle" as a young man in Vienna brought into focus the clash within his own mind of these three cultural-psychological elements. It is essential, therefore, to acknowledge the crucial importance of these influences within his mind as well as in the Western culture he was exposed to. This opens the door, not only to an understanding of the Hitler phenomenon, but to the possibility of meaning in history itself; the primary reason for perpetual anti-Semitism, and why the "Final Solution" to the so-called Jewish "problem" was attempted.

In Chapter I, dealing with Hitler's *mental struggle*, I have tried to depict this struggle against the background of his, and Germany's, excessive attraction to the Greco-Roman world. Obviously, it is not possible to get inside Hitler's mind to describe that struggle in detail, but only as it was reflected in his words and deeds. Since Hitler was fascinated as, for a time, was Germany, by Greco-Roman civilization and, at the same time, bore a consuming hatred of Judaism and Christianity, I felt it was important to record some of the more outstanding examples of the hold that Greece and Rome had on representative Germans, as well as hatred of the Jews and Christianity as expressed in some German writings. The conflict between the Greek, Roman, and Judeo-Christian cultures, that was very much in evidence within German society, found acute and distorted expression in Hitler's mind before it was displayed in politics and war.

I have briefly endeavored to distinguish between the psychology normally associated with Freud, as opposed to what I have termed cultural-psychology. It seems to me that the former is valuable in determining the early emotional influences that predispose an individual's choices in friendships, work, political and other interests. It is one's culture, however, that provides an array of interests from which such choices can be made.

It is one of my purposes to show that the answers to questions raised by psychohistorians, including the question of identity, will be best advanced by merging the psychology of individuals with the study of cultural-psychology. As psychologists often point out, some individuals become so overwhelmed by their personal problems that they cannot meaningfully engage in social and political life while others are able to submerge or redirect their personal problems and interests into work, art, politics, religion, or other social activities. Once in the public arena, however, an individual has to appeal to the public with publicly appealing themes drawn from the prevailing culture.

As I have shown in Chapter II, his *political struggle*, this is what happened to Hitler. Of necessity, I have had to cover much familiar ground in describing his rise to power but, in so doing, I have kept in mind his dominant intention to rid the world of Jews and all that he perceived to have had an origin in Judeo-Christianity. In this way, I believe I have introduced new explanations for often-described events in his political struggle. Among these are the 1923 *Putsch*, the Rohm, Nazi Party, and Fritsch-Blomberg crises.

Believing he had solved the Jewish "problem" in his mind, Hitler sought, in effect, to express that solution politically and, ultimately, as a final solution by the extermination of all Jews. The aim of his political struggle was to achieve absolute power so that he could carry out his intention. Three elements he considered essential to his aim were: (1) the political party of his choice must not have anti-Semitism as just another plank in its platform, but must have it as its foundation, (2) the party's anti-Semitism must insist that Jewry be regarded, not as a religion, but as a race, and (3) the party's anti-Semitism must be "rational" and not "emotional." These were the pillars of Hitler's Nazi ideology that provided a Catch-22 by which Jews would be rendered stateless and helpless. Instead of just thinking and talking about killing Jews, as some Germans and Austrians had done, he would seek the power to actually kill them—not sporadically through "emotional" pogroms, as had been done before in history as a partial solution to the Jewish "problem," but "rationally," i.e., systematically and *en masse* to achieve the

"Final Solution." The Nazi ideology, therefore, did not give rise to anti-Semitism, but was its evil offspring.

Hitler's *military struggle* had two aspects: the first (Part I), a testing period extending from 1933 to 1938 and, the second (Part II), from 1939 to 1945, when he drew the world into war. In this war, Hitler used his army as a veritable bulldozer, clearing territories for his elite SS legions to swoop down on Jews, executing them first, in the field, before careful plans were advanced to transport them to specially-designed genocidal camps for gassing and incineration. Justified as a move to gain *Lebensraum* (living space) for Germans, the real purpose of the military struggle was to gain *Tötungsraum* (killing space). This military struggle was unlike any other in human history, for the winning of battles and the conquest of territories served Hitler's overriding intention to annihilate a people, the Jews, who were seen to be the primary agents of undesirable historical transformation.

Faced with certain defeat by the Russians in the East, Hitler's seemingly irrational "hold fast" military orders were designed to accelerate and complete as much of the "Final Solution" as the shortening time would allow. What he failed to gain on the military front, he was determined to win on the murder front. Hence, just as his National Socialist party became the host to his anti-Semitic political solution, the army hosted the SS's execution of the "Final Solution." And these political and military hosts were but outward manifestations of his mind that had hosted anti-Semitism in the first place. His defeat by the Russians in the East not only short-circuited his plans for the "Final Solution" to the Jewish "problem," but also blocked his plans for a final solution to his problem with the traditionalist army by replacing it with the SS. In this context, the SS's 1934 purge of Stormtroops headed by Ernst Rohm, marked a watershed in Hitler's career. It was then that he had to decide whether to continue his anti-Semitic world revolution with the emotional and zealous Stormtroops or the non-ideological, traditionalist army. It was a decision that haunted him to the end since he was never satisfied that the army was fanatical enough to win the war and achieve the "Final Solution," and there was not enough time to replace the army with the coldly "rational" SS.

In the final chapter, I have, by way of historical reflection, attempted to explain Hitler's *neo-pagan revenge* within the broad context of Christianity's injection of the Judaic spirit into the Greco-Roman world which, over a very long period of time, had the effect of inspiring political movements aimed at democracy, equality, and human rights. (It is wrongly assumed that Greece was "the cradle of democracy" except in form. The democracy that the modern world exhibits in the demand for social and human rights, owes its inspiration not to Greece or Rome, but to Judaism and Christianity.) I have argued that the real reason for anti-Semitism does not follow the usual explanations such as "the Jews were scapegoats," or that they were seen as "Christ-killers," or that they were part of a worldwide conspiracy, or that they controlled much of the Western world's prime institutions. Had that been so, there would have been no Holocaust. The real reason for anti-Semitism is not that the Jews were "Christ-killers," but that they were "Christ-donors." The Jew in the caftan that first aggravated Hitler's mental struggle in Vienna was really the outward manifestation of the Jewish spirit that had been introduced into the Western consciousness through the belief in Christ, the Jew.

But, for the most part, the Western world has shown itself prepared only to accept Christianity in idealized or ritual form (a consequence, in part, of Greek thought patterns) provided it is subsumed by the Greco-Roman substance that dominates the Western world and, to a large extent, Christianity itself. Over the centuries, however, Christian teachings of equality, freedom, and the sanctity of human life, which were often not practiced, were displaced into the secular world of politics, through which they found legislative and revolutionary expression, often without acknowledgment of their source.

Reactionary politics, however, sensed (until Hitler, only vaguely) that the pressure for justice, freedom, democracy, and human rights, had its source in Judeo-Christian ideals. This is the real reason for the virulent spread of modern political anti-Semitism and fascistic, reactionary politics. In the 18th and 19th centuries, this coincided with the emerging emancipation of Jewry from its long history of disabilities. Thus, by virtue of their greater visibility and activity in the social and political life of the West, the Jews were seen to be the historical originators of social democratic pressures. As Hitler would have it, the Jews were the carriers of social democratic "poison." Instead of sporadic pogroms against the Jews that had previously reflected only a partial and religiously-justified "solution" to the Jewish "problem," Hitler directed the "Final Solution" as a response to what he perceived to be the approaching triumph, in secular form, of Judaic and Judeo-Christian-inspired world revolution.

It would obviously take volumes to detail Hitler's mental, political, and military struggles. I have chosen to provide enough material to convey the obsessive current of anti-Semitism and anti-Christianity that runs through his turbulent career. At the same time, I have avoided dealing at length with influences on Hitler that have been flogged to death, such as *The Protocols of the Elders of Zion*. While Hitler made use of this, and other, fallacious material, it was not nearly so important to his intention as the ideas of Nietzsche. The final part constitutes reflections that attempt to give perspective to what Hitler means to those persons who see his reign of terror as constituting a crisis point in history, and especially in light of the continuing democratic world revolution and the reactions it is generating. In this context, it can be said that just as the Roman Empire's adoption of Christianity helped spread Christianity, so the new "Romes" of Britain and the U.S. are spreading democratic ideas around the world. It is my hope that others will pursue in greater depth some of the clues offered here.

While nonspecialist, general readers, may feel some frustration by unfamiliar references, it is hoped that they will be sufficiently stimulated by the book's central themes to pursue further readings. If so, I believe they will be greatly rewarded by a new appreciation of what I perceive to be the inner meaning of history, and the ferment of world revolution. On the other hand, specialists may object to the form of the material since it does not adhere strictly to an academic mode, nor does it fall into a neat category of biography or history, although it contains elements of both.

It seems to me that the writing of history will increasingly have to present a unified world view while avoiding the tendency to become a mere compendium of the findings of varied disciplines. At the same time, our age of mass culture makes it necessary to bridge the gap between the academy and the extramural world, i.e., between town and gown. As it is, and despite the dedicated work of some brilliant scholars, a great deal of lesser published scholarship often finds little outlet beyond the halls of academe and is frequently an elaborate and unctuous form of professorial correspondence. It can even be seen as the unwitting imposition of self-censorship by virtue of a sometimes too rigid, turgid, lifeless, and forbidding style. By contrast, scholars who have written for the opinion pages of major newspapers, can appreciate the challenge that comes from shaping abstract ideas, even if truncated, in ways that are understood by a diverse readership without doing violence to the truth.

My close readings and re-readings of *Mein Kampf*, Hitler's speeches, records of his conversations, and monologues, are among the primary sources for my underlying premise that his meaning is to be found in the peculiar manner in which Western cultural-psychological influences impinged upon his aberrant consciousness. I have relied also on many secondary and tertiary sources, as well as considerable readings in, and reflection upon, Western and world history. The idea for this book followed the publication of my essay, *Hitler: A Clue to History* in the winter 1988 issue of *Judaism* quarterly in New York. I owe a great debt, therefore, to the late Robert Gordis, then editor of *Judaism*, and to Ruth B. Waxman, his managing editor; now editor.

I regret that due to failing health that ended with his death in 1993, William L. Shirer, author of *The Rise and Fall of the Third Reich*, and other works, was unable to read my manuscript. His words of encouragement "from one journalist to another," however, were deeply appreciated.

CHAPTER 1

❦

MENTAL STRUGGLE

In a villa at Berlin's suburban Lake Wannsee on January 20, 1942, fifteen of Adolf Hitler's top Nazis met to coordinate his "Final Solution" to the Jewish "problem." The assembled group discussed transportation, financing and the various methods of achieving the "Final Solution" that all present clearly understood would involve the systematic mass murder of Europe's Jews. The conference lasted less than an hour and a half and was followed by a social gathering that included the serving of drinks and an enjoyable meal in a room overlooking the scenic lake.

How was it possible, one might ask, that plans for the annihilation of an entire people were dispassionately discussed by a group of men meeting as if they were a board of directors considering the assembly-line production of automobiles? Just as it is necessary to look into an individual's past for clues to present conduct, it is essential to search the past history of a people in order to understand their behavior. And just as an individual personality is revealed through word and deed, so a people's history is best reflected in the thoughts and actions of its most representative personalities. Writers and poets, particularly, are often best attuned to a people's spiritual longings and among few European peoples was this more evident than in Germany. There, these longings found distorted political expression under Hitler who showed how an individual aspiring to national leadership draws from the pool of cultural influences to gain power.

One hundred and thirty-one years before the "Final Solution" conference at Lake Wannsee, for example, a young man and woman sat in a room at an inn by that same lake singing, and drinking wine and rum. To an outside observer, it might have seemed as if they were thoroughly enjoying life, and were perhaps a little too merry. Then, by way of sobering up, they drank sixteen cups of coffee, and composed a letter to the woman's husband. Later, they left their room and walked down to the shore. It was late November. They looked out over the cold expanse of lake, then sat facing each other and when they did, the man raised a pistol and fatally shot the woman in the heart; reloaded, and shot himself in the head. The couple were not star-crossed lovers, as might have been surmised, but merely acquaintances and, in response to their hastily delivered letter announcing their intentions, the woman's husband arrived from Berlin to find their bodies by the lake. Soon the world would learn their identities. The man was Heinrich von Kleist, a renowned German author and poet, and the woman was Madame Henriette Vogel, wife of a minor government official. In reporting the tragedy, European newspapers mentioned that Madame Vogel's terminal cancer had generated a wish to end her suffering and this coincided with Kleist's suicidal desire that was prompted by prolonged spiritual distress.

Separated by more than a century, the two Lake Wannsee events have no direct connection and the proximity of their setting is purely coincidental, yet Kleist's murder-suicide pact with Madame Vogel was symptomatic of an anxiety that had been developing among Germans, possibly since the breakup of the medieval world, and certainly since the 18th Century. By the 20th Century, it had reached the point of despair, and this despair was conspicuously reflected in German literature that seemed torn between classical order and the turbulence of romantic idealism. It would be the mark of Hitler's malignant genius to bring these two together in violent union.

Among the symptoms of this despair was an antipathy toward the European Enlightenment. This was prompted by a number of factors including enmity toward the French, who were among the Enlightenment's leaders, but also were associated with Napoleon and his attempt to foist his universalist plan on Europe, prompting the conquered and menaced peoples to identify independence with racial uniqueness. The strongest reaction came from the Germans, for whom internationalism in its various forms would eventually become associated with the Jews that Napoleon had emancipated. German reaction found expression in the Nazi attempt to achieve the "Final Solution" to the Jewish "problem" that ended in the Reichschancellery bunker with the double suicide of Hitler and his wife, Eva, whom he belatedly married the day before.

Kleist's anguish had been reflected in his later plays that veered from a style of high emotion and frenetic brutality to one of cold detachment, and contrasted with his seminal writings that were lyrically optimistic and born of one facet of Enlightenment belief that, through reason, unaided by religion, humans could perfect themselves and society. But after reading Immanuel Kant's works, in which the great German philosopher clearly distinguished between those things that were amenable to reason and those that could only be reached through faith, Kleist suffered a devastating trauma. In a letter to a woman friend, he confided: "...we cannot determine whether what we call truth really is truth, or merely seems so to us." To another friend, he wrote: "The thought that here on earth we know nothing of the truth, absolutely nothing... has shaken me in the very sanctuary of my soul. My *only* purpose, my *supreme* purpose has collapsed; I have none left."[1] Kleist's solution to his problem was suicide, and no more telling symbol of his (and Germany's) split between reason and emotion could be found than in the pistol shots he fired, first into Madame Vogel's heart, then into his own head.

In Britain, the Enlightenment was reflected in the sober empiricism of the philosophers Locke and Hume; in America it culminated in the pragmatic Constitution of the Founding Fathers; in France it was exemplified by the raillery and anti-religious persiflage of Voltaire but, among Germans who, at first, enthusiastically embraced it, a reaction set in that was marked by a pronounced spiritual distress, or *angst* that arose from a complex of historical factors. This was seen in Kleist's writings; in Nietzsche's "death-of-God" philosophy, and in other writers spanning the 18th, 19th and 20th Centuries, who were either blatantly anti-Christian, or tried to reshape Christianity into a Germanic mold. The major historical outcome was that, through Hitler and Marx, Germany became the growing field for two atheistic world revolutions, Nazism and Communism, that sought to supplant Judeo-Christianity and become the heirs to history.

In the 16th Century, the spiritual soil among Germans had already been fertilized by Luther's reforming zeal and was set to receive the seeds of these two revolutions that were blown on French intellectual winds. These carried Rousseau's romantic "noble savagery," with its flight from reason and rediscovery of feeling, and Descartes' rationalism in which human existence became identified with the capacity to think. The first sprouted forth in the *Stürm und Drang* (Storm and Stress) literary movement which, after an initial enthusiasm, was followed by disenchantment, and gave rise to the New Romanticism that the weeds of Nazism were later to choke. The second blossomed into Hegelian transcendental idealism that Marx pruned for his materialist view of history.

Kant and Goethe were significant exceptions, choosing to cultivate their own 18th Century "gardens" by using a humanistic faith and reason. But, in Goethe's case, this was not easy to do as his *Sorrows of Young Werther*, written during what appears to have been a crisis in his youth, and the later *Faust* show. That young Werther's mental stress touched something deep in the German psyche was evidenced by the spate of suicides it triggered among young Germans whose bodies were found either with a copy of *Young Werther* stuffed in a coat pocket, clutched in a hand, or floating on the water where many had drowned themselves. And while the mature Goethe had Faust saved, after reneging on his pact with the Devil, other German writers of the 19th and 20th Centuries ended their versions of the Faustian legend in the dire manner of the first anonymous *Faustbuch* of 1587.

The salvation of Goethe's Faust, however, was effected by the love of a woman and not through God, reflecting Goethe's animosity toward organized religion, particularly Roman Catholicism. Even though *Young Werther* marked the turning point in Goethe's spiritual crisis, his writing of *Faust*, completed just before he died, shows that he was really engaged in a lifelong spiritual struggle that was resolved by the acceptance of the universally human instead of the purely Germanic. Others, such as Kleist, displayed an inward-looking, fiercely nationalistic spirit that even saw merit in the antebellum practice in Napoleon III's hated army, of officers grabbing the chest of an artilleryman with one hand, and with the other pointing a sword to the ground, saying: "You die here," then to a second, third, and all the rest: "Here, here, and here."[2] Kleist died more than a century too soon to see this kind of do-or-die nationalism firmly rooted in his own country. Between the writings of the mature Goethe and Kleist can be seen the dichotomous German elements of order versus chaos that would find expression in politics.

It was the French cult of rationalism, promoted by the Enlightenment and the Encylopedists, that first drew German reaction in the form of the *Stürm und Drang* movement. Inspired by Goethe and Schiller, this movement sought to exalt nature and human individualism. In so doing, it gave rise to the New Romanticism that, in turn, spawned a Volkist anti-Semitic ideology and a fabricated nature mysticism. Combined with social Darwinism, these laid the foundation for Nazi ideas of the "Master Race." Thus, in grossly distorted form, *Stürm und Drang* found its way into politics, and during the twelve years of Nazi tyranny from 1933-45, produced excesses of storm and stress, fulfilling Nietzsche's prophecy of the coming of a "warlike age" in which war would be waged "for the sake of ideas and their consequences." Such an age, he foresaw, would need men whose "greatest enjoyment would be to live dangerously."[3] Indeed, "Storm was a much-used theme of the Nazis. It was expressed in the violence of Hitler's Stormtroops; in the mass exterminations urged by *Der Stürmer* (The Stormer), the Nazi periodical that was Hitler's favorite; in *The Storm*, the Stormtroops' theme song, and in their special brand of cigarettes labelled

STORM. Kleist's tombstone epitaph significantly had described him as a man who lived, sang and toiled in dreary, "troublous times"—a theme of troubles that pervaded a great deal of German literature and was picked up in Stefan George's poem, *The Poet in Troublous Times*, that seemed to anticipate Hitler and his Nazis. Written shortly before Hitler's rise to power, it tells of a race of people that would be led "through storms" by the "only saviour" who could help, "the Man" who would make a "clean sweep," fastening the "true symbol" to the flag of his people, and who would found a new Reich.[4] Hitler filled the bill of all these particulars, and the acute prescience of George's poem indicates the degree to which Germany's longing for identity, unity, and leadership had become part of its *Zeitgeist*. George was but one of many German writers who, like voices crying in a spiritual wilderness, prophesied the coming of a German messiah. But, in George's case, when the "messiah" came in the form of a Hitler, he turned his back on him and fled to Switzerland.

German longing for a salvatory leader points to a crucial tardiness in German development as compared to France and England. Both these countries had achieved unity during the middle ages whereas it was not until the late 19th Century that Germans achieved a national state. Germany was also late in getting representative government and when it did (in 1918), it came heavily burdened. Defeat in war, a bitter peace settlement, a ruined economy, as well as the antidemocratic pressures from industrial and aristocratic interests, gave the fledgling democracy little chance of survival.

Although Hitler's social origins and cultural exposure in provincial Austria, where he grew up, were much less auspicious than the great German writers, he seems, nevertheless, to have osmotically absorbed the tormented

Zeitgeist that some of them represented, or at least he was attuned to German longings for a leader. A more pedestrian view may be that he picked up a popularized messianism from the Volkist and racist material that he voraciously read. But there is clear evidence that his reading was wide, if not deep, and that he drew from a host of writers those elements that best fitted his personal and political needs. His ideas about the "Jewish poison" could have come from many sources ranging from the most vulgar anti-Semitic pamphlets to the writings of the likes of Houston Stewart Chamberlain, the British expatriate and race theorist; the Frenchman, Count Arthur de Gobineau, whose *Essai sur l'inegalite des races humaines*, expounded the thesis of white supremacy; Richard Wagner, the composer, who was much influenced by Gobineau, and, most importantly, Nietzsche. Wagner was particularly useful in reviving German racial myths, but Hitler appears to have drawn the essence of his anti-Semitism from Nietzsche's denunciations of Christianity that were coupled with admiration for ancient Greece.

There is no doubt that Hitler also picked up popularized concepts of Darwin's evolutionary theories such as "survival of the fittest" and "natural selection," that he twisted to his own racist-political purposes. Alfred Rosenberg's *Myth of the Twentieth Century* was another influence, along with the forged *Protocols of the Elders of Zion*. All of these and more would feature in what Hitler would later describe as his mental struggle that was marked, like Nietzsche's introspective battle, by the elevation of the classical world at the expense of the Judeo-Christian. Foreshadowing Hitler's mental struggle was his early passion for Wagner's operas that were permeated, among other things, with classical and Teutonic themes.

One example from Hitler's youth serves to show his lifelong penchant for fixating on those things that reinforced his admiration for Greece or Rome. After attending a production of Wagner's *Rienzi* at the Linz Opera one evening with his boyhood friend, August Kubizek, Hitler behaved as though he had been taken out of himself. In trancelike tones, during a walk up a mountainside after the performance, he told Kubizek that he, too, would one day lead his people just as Rienzi, the medieval tribune, did in the opera. And, in 1939, while Kubizek and Hitler were at Bayreuth as guests of Frau Winifred Wagner, the composer's English-born daughter-in-law, Kubizek later recalled how Hitler told her about the great impact *Rienzi* had on him, noting "In that hour, it began"[5]—an intimation that it was then he realized the high destiny laying in store for him. *Rienzi* was among many Greco-Roman themes that weighed heavily in the resolution of his mental struggle. It was not a struggle in purely personal terms, but one that engaged him with the Greek, Roman and Jewish cultural elements that contributed to the formation of the Western mentality, including his own.

But, in addition to the mystical heights of Wagnerian opera, Hitler's mental struggle was also affected by the lowbrow cowboy and Indian stories of Germany's Karl May that perhaps foreshadowed his attempts to exterminate the Jews. Did he, as a member of the "pure white race," for example, see in the "white" cowboys' slaughter of Indians, his own ultimate desire to exterminate the Jews? Had cowboys versus Indians become transposed, in his mind, as Aryans against Jews?

It seems clear that he did, for he once told his valet that he had ordered every army officer to carry Karl May's books about cowboys fighting Indians, for "that's the way the Russians fight—hidden like the Indians behind trees and bridges, then they jump out for the kill."[6] Since Russians, or Bolsheviks, were among his many synonyms for world Jewry, he no doubt had Jews in mind, too.

9

During his last days in the Reichschancellery bunker, with his hands spasmodically twitching from a nervous disorder, a haggard Hitler came to resemble "Old Shatterhand," one of May's favorite characters whose exploits included single-handedly taking on large numbers of Indians, except in Hitler's case, he had marshalled his entire nation of nearly seventy million against six million Jews, and others who got in his way. Hitler had a full, bound collection of May's books which he read over and over again throughout his life, even during wartime, and he often mentioned that when he first read May's yarns, as a boy, they opened his eyes to the world.

The heroic stories of May, the racist doctrines of Chamberlain, Gobineau, and others, as well as Wagner's operas, and Nietzsche's anti-Christian diatribes, all played a part in the mental struggle that Hitler described in *Mein Kampf*, his autobiography. That struggle ended, he related, when he recognized the role of the Jews in the Western world. Written and dictated in prison after his abortive putsch in 1923, his book strongly suggested that, if the Devil indeed stalks the world, Hitler had made a Faust-like pact with him. But, unlike some of the Devil's legendary "clients" who reneged on their bargains, Hitler kept his to the very end. Echoing Nietzsche, he wrote, that Christianity had destroyed the heathen altars in order to establish its own absolute faith, thus injecting "something that was previously alien to history." Such Christian "intolerance" embodied "the Jewish nature," and had arisen from "specifically Jewish modes of thought."[7] In these and other references can be seen Hitler's mental struggle that engaged the Greco-Roman, or pagan, elements in his mind, and its Judeo-Christian component.

Like many Germans, Hitler shared a Faust-like ruthless striving. In Schopenhauer's *The World of Will and*

Representation (1819), a book that he carried with him during his First World War army service, striving is seen as the essential nature of man and the cosmos. As with other writers such as Nietzsche, Hitler distorted their views. And a hundred years after Schopenhauer, Oswald Spengler, the German historian, was to label Western civilization as "Faustian"—a title that was more applicable to his own country. Even Hitler's propaganda minister Joseph Goebbels acknowledged that "the German soul is Faustian"[8]—a pointed example of how the great river of literature often becomes polluted when it enters political tributaries.

Certainly, if Hitler's manhood could be described as Faustian, and it can, his youth bore uncanny similarities to the neurasthenic young Werther. Like Goethe's fictional character, who is snubbed by his social superiors at Count C_____'s party, Hitler was rejected when he applied for admission to the Viennese Academy of Fine Arts, and except for sketches of buildings that a companion sold to tourists and merchants, he subsequently idled away his time in a flophouse.

Goethe's description of Werther could just as well have fitted the young Hitler. Like Hitler, Werther was a dilettante who sketched a bit and read a bit, and "all the unpleasantness that he had ever faced during his official life, the humiliation at the Count's party, as well as every other situation in which he had failed, now came and went in his mind. Somehow he found in all this a justification for his present inactivity; he felt himself cut off from any prospects, incapable of grasping any of those chances by which one takes hold of the occupations of everyday life..."[9] And elsewhere, Goethe described Werther as being in "constant struggle with himself—a struggle, like Hitler's, that ended in suicide.

The underlying causes of Hitler's mental struggle will never be known since it took place within his mind, and much of the details of his childhood remain unknown. It is only by his words and deeds that we are given an insight into his struggle. It is well-documented, however, that throughout his life, he developed no deep friendships. The little that is known about him comes from his own, sometimes self-serving accounts, and the often sketchy reports of those who knew him. With all of its flaws, therefore, and if read with caution, *Mein Kampf* (My Struggle), remains the best and ultimately most reliable key to his personality. It reveals a man whose sense of his real self was so negligible that he found it necessary to assert an identity that seemed to coincide with the deepest longings of the German spirit.

The "My" in his book's title suggests the personal nature of his struggle and indicates that, even though Hitler was acting in the political arena, he viewed everything he did as part of that struggle. He made his struggle and his people's one, and finally, when he believed they had failed him, he ended his life that had harbored a self-created identity, and if his last "scorched-earth" orders had been carried out, he also would have destroyed the nation he had identified with and which had identified itself with him.

The original title of his book, *A four and One-half Year Struggle Against Lies, Stupidity, and Cowardice: Settling Accounts with the Destroyers of the National Socialist Movement*, also shows that the focus of Hitler's struggle was on world Jewry since "destroyers" was one of his frequently-used euphemisms for world Jewry in all its imagined forms. *Mein Kampf* takes on added significance since it describes the development of an identity that became merged in the unholy trinity of *ein Fuhrer, ein Volk, ein Reich* (one leader, one people, one state). Because there was not much self on which to base an autobiography, *Mein Kampf's* personal content is significantly slight, consequently the focus is on the philosophical-historical themes that attracted him. It is not so much a book about a human being as it is about a human who is willingly becoming—a description of a struggle for an identity that is less personal than it is national and historical.

The development of his identity was provoked when, as a young man, he left his hometown of Linz, Austria, to live in Vienna. There, his identity was defined by those he could not identify with: the "whole mixture" of Czechs, Poles, Magyars, Ruthenians, Serbs, Croats, etc., and "everywhere, the eternal mushroom of humanity;—the Jews, and more Jews."[10] The Viennese Jews in their caftans seemed to have had the greatest impact on his identification, and provide dramatic illustration of how his mind was attracted to the contrasts between the Jews he hated and the Greco-Roman influences in the world that he most admired. For when he saw his first Jew in a caftan, he did not ask himself, "Is this an Austrian?" but "Is this a German?"[11] indicating that even though he was an Austrian by birth and citizenship, he had already identified himself as a German.

This was the culmination of his self-described mental or soul struggle which began when he first came to Vienna in 1907, aspiring to become an artist. It was an unrealistic ambition, neither supported by his talent that focused mostly on sketches of public buildings, nor his educational background that did not include extended and disciplined art training, and he did not have a leaving certificate from the roughly equivalent of an American high school of the same period.

The essence of all good art is spontaneity, and this is something that Hitler apparently lacked except for the expression of violent outbursts of temper, and even some of these were deliberately staged to achieve a particular effect. Everything else, however, seemed calculated, and it is significant that his rejection by the arts academy included the reason: "Few heads," indicating that the drawing of human faces was not a Hitlerian strong point. He was not cut out to be an artist, the academy's director had told him, suggesting instead that he study architecture. But even when he applied to study architecture, he also was rejected.

The suggestion seems to have some merit, however, since most of Hitler's drawings and watercolors were of buildings. During the most difficult times of the Second World War, he would draw, or study, sketches for rebuilding Berlin and his hometown of Linz. He also retained an uncommon relationship with Albert Speer, his chief architect and, later, Minister of Armaments and Production, giving an impression that, through Speer, Hitler vicariously lived out his role as artist-architect.

Even though Hitler's affinity for art and architecture never found full expression, some writers believed his political style had an artistic coloration. As Sebastian Haffner noted, Hitler's conduct "was never that of a public servant (chancellor), but that of an unfettered, independent artist waiting for inspiration."[12] Thomas Mann also saw something of the artist in Hitler. In his 1939 essay, *My Brother*, Mann asked rhetorically: "Must we not, even against our will, recognize in that phenomenon (Hitler) an aspect of the artist's character?"[13] But even if one can detect an artistic element in Hitler's political style, it was always subservient to his most characteristic *modus operandi*, which was that of a prophet with a vision of some future consummation.

Hitler's rejection by the Academy of Fine Arts was among several factors in his life, paralleling that of post-First World War Germany. At the end of that war,

Germany, too, had been rejected by the rest of the world, and was unable to freely practice its political, economic and military arts. After his father, then his mother, died, Hitler was orphaned just as, in the context of the rest of Europe, Germany was, too. In addition, the nation had no strong leader, only the aged Field Marshal-President Hindenburg, its symbolic leader. The First World War had rendered Germany poor, and in his Vienna flophouse, so was Hitler. In defeat, German nationalism was surrounded by cosmopolitan forces just as Hitler had found himself surrounded by cosmopolitan peoples in Vienna.

Before gaining power, Hitler told Hindenburg he needed authority to resurrect "our politically and economically ruined people."[14] And when he succeeded in bringing about this resurrection, he also resurrected himself from being an outcast, a Dostoyevskian underground man, to becoming the self-styled chosen leader of a "chosen race." His relationship to Hindenburg also had some parallels to his relationship with his father. As the uniformed and titular head of the Fatherland, Hindenburg was the premier civil servant, just as Hitler's father, Alois, a uniformed Austrian customs official, was the head of the Hitler household. Hitler's father had wanted Adolf to follow in his footsteps by seeking a civil service career, but this only triggered a conflict with the son who wanted to pursue an artistic career. Hindenburg, too, thought he could induce Hitler into the government along traditional lines, but he insisted on his own terms, which enabled him to destroy the established order, and artfully devise his own. When accepting the chancellorship from Hindenburg, Hitler wore a bourgeois top hat, pin-striped trousers and formal coat, but when he achieved power, he quickly changed into his uniform with Swastika armband.

This Janus-faced ability to appear as one person and to behave as another was illustrated in his youth when he received an "unsatisfactory" school report. One of the few subjects in which he received a satisfactory grade was for moral conduct, indicating that in the classroom he also could behave like any other bourgeois student. He showed his real feelings later by defiantly using his report form as toilet paper.

There is much in Hitler's conduct traceable to his mental struggle that exhibited two major aspects: a personal struggle that may have been linked to his early childhood, and probably stemming from his relationship to his parents; and a struggle in which the cultural-psychological elements of his mind played an even greater part. The first stamped him emotionally as a person of deep hatreds; the second led him to those cultural-psychological aspects of his mind in which he could best find an outlet for his hatreds and at the same time helped him uncover what he believed to be the secret of world history.

The known facts of Hitler's childhood are surprisingly meager and do not provide a sufficiently complete account of what must have been an early personal struggle. At best, the observations of those who knew him as a child are sketchy, merely anecdotal, and sometimes retroactively colored to fit Hitler's later infamy. This much, however, is certain: Hitler was born on April 20, 1889, in Braunau-am-Inn, a small Austrian border town, to Klara Polzl Hitler and her husband, Alois, who was legally her uncle and twenty-three years her senior.

Adolf was the fourth of five children of Alois's third and last marriage. Three older children had died in infancy, leaving Hitler and his sister, Paula, as survivors. Also part of the family were Alois and Angela, two children from the second of Alois's three marriages. There is still some doubt as to who Alois's real father was, for it was not until he was forty that his putative "uncle" Johann Nepomuk Huttler (the family name had a variety of spellings) appeared before the parish priest in Dollersheim and had Alois legitimized on the grounds that he was the son of Huttler's deceased brother, Johann Georg Huttler. Until then, Alois had carried the surname of his mother, Maria Anna Schicklgruber. Much has been written about the possibility that Maria's son, Alois, was the illegitimate child of a Jew in whose house she reportedly had worked, but this has never been pinned down to a certitude. Nevertheless, throughout his life, it was apparently a source of concern to Hitler.

During Adolf's first year of life, his father was posted to Gross-Schonau in lower Austria. At age three he was transferred again to Passau, before being moved two years later to Linz. In 1895, not far from Linz, at a place called Lambach, Alois Hitler bought a ten-acre farm on the site of a Benedictine monastery where young Adolf briefly became a choirboy. But Alois sold the farm in that same year and, at the age of fifty-eight, retired with a pension to Leonding, a small town near Linz.

In January 1903, only eight years after retiring, and following a brief illness, Alois dropped dead while taking a sip from a glass of wine in a Leonding tavern. Adolf had been exposed to his father's influence, therefore, for a little under fourteen years of his life. But they were crucial, impressionable years, and when he was old enough to speak out for himself, there are indications that he and his father came into frequent conflict. One of these conflicts centered on Adolf's desire to become an artist. But neither this conflict nor any of the known facts about his early life would explain the depth of hatred in him which may have stemmed from some severe trauma or great deprivation of affection or combination of both. The insufficiency of information about Hitler's childhood, however, does not make it possible to assert with any degree of confidence the origin of his emotional warp. Whatever the cause, the result was the most diabolical man that possibly the world has ever known, a man who could unfeelingly send millions of men, women and children to their deaths, yet show an inexplicable and bizarre concern for lobsters and crabs. In a decree dated January 14, 1936, for example, Hitler spelled out regulations for the humane preparation of crabs, lobsters and other crustaceans in restaurants by having them dropped one by one into boiling water. Prefatory comments on the decree emphasized that it was intended to strengthen "compassion" as one of the highest moral values of the German people.

In the provincial area of Austria, during the time that Hitler was growing up, and among his family's social class, it is known that the behavior pattern for the male head of household was authoritarian and accompanied by sometimes severe corporal punishment; the role of the mother being that of a noninterventionist who could do little more than secretly comfort a child after the beatings were administered. Some psychologists believe that such a pattern of beatings by the father and affection from the mother can lay the foundations for a sado-masochistic personality. In addition, it can violate that very delicate and crucial process by which a normal child tends to achieve an identity through its parents, and which leads to an expanded identity when the child is exposed to the cultural influences of religion, education, tradition, etc.

There is, in fact, substantial evidence that Hitler's household was excessively authoritarian. Frau Horl, who worked for Alois after his second wife died, characterized him as a very strict man with a "terrible temper." His customs-house colleagues and village cronies also talked about his temper that would flare for no apparent reason.[16] Brigid Hitler said her husband, Alois, Jr., told her about the beatings that his father would give to his children, his wife, Klara, and the family dog. And when he wanted Adolf, he would whistle through two fingers in his mouth just as he would when calling his dog.[17] In conversations with some of his staff, Hitler, too, would tell about the whippings his father gave him. In *Mein Kampf*, however, his references to his parents are generally positive, possibly because he wanted to go on public record with a more acceptable family image. But it is also possible that he retained a filial respect for his parents despite whatever abuse he may have suffered. This is certainly true of his mother, whose photograph he always displayed in his living quarters and which he had beside him when he committed suicide.

Nevertheless, the kind of authoritarian parentage Hitler most likely had, often results in an inferiority complex that can harbor a suppressed rebellion that exhibits itself in a fantasy world of superiority resembling the authoritarianism that the young person has been exposed to. Very often the overthrow of the father is achieved in the eyes of the child, and this can be accompanied by the simultaneous overthrow of the higher father (God) that the authoritarian parent and/or society has led the child to believe in. Consequently, the child can become a father and a God to himself, and this can be expressed as megalomania. Thus, events that would pass without notice, or comment, in the lives of normal persons, become greatly exaggerated by the megalomaniacal personality, and take on a larger-than-life importance. To set oneself up as both father and God is one of the greatest burdens that a person can shoulder, and it is freighted with the utmost danger. For if reality persistently contradicts one's megalomaniacal fantasies, as it inevitably does, life can become insupportable and end in hopeless madness, or suicide.

During his climb to power, Hitler did meet with a number of reverses that prompted threats of suicide. And when he no longer could sustain his fantasies in the face of such realities as allied bombings, his retreating armies, and Russian soldiers advancing to within hundreds of yards of his headquarters, he finally ended his life.

All that is known about Hitler, particularly during his public life, supports the characterization of him as a megalomaniac. But allowing that, just as paranoids can have real as well as imaginary enemies, megalomaniacs can also have real as well as fancied talents. There is no doubt that Hitler showed some astounding political and military skills. But he also sounded off on many topics where his competence did not match his confident assertions. In innumerable monologues that his staff were often subjected to, he would expound on history, religion, art, architecture, and almost any conceivable subject with an air of omniscient authority such as he insisted upon asserting as both leader of his people and commander of his armies. He not only became a father and God to himself, but a father-God to his people.

To achieve that Godlike role, he struck an empathetic chord; appealed to some deep-rooted need among a nation of nearly seventy million people, and this is one source of constant bafflement to historians, psychologists, and others, who can, on the one hand, come to grips with the pathology of one individual but, on the other hand, find it beyond their comprehension, how a whole nation could have become accomplices to Nazi irrationality. What makes it even more difficult to understand is that there were plenty of overt signs that a once highly-civilized country had been taken over by thugs and murderers. There were wreckings and burnings of Jewish-owned shops and synagogues; brutal beatings and killings by the Stormtroops; the euthanasia of deformed and deranged

Germans, and Hitler's hate-filled speeches that, among other things, prophesied the annihilation of an entire people. And one has to ask how a nation came to support a regime that took pride in the elite legions of black-uniformed men wearing the ominous skull and crossbones or runic SS symbols as their insignia.

Part of the answer to the horrifying symbiosis of leader and people may lie in the German past in which efforts to achieve unity were greatly frustrated by a succession of historical events that caused the Germans to lag behind in the advancement toward the modern age. Efforts at monarchical stability were blocked in the early 11th Century; attempts at unity of principalities were halted in the mid-13th Century; middle-class development was curbed by the Thirty Years War; self-government was discouraged by the Constitution of 1871, and when representative democracy was introduced at the close of the First World War, it was heavily-loaded with social, economic, and political obstacles.

Just as Hitler struggled to establish his identity, Germans had fought for their identity in numerous wars—the most recent being the First World War of 1914–18 for which Germany was severely punished and ostracized. Its defeat and the subsequent imposition of restrictions and reparations under the Versailles Treaty, helped create psychological responses among the Germans similar to those that Hitler experienced acutely in his own personality. His life, and Germany's, became intersected like the two twisted branches of the Swastika that were emblematic of both, as well as an esoteric symbol of the attempt to supplant Christianity's cross with the crooked cross of the "New World Order." On the basis of personal and societal humiliation alone, Hitler could not have merged his struggle and his nation's to such a complete degree. There had to be other impelling factors, and it is part of his wayward genius that he discovered the cultural-psychological source of these factors that go to the heart of the Hitler phenomenon. These will be dealt with later, but for now it is important to note that Hitler's mental struggle, involving the cultural-psychological elements in his psyche, led to an acute identity crisis that he sought to solve by banishing the Jewish constituent in his mentality that he perceived to be, not only the source of his personal conflict, but also of Germany's and the world's.

For the most part, historians taking a psychological approach to history have tended almost exclusively to focus on the unconscious factors in the behavior of major historical figures. In Hitler's case, this has resulted in highly complex rationalizations for his presumed unconscious dynamics, and often these are more fanciful than historical or psychological, and lack the clinical evidence that is an essential part of any meaningful psychoanalysis. As Isaiah Berlin says, conscious human choices come into play in history more than is "usually and complacently supposed." He also remarked on the tendency to attribute too much to unavoidable operations of natural and social laws as the workings of the unconscious, or unalterable psychological reflexes..."[18]

Using a psychological approach to the Nazi era, some historians have not only allowed the Freudian writ to run, but to run away with them. In so doing, they have ignored very important cultural-psychological factors— an ignorance that is, in itself, of psychological interest. A large part of the problem may stem from the habit of many psychologists and historians of signing "The Unconscious" on bad checks written against a greatly overdrawn psychological account. Indeed, many who do so would no doubt feel greatly depreciated if it was suggested that their own long, arduous and conscious efforts, that brought them to prominence in their professions, were to be ascribed to some unconscious psychological complex.

There may be a role for Freudian, and post-Freudian, psychology in any consideration of Hitler, particularly when it encompasses childhood, or unconscious factors that are based on solid evidence, and which may have affected Hitler's emotional and mental disposition. But the disposition that led him to hatred instead of love did, in fact, find expression through given cultural-psychological forms in however distorted ways, and particularly so since he was operating in the public arena. It could certainly be argued that an excessive focus on the "unconscious" has tended to retard the understanding of history, for while Freud claimed to have originated a scientific method for exploring the unconscious, a great deal of confusion still surrounds that concept, even to the extent of calling into question the "science" that deals with it.

The term itself suggests experience that, for one reason or another, has not yet become conscious or clothed in language. The difficulty inherent in the concept becomes apparent when psychologists and historians use such self-contradictory terms as "unconscious goals," "unconscious motives," or "unconscious demands." Goals, motives, and demands belong in the province of the consciousness; they imply willful direction, and since the will is never blind, this must necessarily involve the intellect. It is not possible to speak of the will without giving it a focus, and this is seen in such terms as "will-to-live" and "will-to-power." It is impossible to assume a will's autonomy; it has to be conceived with reference to a directive capacity, and would have to involve will, intellect, and subject, hence it could no longer be called "the unconscious." It may be, however, that since the constituents of the consciousness have been transmitted through culture, traditions, education, religion, etc., that most individuals are, in this sense, unconscious or only vaguely aware of the source of these constituents. How many people, for instance, see themselves as a psychological composite of Jewish, Greek, and Roman influences? And yet the main constituents of the Western consciousness come from these three cultural-psychological sources.

This is seen in many small ways as when looking up words in a dictionary one finds their origin in Greek, Roman or Hebrew languages or the polyglot of languages that in lesser ways also have contributed to the Western ethos. The Roman Catholic Church, with its now selective Latin masses, is another reminder of the Roman influence (not to speak of its administrative structure and doctrinal development) as is the Latin terminology used by lawyers in their legal briefs, or the Greek source of terms used by doctors in their diagnoses and physicists in their mathematical calculations. In larger ways the influence of Greece, Rome, and the Jewish spirit have been woven into the very fabric of Western civilization; the Judeo-Christian spirit being most evident in our time in the passionate, and sometimes revolutionary appeals for justice, freedom, equality and human rights. Without the Judeo-Christian influence, Martin Luther King's civil rights speeches, for example, would just not have been possible, including his last one when he spoke of having been to the top of the mountain and "seen the Promised Land." And while Gandhi's asceticism was greatly influenced by Hinduism, the moral thrust of his movement to uplift his people owes more to the passion for justice and human rights that is the inspiration of Judeo-Christianity.

But individuals are often so engrossed in a quest for personal salvation that they fail to see how Judeo-Christianity has infiltrated the realm of politics and is trans- forming the world. In our time, politics is really spilt religion that often leaves many stains of bloodshed. Religion's influence on politics is often unacknowledged, as in Marxism, when it is clear, for instance, that in the development of his Communist theories, Marx owed a great deal, not only to Hegel, but to Ludwig Feurbach's *The Essence of Christianity*, as well as his own Judaic back- ground. Not only are poets the "unacknowledged legislators" of the world, as Shelley would have it, but so are the religious, philosophers, writers, and even com- posers. But it is religion that provides all the others with their cues even when their works are antireligious. This inability of many people to see the influence of religion may stem, in part, from the separation of church and state in much of the world that blinds many to the fact that separation of church and state *as social institutions* does not mean the severance of individuals from their moral conscience which it is religion's vocation to cultivate.

Even Freud, on occasion, recognized that in addition to examining the unconscious through a microscope, as it were, it is also necessary to use field glasses to scan the broader influences of religion and culture on the human consciousness, and this indeed seems to be part of what he understood by his concept of superego. In the psychologi- cal study of Woodrow Wilson that he and William C. Bullitt conducted, Freud noted: "The civilization in which a child is educated nevertheless influences his character. It deter- mines, at least, the style of the clothing in which his desires must be dressed in order to appear respectable. The child breathes in from the atmosphere of his home and his com- munity, ideas as to the gentleman-as-he-should-be, and determines the form of his consciousness."[19] Apart from this incredibly bourgeois acknowledgement of the "respect- able" influences of civilization, home, community, and ideas on the "form" of human consciousness, one has to ask how the "unconscious," that Freud believed provided the source for much human motivation, could move in any direction without the conscious tools of will and intellect as directing agencies. A nonpolitical mass killer, for example, does not need to dress his desires in respectability in order to express his hatred, he has only to climb to the top of a high building with a rifle and start shooting at passersby. But a mass killer who seeks public office and power has to conceal his hatred under the intellectual and moral cloak of his culture. This, indeed, was the big lesson that Hitler learned when, in 1923, he unsuccessfully tried to take the direct road to power through force.

Hitler shared with all Europeans a mentality that was cultivated through religion, education, tradition, and other influences. There is now more than sufficient scholarship to establish that the main elements in the cultivation of the Western mind are of Jewish, Greek and Roman origin. Just as, in ancient times, individual Jews, Greeks and Romans found it difficult to agree on life's fundamental issues, so these three cultural types are in perpetual confusion within the Western psyche as reflected in the neurosis of Western (now universal) political life. The Jewish spirit is marked by religious prophecy, the Greek by metaphysics, and the Roman by pragmatic jurisprudence, and the struggle for survival of each within the European psyche is demonstrated in the realm of politics. As so many scholars have pointed out, the Greeks were preeminently contemplative and artistic; the Romans were the conquerors, the administrators, the builders of roads, bridges and aqueducts; the Hebrews were religious with a long line of prophets providing moral vision and emotional reaction to excessive legalism and organization.

If, for example, two thousand years ago an individual Jew, Greek and Roman had come together to discuss the fundamental issues of life, it is likely that the Greek would veer into speculations about the ideal, only to be brought back to earth by the practical Roman, concerned with the most direct way of solving problems. But the Jew would find fault with both the Greek and Roman views, calling attention to his belief that there is a God who has a personal relationship with human kind through which he communicates, not just what is ideal or practical, but what is moral; what is right and what is wrong. During debates in Congress and other governmental bodies, it is instructive to see the expression of these fundamental spirits depending upon the dominance of one or another in the minds of the individual speakers. Indeed, the debates of the Founding Fathers present one of the best examples of how a balance was sought between the ideal and the practical (the Federalist Papers show this most clearly) but, as it turned out, the Bill of Rights, something of an afterthought, contains the Constitution's strongest moral, therefore Judeo-Christian, component. (A history of the Civil War has yet to be written that traces the predominance of the Greek spirit in the South as opposed to the more practical Yankee (Roman) spirit combined with Judaic Puritanism in the North.)

Just how the Jewish, Greek and Roman elements became part of the Western cultural-psychological inheritance is, of course, a matter of familiar history. Greek civilization was incorporated into the Roman imperium, and later, under Constantine, the Jewish moral and prophetic traditions became part of the Western heritage when Christianity became the official religion of the Roman Empire. The consequence for Western people has been a psychological *confusion* of these three antinomial elements within the one consciousness, and the efforts to

27

reconcile these differences has resulted in many an individual neurosis and, socially, has exploded in innumerable bloody conflicts and upheavals that are part and parcel of what we call history—and no longer just Western history, but also universal history.

It is easy enough to recognize these three elements as symbolically found in architecture, as we do in the many buildings throughout the Western world, some of which have Christian spires (one aspect of the Jewish spirit) superimposed, sometimes extraneously it seems, on Greco-Roman structures. But it is much more difficult to discern them in our minds, since they do not always operate in their own separate ways but in a confused interplay. They are part of what Marx called the "world-historical necromancy" that brings us all into involuntary involvement in history—the tradition of all the dead generations that weighs "like a nightmare on the brain of the living."[20] Or, to quote Isaiah Berlin again, we all inherit from our ancestors "ancient spectacles through which we are still looking."[21] Most people, however, are unaware of these psychological "spectacles." They do not know the origin of the constituents that inhabit their consciousness, and this may have been what Christ had in mind when he said, "Father forgive them for they know not what they do."[22] Those who have some awareness of their "psychological spectacles" include individuals who are moved to explore the meaning of human life, and those, like Dostoyevsky, Nietzsche, and Hitler, who experienced a crisis of the spirit. For Hitler, as for all Europeans, whether they recognize it or not, these psychological spectacles are Jewish, Greek, and Roman trifocals. Hitler would have preferred them to be Greco-Roman bifocals tinted with pseudo-German mysticism, and social Darwinism.

Hitler's mind offers an opportunity to see, in exaggerated form, the tensions among these three antagonistic constituents in the Western consciousness, and this makes him the best clue to history that has so far been disgorged. For him, the Jewish spirit was evident in all things international such as finance, trade, social democracy, liberalism, Communism, etc., and all these he perceived to be antithetical to German nationalism and culture. What appears to have transpired, judging by his own account of his "mental struggle," was a sort of psychological provocative contradiction in which the more he was provoked by the Jewish spirit, the more his German nationalism was stimulated. And since the emotional disruptions of his childhood had disposed him toward hatred, he could not find an adequate outlet for that hatred in Judeo-Christianity—the religion that, even if imperfectly practiced, nevertheless preaches love, mercy, and universal community. His hatred led him, therefore, to discover that the source of social pressure for freedom, equality, and the transcendence of national sovereignty, came from the Jewish spirit through Christianity. "The heaviest blow that ever struck humanity," he once said, "was the coming of Christianity," which was the first creed in the world to "exterminate its adversaries in the name of love."[23] Without Christianity, he believed, there would also have been no Islam, Bolshevism, or social democracy, and under German influence his much-preferred Greco-Roman-type empire would have achieved world domination. Christianity had brought about the collapse of the Roman Empire, he asserted, and a "night that lasted for centuries."[24] In an inversion of what the Western world had come to believe, he saw Christianity as inaugurating darkness and extinguishing the light of Roman imperialism. And since Christianity was of Jewish inspiration, Hitler saw the Jews as the carriers of this darkness, or as he often labeled them, "a poison."

The tensions stimulated by the Jewish spirit have been noted in literature by Edmund Wilson and others. "...the strong Hebrew strain in English," Wilson wrote, "is to some extent at variance with the influence of the Greek and Roman tradition" and where there is an inclination toward the Greco-Roman tradition, "one is likely to resent the other."[25] Matthew Arnold and American philosopher William Barrett, wrote at length on the contrasts between Hebraism and Hellenism, but unaccountably did not include the Roman influence in their considerations. Nor did they look upon these polarities in their psychological interplay *within* the Western consciousness, but only as *external* cultural phenomena. George Eliot's *Romola* provides probably the best literary exploration of this disturbing psychological triumvirate, but the full implications of the psychological interplay of Greek, Roman and Jew in the Western psyche have received the most astute recognition from British thinkers John Macmurray and Fredrick Lohr. Both men saw the clash of the antagonistic Jewish, Greek, and Roman spirits as central to an understanding of history.

Indeed, the savagery with which Hitler's Germany sought to eradicate the Jews presents the most compelling evidence of the dynamic psychological tensions generated in the Western world by these three spirits. It is these tensions that make it difficult for individuals to achieve an identity that can bring about a psychological integrity, and sometimes pushes them into identifying themselves with chauvinistic nationalisms or chiliastic universalisms.

In our day "identity crisis," notwithstanding its use in a popular and often frivolous sense, has become a familiar term for the condition that many individuals increasingly find themselves in. And there are few serious works of history, philosophy, and psychology these days that do not take up the identity question. Perhaps the best known attempt to grapple with the problem has been that of psychoanalyst Erik Erikson. In his study of Martin Luther, Erikson observed that some people reach a crisis in their lives; a sort of "second birth" that can be aggravated by widespread neuroticisms or by pervasive ideological unrest." And some individuals, he notes, will "succumb to this crisis in all manner of neurotic, psychotic, or delinquent behavior; while others will resolve it through participation in ideological movements passionately concerned with religion or politics, nature, or art..."[26] Erikson also referred to Luther as having acquired a historical identity after going through a psychological struggle very much like Hitler's. And it is one of the merits of Erickson's work that he has corrected some of the overkill that historians, psychoanalysts, psychologists and others have directed at "unconscious forces" instead of the historical factors that influence the formation of identity. The great weakness in Erikson's otherwise pioneering studies, however, stems from his failure to properly explain what he means by "identity" that he seems to link too closely with Freudian concepts. For insofar as an identity is a willful representation that an individual asserts, it cannot represent one's true self, but what one sees oneself as being; the true self being unknowable except in relationship with others. When, for example, a person asserts, "I am an American," "I am a Communist," or, as in Hitler's case, "I am a German," these do not represent the person's true personality that remains unchangeable despite identity change. Joe Smith will always be Joe Smith whether he considers himself to be a Communist, an American, or a Christian. Such identifications point to historical sources, not to mysterious factors in the unconscious. This is recognized, for example, in Barrett and Yankelovich's study of ego and instinct in which they record that a person's identity might seem to be the most individual, unique, and private thing about a person, but "since this identity is developed both from and within culture, it is always essentially related to social and historical factors."[27]

Hitler's attempts to fasten onto an identity took place in Austria where he was exposed to Pan-German nationalism. His chosen identity was as a German, and he latched onto it with a zeal that is often exhibited by naturalized citizens, or converts to a new faith. He became a *super* German, evading the draft in Austria, but willingly accepting army service in Germany. It is a common feature in personalities, whose sense of real self is very weak, that they must assert their identities more strongly than persons with a sound sense of self.

Hitler's efforts to identify himself as a German were greatly bolstered during the First World War when he received the Iron Cross, both first and second class, a singular accomplishment for someone holding a lance-corporal's rank. But this triumphant reinforcement of his German nationality was dealt a great blow by the socialist revolution of 1918 that preceded Germany's humiliating surrender to the Allies. He saw the revolution, and the defeat, as being due to the Jewish "enemies" who were responsible for everything that worked against German nationalism and, therefore, against his own strong German identification. For Hitler, all internationalism represented a will-to-identify with humanity that ran counter to his will-to-identify with Germany.

As with all national identifications, however, Hitler's was bound to find expression through the Western world's cultural legacy which, as previously noted, is predominantly Jewish, Greek, and Roman. As Simone Weil saw clearly, "everything that shocks us about Hitler's methods is what he has in common with Rome," and any specifically Germanic frills that he added to the Roman tradition, she thought, were "pure literary and mythological patchwork."[28] Despite the pseudo-Aryan mythology that the Nazis cloaked their ideology in, German society was really permeated by influences that could be traced *only* to classical antiquity, and which were set up in opposition to Judeo-Christianity. For while Judeo-Christianity was a source of hope for many in the Western world, and provided pressure for equality, freedom and brotherhood, it was, to Hitler, a "poison." He consequently fought back against this pressure, extolling instead the Greco-Roman elements of his consciousness.

In so doing, he was fulfilling an expression of German nationalism that had been long adumbrated by more than one German writer. Theodor Mommsen, 19th Century Germany's premier Roman historian, for instance, saw in the growing German nationalism a resurrection of the Roman republic. Others, such as novelist William Raabe, said of Bismarck's Reich that "We (Germans) are now asked to become Romans," and Schiller saw 19th Century Germany as a new Greece or a new Rome, or a combination of both. Rainer Maria Rilke thought the "Roman idea" was one that could acquire universal value. He had Italy in mind when he said it, rather than Germany. Nevertheless, Mussolini's Italy was imbued with the Roman idea, and the Third Reich expressed the German version of the same thing with Greek themes thrown in. Simone Weil went so far as to say that, in Hitler, the Romans never before had such a "remarkable imitator, if indeed he is an imitator and has not independently rediscovered their system."[29]

That the resolution of Hitler's mental struggle caused him to fixate on the Greco-Roman constituents in his mind while rejecting the Judeo-Christian, can be seen from the unstinting admiration he often expressed for Greek and Roman antiquity. "...we must not be deterred from the study of antiquity. Roman history...is and remains the best mentor, not only for today, but probably for all time." Elsewhere, he said, "The Hellenic ideal of culture should also remain preserved for us in its exemplary beauty...The struggle that rages today is for very great aims. A culture combining millenniums and embracing Hellenism and Germanism is fighting for its existence."[30] Unmistakably, these statements show that, despite Nazi rantings about an Aryan past, the real model for Nazism was Greco-Roman civilization. And, apart from whatever significance psychologists might also draw from it, Hitler's fascination for wolves may have been linked to his admiration for Rome that legend says was founded by the twins, Romulus and Remus, who were suckled by a she-wolf after they had been abandoned. "Wolf," for example, was the name Hitler gave to a pup of his pet dog, Blondi, an Alsatian or German wolfhound, and his various wartime headquarters were named *Wolfsschlucht* (Wolf's Gulch), *Wolfsschanze* (Wolf's Lair), and *Werwolf* (Manwolf). As a young politician, Hitler preferred to be called "Werewolf," and he liked his first name, Adolf, believing it to be an old German compound of Athal (noble) and Wolfa (wolf).

Many times Hitler had expressed the view that Christianity had ended Greco-Roman civilization, and he wanted to restore it; he wanted to build a "New World Order" that was really founded on the old pagan world order. And to do that, he had to eliminate Christianity *and* the Jewish people, the latter representing the *corpus materiale* that provided the Christian *corpus mysticum* with living testimony. But, in trying to restore a neoclassical world order, Hitler was not attracted to the Greece of high reason, but by militant Sparta with its six thousand elite dominating more than three hundred and fifty thousand Helots. Such domination was possible, Hitler thought, because of Sparta's systematic race preservation in which sick, weak and deformed children were put to death just as the mentally defective and deformed were among the first to be exterminated by the Nazis. "Sparta," Hitler said, "must be regarded as the first Volkist state,"[31]—a clear indication that he believed his Third Reich to be the second Volkist state. But his "Master Race" concept could also have been plucked right out of Plato's *Menexenes* where Aspasia orates over those who have died in battle. "No Pelopes nor Cadmians, nor Egyptians, nor Dauni, nor the rest of the crowd of born foreigners dine with us; but ours is the land of pure Hellenes, free from admixture."[32] To distinguish themselves from any foreigners, Athenians wore brooches shaped like golden grasshoppers, signifying that they were children of Attica who had come direct from her soil. The Nazis gave a new twist to this method of discrimination when they forced Jews to wear yellow stars as a symbol of their separateness from, and "inferiority" to, the "Master Race" of Germans that was rooted in blood and soil.

The influence of Greece, in particular, on 18th and 19th Century Germans was so great that British historian Edith Butler referred to it as the "tyranny of Greece over Germany." Germany, she wrote, was surrounded by Greek myths deriving from Goethe and Nietzsche: "national heroes for the most part transformed into supermen," and these were still further mythologized in prophets and forerunners of Hitler "not gradually and slowly by popular accretions and superstitions, but violently, willfully by highly intellectual if much-bedazzled minds."[33]

Beginning with Johann Winckelmann's "discovery" of the lost beauty of Greek art in the 18th Century, Germany produced a whole line of devotees to classical antiquity that included Lessing, Goethe, Schiller, Holderlin, Heine, Nietzsche, Spitteler, George, and Schliemann; the latter quite literally digging up the Greek past. Winckelmann's singular fascination with the *Laocoön* sculpture marks a milestone in German absorption with things Greek and Roman. This Greek sculpture depicts Laocoon, the legendary Trojan priest and his two sons being mangled by two huge sea serpents after Laocoön warned the Trojans against the Greeks' gift of a wooden-horse decoy. For Winckelmann, *Laocoön* was the perfect expression of art in which "greatness and composure of soul" was shown amidst intense suffering. He compared it to the depths of the sea that are always calm, however wild and stormy the surface might be. He saw a perfect balance between the pain, shown in the tightening muscles of arms, legs and abdomens of the *Laocoön* bodies, and the composure and nobility of soul showing on Laocoön's face. "Laocoön suffers," Winckelmann wrote, "and his misery pierces us to the soul; but we should like to be able to bear anguish in the manner of this great man."[34]

One likes to think that Winckelmann would have been horrified had he but seen this kind of ultra-stoicism transposed into twisted reality as when Gestapo Chief Heinrich Himmler addressed a group of SS generals in 1943 on the annihilation of the Jews and other peoples. "Most of you must know," he said, "what it means to see a hundred corpses lie side by side, or five hundred, or a thousand. To have stuck this out and—excepting cases of human weakness—to have kept our integrity, this is what has made us hard. In our history, this is an unwritten and never-to-be-written page of glory..."[35]

So much for the "glory that was Greece" and the grandeur that was Germany. As Lucy Dawidowicz perceptively noted, the Germans held counter-images of themselves that were "dual and inconsistent." On the one hand, they were the wholesome, vigorous supermen, invulnerable to the "Jewish poison," but in accordance with their other image, they were "latter-day Laocoöns in the grip of a death struggle."[36]

There is no record of what Hitler thought about the *Laocoön* sculpture or whether he thought about it at all. He had a penchant, however, for a certain kind of art that seemed to resemble a debased Germanic version of Greek art. Among his favorite artists was Franz von Stuck, whose paintings featured naked women in various poses with huge serpents slithering between their thighs and wrapping around their bodies. They bore such titles as *Sensuality, Depravity, Sin* and *The Siren*. The eyes of a Medusa reminded Hitler of his mother's. "Those eyes!" he exclaimed, "those are the eyes of my mother!"[37] And while the eyes do have a remarkable resemblance to his mother's, they do not express her look of melancholy and pain. They are fierce and penetrating like Hitler's during his frenzied speeches when he worked himself into orgasmic-like climaxes, and secreted sweat like it was surrogate semen. More than one writer has described the sensuality of Hitler's speeches as when he waited to get the "feel" of the crowd that he regarded as feminine. Or, as Susan Sontag wrote after seeing Hitler in Leni Riefenstahl's film, *Triumph of the Will*, "the expression of the crowd is one of ecstasy: the leader makes the crowd come."[38] Hitler owned and hung some of Stuck's brothel-like art in his rooms—an unwitting indicator of his own perverted sexual preferences that reportedly included the desire to have women kick, defecate and urinate on him. Several women, who may have been intimate with Hitler in this fashion, either committed suicide or attempted to, possibly out of guilt for their depraved actions, and/or through disappointment in the exhibition of private weaknesses in a publicly powerful man.

Hitler's artistic preferences, as reflected in Stuck's paintings and the monolithic Greco-Roman-type buildings he planned for Berlin and Linz, were conspicuous signs of how far Germany's artistic taste had declined from the time of Goethe, who saw the nobility and serenity in Greek art that had first attracted Winckelmann. But, having gone through his unnerving *Stürm und Drang* period, he sensed the danger of an excessive German identification with the antique world particularly if, as an ideal, it was filtered through the German mind. In addition to its nobility and serenity, Goethe was aware of another aspect of Greek art: a demonic spirit that he had spent a good part of his life struggling against. This spirit, and an excessive Roman-type patriotism, were the Scylla and Charybidis that Goethe felt Germany should avoid. In conversations with his friend, Eckermann, and perhaps drawing too optimistically from his own achievement of humanistic balance, Goethe saw Roman history as no longer suited to Germans. "We have," he said, "become too humane for the triumphs of Caesar for them not to be repugnant to our feelings. Neither are we much charmed by the history of Greece..."[39]

Goethe had in mind Greek and Roman history and not their art. But in any event, Hitler's Nazi regime proved him disastrously wrong. With its strutting legions and *Sieg Heils*, it bore many of the hallmarks of the Roman world, and at the same time sought to settle once and for all the battle between paganism and Judeo-Christianity. In one way or another, this battle had engaged some of Germany's greatest minds. The poet Heinrich Heine, for instance, was one of those who had an inkling of what was in store. "Don't worry German Republicans," he predicted, "your German revolution will be no gentler or milder because it has been preceded by the *Critique* of Kant, the transcendental idealism of Fichte, and even the philosophy of nature." Such doctrines, he added, give birth to revolutionary forces which only wait, for the day, to erupt and fill the world with terror and amazement."[40]

Little did Heine, a Jewish-German, who was more German than many Germans, realize how much "terror and amazement" would fill the world. The Germany of Goethe, Lessing, Schiller, and Kant, that the world had come to regard as "the new Athens" of reason and beauty, was transformed into a hellish place that out-Neroed Nero's Rome. Its conquered territories became a diabolical Sparta in which an elite few, not only kept millions of latter-day Helots in slavery, but also murdered millions by assemblyline methods that made all past historical atrocities pale by comparison. There seems little doubt that had Heine been alive during the Nazi era, he would have been dispatched to the extermination ovens. All of his passionate poems and writings, extolling the virtues of the German race, would have fallen on deaf ears and stone hearts.

"In what other country," Edith Butler felt compelled to ask, "would the discovery of serenity, simplicity, and nobility in art have brought about such dire results?" The baffling quality of the Germanic temperament "stares out at us..." she added, "but one thing at least is certain; only among a people at heart tragically dissatisfied with themselves could this grim struggle with a foreign ideal have continued for so long." To an Anglo-Saxon mind, Butler wrote, "it seems wasteful, deplorable and almost perverse that the beauty of Greek art and poetry have caused so much frantic pain and so little pure pleasure.[41]

The *Laocoön* group may offer a clue to this "frantic pain." It is believed to have been carved in Rhodes about 25 B.C.E., long after the golden age of ideal Greek art that displayed an eternal calm. Such tensions, as shown in *Laocoön*, were inadmissible then, and such art as the *Laocoön* really expresses a great tension between reason and emotion that one has come to associate with the baroque. As Gilbert Highet has carefully explained, the word "baroque" comes from the Spanish *barroco*, a large irregular pearl that contrasts with a regular pearl's perfect spherical shape; it is straining outwards almost to bursting point—"a beauty compressed but almost breaking the bounds of control."[42]

The age of baroque could have been seen as a warning that the long-lasting influence of the Western world's classical stoicism was about to be challenged; that in neither life nor art could emotion much longer be kept under the restraints of reason as it had been, off and on, since the breach of the Roman Empire by Christian faith. It was precisely under Marcus Aurelius, the otherwise sensible and highly tolerant Stoic emperor, that Christians were brutally persecuted.

The singular relationship of Germans with Christianity is evident in their Gothic cathedrals that are among the most colossal of any in Europe, appearing as though they had been built by immigrant classical craftsmen reluctantly instructed in the Christian catechism. And while, throughout the Latin countries, baroque art retains a stoic emotional submission to reason, among Germans it is on the verge of casting off rational restraints. The first great social display of European unbalance, however, came not from the Germans, but from France. Just when it seemed that, through the Enlightenment, reason had triumphed, France erupted in a shocking emotional reversal in which heads were chopped off. The Revolution seemed like a symbolic triumph of heart over head, darkness over the Enlightenment. Somewhat tardy, but not to be outdone, suppressed German emotions finally exploded in the 20th

Century's Incremental War, i.e., the First and Second World Wars that were really part of Germany's one struggle for identity and a place in the sun. The continuity of the two wars was well-symbolized by the First World War Iron Cross that Hitler always wore on his uniform, along with the Swastika; the Iron Cross evolving, as it were, into the crooked cross.

With this two-phase war, the "New Athens" of Goethe, Schiller and others was transformed into the "New World Order" of Nazi havoc and chaos. The demonic spirit Goethe had feared in himself, and observed in young Kleist's frenzied works, had finally found social expression under Hitler. No longer was emotion suppressed by, but overthrew reason, making it a slave to emotion and an expression of total irrationality; the burning of proscribed books after the Nazis came to power, presaged the burning of bodies in crematoria. From a fascination with Laocoön's serenity when confronted with suffering and certain death, Germany, as reflected in the tastes of its leader, had turned to Stuck and the kind of art that seemed to suggest a lascivious death wish. Where Faust had been a perpetual German literary legend, in Hitler he stepped onto the world stage to keep his pact with the Devil, and did so with such zeal that one could suspect that he was really the Devil incarnate come to combat the Christian God incarnate.

The portents of the arrival of a Hitler-type leader, and the power and fury he would bring in his wake, were so many and spanned such a long period of time that it forbids one to look for an explanation of Hitler in isolation from German culture and German culture separate from European culture, for apart from regional colorations that all nations have contributed to Western civilization, Germany was part of that civilization. And the cultural-psychological impact of the Greek, Roman, and

Jewish spirits on the Western mind and institutions, and on Hitler and his compatriots, is much too great to be displaced by the argument that all Hitler's doings were due to the workings of the unconscious. If such were the case, then Hitler could more easily have found an outlet for his unconscious desires in any one of a number of quick and murderous ways, rather than launching his long and arduous political and military struggles that involved millions in his own country and around the world.

He would not, for example, have needed the inspiration of Richard Wagner who, along with Nietzsche, was one of the most significant foreshadowers of Hitler's coming. For a time, Wagner also dabbled in politics in the belief that therein lay his vocation, but when he realized it was not, he turned instead to music, a reversal of Hitler's life pattern in which he set out to become an artist, then turned to politics when he failed. As a composer of grand operas, all Wagner's stage was a world whereas, for Hitler, all the world was a stage. But in their separate ways the composer and the politician expressed similar themes of anti-Semitism, racism, classical antiquity, and pseudo-Teutonic mythology. No wonder that the operatic shrine that Wagner built at Bayreuth held such a fascination for Hitler whose annual pilgrimages there made of it also a shrine of National Socialism.

By Hitler's own admission, Wagner's operas had a great influence on him, and there was also Wagner's writings that urged "emancipation from the yoke of Judaism." This seemed to him the "foremost necessity," requiring nothing less than a "war of liberation against the Jews."[43] Other portenders of Nazism, like Rilke, were obsessed by the antique world and the "Roman idea" that Rilke thought could acquire universal value, or that George predicted would inaugurate a "New Reich" modelled on Greece and Rome. There was also Hermann Lons who expressed the anti-Christian component that many other Germans were espousing. "We Germans," he wrote, "pretend that we are Christians, but we are nothing of the sort and never can be. For Christianity and race consciousness are incompatible, as are socialism and culture."[44]

Over and over again, and spanning a long period of time, numerous writers manifested their anti-Semitism, anti-Christianity, racism, and adoration of Greco-Roman civilization. Hitler stirred all of these themes in a witch's cauldron and brewed the deadly potion that the world came to know as Nazism. The heady effect was that, in Canute fashion, Germany stood up and tried to turn back the tide of Judeo-Christianity so that it could be replaced by an ersatz classical "civilization" tinted with a pseudo-Germanic mysticism and social Darwinism. The emphasis of the latter on man as a biological creature was particularly well-suited to the Nazi ideology that saw humankind *only* as a biological species in a struggle for survival that pitted the best-fitted against the least-fitted.

And it is one of the many astounding paradoxes of Nazism that its leader was totally unlike the Nazi ideal of the tall, blond, physically superb specimens of manhood who were supposedly best-fitted to survive. When Hitler first came to power, he weighed about one-hundred-and-fifty pounds and was less than five-feet nine inches tall, and he was neither blond nor physically distinguished. He had an unprepossessing torso, proportionately too long for his short legs, and his nose was so long that he grew a mustache to make it appear less noticeable. Instead of Nordic-blond, his hair was dark brown, and he was a monorchis—a possible indicator of sexual impotency.

When American columnist Dorothy Thompson first saw him, Hitler seemed anything but a superman. To her, he was "formless, almost faceless, a man whose countenance is a caricature, a man whose framework seemed cartilaginous..." He was "the very prototype of the Little Man."[46] This, and many other descriptions, strongly suggest that it could not have been the message-carrier that appealed to the German people, but the message and, since it was so powerful and welcome, after awhile its bearer's glaring personal defects were transmuted by his audiences into the most enthralling attributes.

Consequently, any study of Hitler must ultimately come to grips with his message whose essence, time and time again, he emphasized, was the need to root out the "Jewish poison," first from the German homeland and then from the rest of the world. It is the message that began formulating in his mind in Vienna after he saw his first Jew in a caftan. Until then, he claimed, he had been offended by anti-Semitic attacks in the Viennese press. But now, he began to think more and more about Jews and to read anti-Semitic books and pamphlets. He came to "recognize the Jew as the leader of social democracy."

He related how the scales fell from his eyes and "a long soul struggle had reached its conclusion."[47] Once this soul, or mental struggle had ended, Hitler ceased to be a "weak-kneed cosmopolitan and became an anti-Semite."[48] And since he had come to associate all things liberal-democratic with the Jewish spirit, he was, in effect, trying to kill this spirit from within his own mind and which he, along with all Europeans, had inherited in its Christian form. The essence of this spirit is the moral conscience which cuts across limiting ideas of soil and race that were the underpinnings of the identity Hitler acquired from Greek and Roman models. "Conscience," he declared, was "a Jewish invention" that he vowed to wipe out.[48]

From the end of his mental struggle, Jew hatred became his life's dynamic, propelling him on a mission to obliterate from the world all vestiges of the Jewish spirit as he believed he had done in his own mind. He was like a *Laocoön* come to life, but instead of stoically accepting his fate, he launched into a death struggle with the serpent in the form of a deadly poisonous world Jewry that he believed included not only the Jews, but Christianity, Communism, Freemasonry, international finance, and social democracy. Having ended his mental struggle, Hitler left Vienna for the quintessential German city of Munich where his political struggle would begin. Instead of just thinking and talking about killing Jews, as so many Germans and fellow Austrians had done, he would seek the power to actually kill them—not sporadically through emotional pogroms as had been done before in history as a partial solution to the Jewish "problem"—but systematically and "rationally" to achieve the "Final Solution."

But before he could translate his mental struggle into a political struggle, the First World War began. Hitler was among the thousands who crowded Munich's Odeonsplatz on August 1, 1914, to cheer the announcement that Germany would go to war. And despite the fact that he had evaded the draft in Austria, Hitler volunteered for service in the German army. Two days after he stood cheering in the Odeonsplatz, he petitioned Bavaria's King Ludwig III for permission to join a Bavarian regiment. The next day he received an affirmative reply with orders to report for duty with the List Regiment. After less than ten weeks of training, he was sent to the Front where he witnessed the Battle of Ypres, one of the bloodiest engagements of the war. It was a crucial battle in which the German High Command sought to make a breakthrough to the English Channel. But after four days of fighting, the British held off the Germans, and the List Regiment alone lost half of its 3,500 men.

Throughout the war, Hitler was a runner who carried dispatches and mail from regimental headquarters to frontline positions, and sometimes, much to his annoyance, his duties were carried out during daylight instead of at night. He later speculated that some twenty thousand runners were "uselessly sacrificed" on missions that could have been accomplished at night with less danger. "How often I had to face a powerful artillery barrage, in order to carry a simple postcard,"[49] he complained.

Various legends have survived about Hitler's bravery, and there is little reason to doubt them. But the specifics of his heroic acts are open to question. One of the most persistent stories is that while carrying dispatches he came across fifteen French soldiers in a trench near Montdidier, and succeeded in single-handedly capturing them, and bringing them back to his command post. But whatever the circumstances of his valor may have been, the record is clear that in December 1914, only a few months after enlisting, Hitler was awarded the Iron Cross second class, and in May 1918, he received a regimental certificate for bravery. Again on August 4 of that same year he received the Iron Cross first class, a rare honor for an enlisted man. Historians have searched in vain for details as to why he received these honors, and compounding the mystery is the fact that a noncombatant runner would have fewer opportunities to display heroism than combat soldiers. Ironically, too, Hitler had been considered several times for promotion to noncommissioned officer, but was turned down because it was felt that he had no leadership qualities.

In October 1916, Hitler was slightly wounded on the left thigh while exposed to action at Le Barqué, and he was sent to Beelitz Hospital in Berlin. He remained in Germany until March 1917, and was enraged at the defeatist attitude he observed among civilians and fellow soldiers being treated at the hospital. His anger at such attitudes had already been provoked by letters his comrades at the front had shared with him, and was reflected in letters he wrote to acquaintances in Germany. In one of these, addressed to Ernest Hepp, an assistant judge in Munich, Hitler described how he and his army comrades wished that they might get a chance to "even scores with *that crew*, to get at them no matter what the cost, and that those of us who are lucky enough to return to the Fatherland, will find it a purer place, less riddled with *foreign* influences, so that the daily sacrifices and sufferings of thousands of us and the torrent of blood that keeps flowing here day after day against an *international world of enemies* will not only help to smash Germany's foes outside but our *inner internationalism*, too, will collapse..."[50] (My italics.)

The significance of this letter has not been fully appreciated. It was written during the early stages of war when hopes were still high for a German victory, and long before the harangues would mount about a "stab-in-the-back" by Germany's supposed "internal enemies." More importantly, however, is that the letter, dated February 15, 1915, contains, in general form, the basic ingredients that would be reiterated in *Mein Kampf*, in speeches, monologues, and conversations throughout Hitler's life. "Purer place" incorporated his "master" or "pure race" notions, and "foreign influences," "that crew," "international world of enemies," and "inner internationalism" were synonyms for Jewry in all of its real and imagined forms, which he would later set out to "smash" both inside and outside of Germany. Some of Hitler's comrades who were "lucky enough" to return to the Fatherland were among those who provided the Stormtroop nucleus for smashing Germany's internal foes. As Hitler said on many occasions, he carried with him throughout his life the basic views he had developed as a consequence of his mental struggle in Vienna, and the Hepp letter clearly indicates that such was the case.

The hatred against international Jewry, that had been germinating since his Vienna days, was aggravated by his war experience. As a first-class private, or lance corporal, Hitler placed his confidence in the generals to achieve Germany's victory over the "international world of enemies." And, unlike most army privates whose thoughts and feelings are often centered on private matters such as a letter from wife or sweetheart, family, or friends, or when they are going to get their next beer or cigarette, Hitler served out his time, friendless, beerless, and fretting about the larger, general concerns of the generals and politicians. He had no wife or sweetheart that he could correspond with, and he could expect no letters from his parents since they were both dead.

There can be no question that, for Hitler, his army service was an important experience. Unlike the rejections he had received in Vienna from the fine arts academy, the army had given him his first major psychological reinforcements through the Iron Cross and other awards. The army became his "irreplaceable school," and it was to it that Germany owed everything; it was the guardian of the race against the rapid encroachments of internationalism, as exemplified in the stock exchange, communism, and world Jewry. The army had trained men for unconditional responsibility at a time when this quality had become rare, and was becoming more so because of the "model prototype of all irresponsibility, the parliament..." The army was the school that still taught the individual German not to "seek salvation of the nation in the lying phrases about an international brotherhood of Negroes, Germans, Chinese, French, etc., but in the force and solidarity of our own nation."[51]

That the army was no match for the "insidious battle" being fought by the "international world of enemies," became clear to Hitler soon after he was temporarily blinded by gas during the Battle of Flanders in October 1918. South of Ypres on October 13, the British launched a gas attack that lasted for several hours. The next morning, when Hitler arrived at his command post, his eyes were burning "like glowing coals," and he could not see. He was sent to Pasewalk Hospital in Pomerania where, on November 10, 1918, he and his comrades learned from the hospital pastor that the imperial House of Hohenzollern had been overthrown and replaced by a social democratic republic. To Hitler, this was "the greatest villainy of the century" and the pastor's announcement caused everything to go black before his eyes. "I tottered and groped my way back to the dormitory," he recorded, "threw myself on my bunk, and dug my burning head into my blanket and pillow. Since the day I had stood at my mother's grave, I had not wept." In the nights that followed, Hitler recounted, "hatred grew in me, hatred for those responsible for this deed."

Hitler would bitterly reflect that Kaiser Wilhelm II was the first German emperor to hold out a conciliatory hand to Marxist leaders who, while shaking the imperial hand in theirs, reached for a dagger with their other hand. "There is no making pacts with Jews," Hitler noted, "there can only be the hard: either—or. I, for my part, decided to go into politics."[52] Thus, from the very beginning, the Jews were irrevocably linked with Hitler's political intentions.

As it turned out, the Army not only helped clarify his political views, which received their "granite foundation" during his mental struggle in Vienna, but helped in the transition from his mental to his political struggle. Hitler's *Reichswehr* (army) superior had ordered him to prepare a report in response to questions posed about Jewry by one

49

Adolph Gemlich. Submitted on September 16, 1919, during the aftermath of war, the report encapsulated the ideas that had been fermenting in Hitler's mind since his mental struggle in Vienna had ended. The Gemlich report predated by six years the publication of the first volume of *Mein Kampf* in 1925, and shows that Hitler's political intention had been clearly formulated by at least 1919; actually earlier when one considers the Hepp letter of 1915. This is further supported by his own statement that the "granite foundation" of his philosophy had been set in Vienna even before the war.

The Gemlich report contains his insistence that the Jews are a race, and not a religion, as well as the distinction between a "rational" as opposed to an "emotional" anti-Semitism. In Hitler's mind, all prior historical expressions of anti-Semitism had given rise to emotional pogroms which were merely partial solutions to the Jewish "problem." He sought to forge a "rational" anti-Semitism that would result in the "Final Solution" to the Jewish "problem."

The report constitutes what would become the cornerstone of Hitler's political philosophy, and shows that Nazism did not give rise to anti-Semitism, but was its evil offspring. As his report expressed it: "...anti-Semitism very easily; acquires the character of a mere manifestation of the emotions. And this is not as it should be. Anti-Semitism regarded *as a political movement*, should not and cannot be understood in emotional terms but only through a knowledge of the facts. The *Final Aim* must be the deliberate removal of the Jews. Both (objectives) are only possible through a government of national strength, not a government of national impotence."[53] Containing, as it does, the seed ideas for achieving the "Final Solution" to the Jewish "problem," the Gemlich report was the outcome of Hitler's mental struggle in Vienna that became clarified during his army service. It also owes a debt to two Austrian political parties that Hitler had studied in Vienna. In *Mein Kampf*, he describes his attraction to the Pan-German party of August Georg von Schonerer and Karl Lueger's Christian Socialist Movement. But even though there were aspects of Lueger's party that he admired, Hitler thought that Lueger did not really understand the Jewish "danger" because his anti-Semitism was founded on a view of Jewry as a religion, and not as a race.

Hitler felt that Lueger made the mistake of playing down racial issues in order to win over a large mass of people from Austria's many ethnic groups, and at the same time opposing the Jews on purely religious grounds. To Hitler, this method of combating the Jews would give no cause for concern since "If the worst came to the worst, a splash of baptismal water could always save the business, and the Jew at the same time." But, if the Jews were regarded as a race, such a conversion would not be possible. Lueger's whole movement, therefore, came to "look more and more like an attempt at a new conversion of the Jews, or perhaps even an expression of a certain competitive envy. Hence, the struggle lost the character of an inner and higher consecration...Lacking was the conviction that this was a vital question for all humanity, with the fate of all non-Jewish peoples depending on its solution."[54] In other words, the Jews were a "problem," not only for Germans, but for "all humanity," and it would be necessary to block the escape of the Jews by means of religious conversion that had been open to Jews in medieval times. If only as a political tactic, therefore, it was essential to insist they were a race and not a religion.

Clearly, Hitler already had the "Final Solution" strategy worked out in his mind. For this reason, he felt that Schonerer's Pan-Germans had based their anti-Semitism on "a correct understanding of the importance of the racial problem, and not on religious ideas."[55] The essence of much that Hitler thought, said, and did is contained in the distinction he made between race and religion. It represents the political counterpart to the ideas of 19th Century natural and physical sciences in which the human mind was seen as rooted in biology and physiology. Books on the physiological basis of the mind were commonplace and, with Darwin's *Origin of the Species*, were popularly perceived as a denial of human spirituality and God-created uniqueness. One writer whose works are known to have been read by Hitler was Ernst Haeckel, a biologist and philosopher, who wrote that nobody "speaks any longer of a 'moral order,' or a personal God, whose 'hand has disposed all things in wisdom and understanding'...Darwin, by his theory of selection, has shown that the orderly processes in the life and structure of animals and plants have arisen mechanically without any preconceived design, but he has taught us to recognize, in the 'struggle for existence,' the powerful force of nature..."[56]

Literature, too, held out many examples of this way of thinking. One of these being Turgenev's *Fathers and Sons* in which the young biologist, Bazarov, sees nothing spiritual in man, and yet finds himself caught in an inexplicable emotional turmoil when he falls in love which, as a scientist, he cannot explain in scientific language. He tells two houseboys "I'm going to split the frog open to see what's going on inside of him; since you and I are no different from frogs, except that we walk on our hind legs, I'll find out what's happening inside of us too." By scientific dissection, Bazarov believes it is possible to discover *what* a frog or a human is and yet, Anna Odintsova, the woman he comes to love, observes that Bazarov does not know *who* he is.[57] (My italics.)

Like Bazarov, Hitler, too, saw no difference between humans and all other animals, and he noted that "recent experiments make it possible for one to wonder what distinguishes live bodies from inanimate matter."[58] He saw the "myths of religion crumbling with the advance of science" until all that would be left "is to prove that in nature there is no frontier between the organic and the inorganic."[59] Armed with such superficial understanding of what the new sciences were discovering, Hitler saw race as the supreme value which he linked to blood, and a crude version of the Darwinian struggle for survival which, with humans, took the form of politics.

As he expressed it, "politics is, in truth, the execution of a nation's struggle for existence...consequently politics is always the leader of the struggle for existence..."[60] This ties in with Hitler's view of the state as being a fixed, or static, thing whereas politics was movement and struggle. Presumably this struggle would end only when the German national revolution was extended throughout the world, and all Jews and Jewish influences had been extirpated. When Germany finally dominated the world and ushered in a new world order, there would be no more struggle for survival since all other races would have been mastered by the "Master Race" and, under Hitler's leadership, Germany would have succeeded, where no other race had, in transcending Nature's "unbreakable" laws.

But just how one could be subservient to Nature's laws and above them at the same time is one of the innumerable contradictions that Hitler never addressed himself to. Indeed, it was habitual for him to hold mutually contradictory views. "Nothing that is made of flesh and blood," he said, "can escape the laws which determined its coming into being. As soon as the human mind believes itself to be superior to them (Nature's laws), it destroys that real substance (the body) which is the bearer of the mind."[61]

In the struggle for survival, Hitler believed that Jewry had inspired social democracy, communism, parliamentarianism, and other devices by which the weak banded together to defeat the naturally strong, and thus tried to upset the natural order. To counteract this, a philosophy of life had to be developed to reject the democratic mass idea and "give this earth to the best people, that is, the highest humanity," and must "logically obey the same aristocratic principle within a people and make sure that the leadership, and the highest influence of this people fall to the best minds. Thus, it builds, not upon the idea of majority, but upon the idea of personality."[62]

There was, of course, nothing "logical" in Hitler's so-called "aristocratic principle." As with much that he espoused, his ideas were loaded with gross inconsistencies, not the least of which was his assertion that nature determines everything in the universe through the struggle for survival it implants in its creatures. If that were the case, he did not explain how the Jews, or anyone else, could escape from nature's rigid laws to correct them, or how the Nazis could hope to rise above those laws. In addition, if one were to accept his description of the near domination of the world by Jewish influences, one would have to concede that not the Germans, but the Jews, were at the highest level of evolutionary development. But, since the Jews represent a minuscule proportion of the world's people, it is even more incredible that, *as a race*, they could have influenced the world to such a degree as he asserted; if they had, there would have been no Holocaust. It is only when Jewry is considered as a *spiritual* or *religious* influence that such an idea would be understandable, yet it is precisely this consideration which Hitler overruled when he categorically insisted that Jewry represented a race and *not* a religion. His assertion, however, should not be taken at face value, but must be viewed as a tactical device. He had to insist that the Jews were a race in order to exterminate them. To admit that they were unified by their religion and not by race would have undermined his whole political philosophy based on race and leadership. Furthermore, Hitler's idea of fusing the mass of people in allegiance to one person (himself) reflects, in a way that democracy does not, the very principle he denounced of the weak deriving strength from the group. Despite what he claimed, democracy, even with its imperfections, opens up the possibility for the exploration of individual talents through the exercise of freedom. Instead of submitting one's personality to a hero-leader, democracy prepares the economic, political, and cultural climate that allows more individuals to become their own heroes.

The key to Hitler's view of the human species is contained in his concept of race which not only defies rational explanation, but is totally unsupported by historical and biological evidence. It is possible, however, that either consciously or unconsciously, he also saw in the race concept a device for unifying his people. Linked as it is to blood and soil, the race concept is inextricably bound to nature and the organic. The problem arises, however, when people do not act as an organic whole in the inexorable way they are supposed to. Hitler got around this difficulty by asserting that once in a while a rare individual, a personality of genius, emerges to lead the race in its struggle for survival. The biological mechanism by which this genius is produced is dogmatically asserted, but never explained, and since the genius is self-designated, there is none other at his level to refute him. Under this strange "organic" concept, totalitarianism becomes its most fitting political expression with the Fuhrer (the head) directing the movements of the rest of the body.

Under normal circumstances, as an organism struggling for survival, the German volk, by Hitler's theory, would function naturally and holistically, as supposedly it did in the remoteness of its Teutonic past, but if invaded by a germ, then the Volk would react like any other organism and become diseased, perhaps fatally, unless the germ was destroyed under the genius personality's leadership. This is precisely how Hitler viewed not only Germany, but the entire "Aryan" race (a term he used in a most unscientific way), as being poisoned by the invading germ of world Jewry in its many avatars. Before he could reinvigorate the folkish state, his first task would be to "eliminate the existing (all-pervasive) Jewish one."[65] Such were the ideas that he first worked out during his mental struggle in Vienna, clarified during his army service, and prepared him for his political struggle.

CHAPTER ONE: BIBLIOGRAPHY

1 Heinrich von Kleist, *The Marquise of O and Other Stories*, tr. David Luke and Nigel Reeves (New York: Penguin Books, 1978) 80.

2 Konrad Heiden, *Der Fuehrer* (Boston: Houghton Mifflin, 1944) 214.

3 Friedrich Nietzsche, *A Nietszche Reader* (London: Penguin Classics, 1977) 283.

4 Stefan George, *The Poet in Troublous Times* as cited by E.M. Butler in *The Tyranny of Greece Over Germany* (Boston: Beacon Press, 1958) x.

5 Robert Payne, *The Life and Death of Hitler* (New York: Praeger Publishers, Inc., 1973) 53.

6 Robert G.L. Waite, *The Psychopathic God* (New York: Basic Books, Inc., 1977) 10.

7 Adolf Hitler, *Mein Kampf* (Boston: Houghton Mifflin Co., 1971) 454.

8 George Mosse, *Nazi Culture* (New York: Grosset and Dunlop, 1973) 105.

9 Johann Wolfgang von Goethe, *The Sorrows of Young Werther*, tr. Elizabeth Mayer and Louise Bogan (New York: Vintage Books, 1973) 132.

10 Hitler, *Mein Kampf* 123.

11 Hitler, *Mein Kampf* 56.

12 Sebastian Haffner, *The Meaning of Hitler* (New York: Macmillan Publishing Co., 1979) 6.

13 Nigel Hamilton, *The Brothers Mann* (New Haven Press, 1979) 305.

14 Werner Maser, *Hitler's Letters and Notes* (New York: Bantam Books, 1976) 175.

15 Waite 45.

16 Waite 153.

17 Waite 155.

18 Isaiah Berlin, *Concepts and Categories* (New York: Penguin Books Ltd., 1981) 178-77.

19 Sigmund Freud and William C. Bullitt, *Thomas Woodrow Wilson: A Psychological Study* (Boston: Houghton Mifflin, 1966) 106.

20 Karl Marx, *The Portable Marx* (New York: Viking Penguin, Inc., 1983) 288.

21 Berlin 171.

22 *New Testament*, King James version (New York: The World Publishing Co., 1948) St. Luke 23:24.

23 H.R. Trevor Roper, intro. *Hitler's Secret Conversations* (New York: Signet Books, 1961) 37.

24 Roper, 37.

25 Edmund Wilson, *A Piece of My Mind* (New York: Farrar, Straus & Cudahy, 1956) 88.

26 Erik Erikson, *Young Man Luther* (New York: W.W. Norton Co., Inc., 1956) 88.

27 William Barrett and Daniel Yankelovich, *Ego and Instinct* (New York: Random House, 1970) 436.

28 Simone Weil, *Selected Essays* (London: Oxford University Press, 1962) 119.

29 Weil 119.

30 Hitler, *Mein Kampf* 423.

31 Telford Taylor, intro. *Hitler's Secret Book* (New York: Bramhall House, 1986) 18.

32 B. Jowett, *The Dialogues of Plato*, 4 vols. (New York: Charles Scribner's, 1871) 575.

33 Butler 333.

34 Butler 46.

35 William L. Shirer, *The Rise and Fall of the Third Reich* (New York: Simon & Schuster, 1960) 966.

36 Lucy S. Dawidowicz, *The War Against the Jews* (New York: Holt, Rinehart & Winston, 1975) 165.

37 Payne 5.

38 Susan Sontag, *Under the Sign of Saturn* (New York: Farrar, Straus, Giroux, 1980) 102.

39 J. Oxenford, *Goethe's Conversations With Eckermann* (London: George Bell & Sons, 1898) 97.

40 Hans Kohn, *The Mind of Germany* (New York: Charles Scribner's, 1960) 117.

41 Butler 335.

42 Gilbert Highet, *The Classical Tradition* (New York: Oxford University Press, 1971) 289.

43 Kohn 203.

44 Kohn 234.

45 Marion K. Sanders, *Dorothy Thompson* (Boston: Houghton Mifflin Co., 1973) 168.

46 Hitler, *Mein Kampf* 60.

47 Hitler, *Mein Kampf* 64.

48 Alan Bullock, *Hitler: A Study in Tyranny* (New York: Perennial Press Library, Harper & Row, 1971) 216.

49 Roper 80.

50 Maser 88.

51 Hitler *Mein Kampf* 280.

52 Hitler *Mein Kampf* 203-206.

53 Payne 130-131.

54 Hitler *Mein Kampf* 120.

55 Hitler *Mein Kampf* 120.

56 Ernst Haeckel, *Die Weltrathsel* (Bonn: 1900) 121, 311, 14.

57 Ivan Turgenev, *Fathers and Sons*, tr. Barbara Makanowitzky (New York: Bantam Books, 1963), 16.

58 Roper 106.

59 Taylor 7.

60 Taylor 5.

61 Hitler, *Mein Kampf* 443.

62 Hitler, *Mein Kampf* 453.

CHAPTER 2

❧

POLITICAL STRUGGLE

"I had no intention of joining a ready-made party," Hitler related in *Mein Kampf*, "but wanted to found one of my own."¹ But after giving a spontaneous and fiercely anti-Semitic speech in the fall of 1919 at the small *Deutsche Arbeiterpartei* (German Workers' Party), its founder, Anton Drexler, thrust a booklet into his hand entitled *My Political Awakening*. It described Drexler's development as a nationalist, and reminded Hitler of his own mental struggle and awakening in Vienna that would set him on the path to "awaken Germany." ("Germany Awake" would later become a familiar Nazi rallying cry).

A few days later, Hitler received a postcard advising that he had been made a member, and inviting him to the party's next committee meeting. Bemused by this method of recruiting members, and despite his aversion to joining a "ready-made party," Hitler decided that this "absurd little organization" was not yet fixed, or big enough that it could not be molded into the "proper form." Its goal could still be determined "in a way that would be impossible in the existing major parties..." He was convinced that through "such a little movement the rise of the nation could some day be organized, but never through the political parliamentary parties which clung far too greatly to the old conceptions, or even shared in the profits of the new (republican) regime. For it was a new philosophy and not a new election slogan that had to be proclaimed." It was, he acknowledged, a "grave decision to begin transforming this intention into reality."[2]

The German Workers' Party (GWP) was one of many fiercely nationalist, right-wing organizations in Munich, most of which were laced with anti-Semitism to greater or lesser degrees. Drexler, a Munich locomotive yard locksmith, founded the party on January 5, 1918, at the *Furstenfelder Hof*, a small beer tavern where he attracted more than twenty persons, most of them locomotive workers. The GWP was an outgrowth of the *Politscher Arbeiter-zirkel* (Political Workers' Circle) that Drexler had formed with Karl Harrer, a journalist from the rightist *Müncher-Augsburger Abend-Zeitung*. Even after the GWP was formed, the circle continued to meet, at least until late in 1919, as a kind of inner group of the party. Membership numbered roughly two hundred, but attendance at regular meetings was usually about thirty or forty, and in order to give the impression of being a much larger party, its membership numbers were greatly inflated. Thus, when Hitler joined, his membership card listed him as Number 555, and as a committee member, he became Number 7. A similar deception was practiced by referring to the "Munich branch" of the party with the clear implication that it was only one branch of a multi-branch national organization.

When Hitler joined the party in September 1919, he was still in the army and was assigned to give "citizenship courses" to *Reichswehr* (regular army soldiers) which were really rightist propaganda lectures. A constant theme of the talks was the condemnation of the Versailles (peace) Treaty, viewed by many Germans as excessively punitive even though republican Finance Minister Dernberg wrote in the *Berliner Tageblatt*, "Not one, no not one of the rapacious and oppressive clauses (in the treaty) is without its precedent in the proposals which the (German) right and many national liberals made during the war in anticipation of a German victory."[3] Dernberg's observation was supported by the Brest-Litovsk Treaty that Germany imposed on Russia on March 2, 1918. Under this treaty, Russia was forced to give up territory as large as Turkey and Austria-Hungary combined and with a population of fifty-six million. In addition, it was required to donate a third of its railroads, 73 per cent of its iron ore, 89 per cent of its coal, more than 5,000 factories and industrial units, and six million marks as an indemnity. In Eastern Europe, Hitler, who liked to refute accusations that Brest-Litovsk was more excessive than the Versailles Treaty, demonstrated a brutality and severity that went far beyond either and, had he won the war, would have meant total terror and subjugation for all conquered peoples.

Hitler's charges of a "stab-in-the-back," resulting in Germany's surrender, were also unfounded. Field Marshal von Hindenburg, chief of the army's high command, and General Erich von Ludendorff, the quartermaster-general, both realized months before war's end that it could not be won, and they were preparing for peace before the social democratic revolution took place. Nevertheless, it was Hindenburg who, without justification, first raised the cry of "stab-in-the-back," that Hitler so frequently used. It had the effect of preserving the army's reputation while heaping the blame for defeat on the social democratic government whose representatives were given the ignominious job of signing the instruments of surrender. The truth is that the caste-consciousness of the Junker officer corps resulted in the army going to war with fewer men than it should have. In 1913, the year before the war began, the army's "old guard" rejected a general staff proposal for the formation of three new army corps. This, however, would have meant the recruitment of officers from the bourgeois class, and that was something that the military's traditionalist nobility would not accept. It was a classic example of "for want of a nail a shoe was lost, and for want of a shoe, the horse was lost."

Even before his discharge from the army in March 1920, Hitler had already taken steps that would turn the GWP into a "party of my own." A measure of his rapid influence was that within four months of joining the party, he was already proposing drastic reforms that focused on granting the executive committee a great deal more authority. It was his first bid for that absolute control that he felt was essential to his political struggle. His attempts in this direction were at first rebuffed, but Hitler soon found other ways to assert his will.

As the party's propaganda director, he won majority support for expanding propaganda activities under the justification that this would attract more members and more money for the party treasury. Harrer, who liked to think things out before making a decision, disliked Hitler's impulsiveness, and abhorred his hate-filled oratory. He opposed Hitler on the propaganda proposal, and when he was outvoted, he resigned from the party, the first casualty of Hitler's political struggle, and the first example of how the democratic procedure of voting, that Hitler so much despised, would be cynically used to his benefit.

Partly, or according to Hitler, largely because of his propaganda skills, the party was soon in a position to rent an office, acquire basic materials, and hire a full-time business manager. And since he was in charge of propaganda, he was authorized to do the hiring. In an obviously opportunistic move, he hired Rudolph Schussler, a regimental comrade, who was among the first of many *Reichswehr* veterans and *Freikorps* (Free Corps) members that Hitler would recruit for the party because they shared his nationalist and anti-Semitic views, and enhanced his power and influence within the party. The *Freikorps* were armed bands, mostly veterans who were excluded from the *Reichswehr's* postwar strength under the Versailles Treaty's limitations. In the immediate postwar years, *Freikorps* units sprouted throughout Germany, and provided the foundation for cadres of bullies who would use terrorist tactics to help Hitler gain national power. They provided the nucleus for the Stormtroops (*Stürmabteilung*) or SA, which, along with the *Schutzstaffel* (SS), or guard detachment, would forever become infamously associated with Nazism and mass murder. Deprived of its link to the monarchy, and faced with serving a republican government it could not stomach, the army began to see in the Nazis the only hope for national revival. Consequently, despite the army's elitist disdain for some of the Nazi rabble and their "Bohemian corporal" leader, increasing, and usually secret, support was provided for the upstart party. The underlying and mistaken assumption was that by aiding the Nazis, the army would be in a position to control them.

Confronted with the GWP's "absurd little organization" that he thought was little more than a debating society, Hitler developed several strategies that he felt were essential to molding it into a mass movement. He had to gain control of the party, then abolish its parliamentary form which he associated with social democracy and world Jewry. As he put it, parliamentary democracy, and the popular press, were among the Jewish-inspired means by which "cattle become masters." But, before achieving his aims, Hitler would make himself indispensable by proving that he could appeal to the masses.

In this he was fortunate that Captain Karl Mayr of the Munich *Reichswehr* singled him out to conduct propaganda courses because he was impressed with Hitler's rhetorical skills, as well as his political orientation. This, and the impact he had on the GWP when he gave his first impromptu speech to its members, had convinced Hitler that his greatest asset was his oratory. Since joining the GWP, he also had been speaking to larger audiences. Before he joined the party, the audiences numbered in the thirties and forties, but by November 1919, only three months after he joined, the party was attracting up to three hundred people.

Hitler gave the clear impression that the increased numbers were solely due to his speeches, but the fact is that he was sometimes only one of several speakers who often preceded him on the platform. He also took credit for planning the party's first truly mass meeting on February 24, 1920, in the two-thousand-seat *Hofbrauhaus*. At this meeting, the party's twenty-five point program was presented. Drexler who, with Hitler and others, had hammered out the final program, would record that it was he, and not Hitler, who had proposed the *Hofbrauhaus* meeting over Hitler's objections.

Always sensitive to dramatic effects and the right psychological moment, Hitler reportedly was fearful that the party could not fill such a large hall. It is more likely that his greater fear was that he would fail to spellbind his first mass audience. But whatever the reason for his hesitancy, it is obvious from his description of the event that he considered it an important milestone in his political struggle. Certainly it was the largest audience he had faced until that time, and it was also the occasion for publicly making known the party's main goals which called, among other things, for the denial of citizenship to Jews on the grounds that they could not be "racial comrades" because they were not of German blood. As for the Jewish-materialistic spirit "within and around us," this would have to be combated by the party as it struggled to establish the union of all Germans in a Greater Germany. The peace treaties of Versailles and St. Germain would, of course, be scrapped.

The beerhall meeting was certainly the largest that Hitler had faced until that time, and it was also a test of his drawing power as a speaker, as well as the strength of support for the party's platform. It was also crucial to his struggle for party leadership. In the *Festsaal* of the Munich *Hofbrauhaus*, he related, "the twenty-five theses of the new party's program were submitted to a crowd of almost two thousand and every single point was accepted amid jubilant approval."[4] And, in his bloated writing style, Hitler noted that these "first guiding principles and directives were issued for a struggle which was to do away with a veritable mass of old traditional conceptions and opinions and with unclear, yes, harmful aims. Into the rotten and cowardly world and into the triumphant march of the Marxist wave of conquest a new power phenomenon was entering, which at the eleventh hour would halt the chariot of doom."[5]

Naturally, Hitler's account of the event spotlights his own speech with the implication that it was the only one that really mattered. But, in fact, he was preceded by a homeopathic physician, who was billed as the main speaker. Four others were on the platform as well. A police report described the meeting as verging, at times, on a riot because of the presence of about a hundred socialist and Communist hecklers who drowned out some of

Hitler's words. Hitler's version is that when he took to the floor, there were violent clashes between the party's Stormtroops and the reds, who were quickly subdued, and the meeting was again brought to order. But, as Hitler went over the twenty-five points, the audience accepted them "one after another with steadily mounting joy… and when the last thesis had found its way to the heart of the masses, there stood before me a hall full of people united by a new conviction, a new faith, a new will." The principles of a movement which could no longer be forgotten "were moving among the German people."[6]

Munich's newspapers were much more brief and pedestrian in their accounts of the beerhall meeting and their focus was not on Hitler's speech, but on the homeopathic physician's. The advent of a German messiah or the birth of a new secular faith was not recorded. However inflated Hitler's account of his part in the *Hofbrauhaus* meeting might be, it is clear that he saw it as being of great significance in his climb to power. He may have been impressed, on the one hand, by his ability to hold the attention of a mass audience and, on the other hand, he undoubtedly saw the necessity for a dedicated band of strong-arm men to keep the opposition in check—a combination he would use successfully throughout his political struggle. He may have seen, in the clash between the Stormtroops and the reds, a foreshadowing of the ultimate clash between nationalists and international socialists that was to come to Germany and Europe.

Following the *Hofbrauhaus* meeting, Hitler was foremost in urging larger and more frequent meetings, and he worked tirelessly so that he could make himself indispensable to the party. As a consequence, by early 1921 when the party had grown to about 3,000 members, and held its largest rally to date in the 6,500-seat Krone's Circus, Hitler and Drexler were no longer seeing eye-to-eye on the party's aims and future. The showdown was triggered during Hitler's absence in Berlin. Drexler had taken moves that appeared to be aimed at merging the party with another nationalist, but more truly socialist, group in the Hanover region of northern Germany.

Drexler, a weak-willed alcoholic, might have hoped that by merging with another party, Hitler's support from his ex-army comrades and *Freikorps* members would be offset by the newcomers. If that were so, it was a gross miscalculation of Hitler's ruthless determination to gain absolute control, as well as a failure on Drexler's part to recognize that he did not have the backbone to stand up to Hitler. Furthermore, the merger proposal had been bandied about for months, and Hitler's strenuous opposition to it was well known. Apart from the possibility that the Hanover group's merger with the GWP would dilute his power, Hitler felt that its members were not fanatical enough, particularly in their anti-Semitism, the same fault he would find later in the army during his military struggle.

After returning to Munich on July 11, 1921, Hitler resigned, but left the door open for his return by submitting a lengthy letter that spelled out the conditions under which he would rejoin the party. These included the abandonment of the merger plan, the resignation of the executive committee headed by Drexler, and most important of all, the assignment of dictatorial authority to himself. It was one of those skillful tactics that were to become his hallmark and, in which he would gamble all on an intuitive assessment of his strength in relation to the opposition. Within a day of receiving Hitler's letter, the committee accepted his conditions and offered only feeble rebuttals to some of his assertions. The entire committee welcomed his dictatorship and acknowledged his "immense knowledge, exceptional oratorical skills, and rare self-sacrifice."[7]

Hitler quickly followed up on this victory. On July 29, before a meeting of more than 500 party members in the *Hofbrauhaus*, he announced that he was ready to assume the party leadership, and after clearly stating his political views and aspirations, he urged anyone who disagreed with him to leave the party. And, in what was to be the party's last parliamentary act, the members gave Hitler dictatorial power by a vote of 543 to 1. As the party later expanded and became a truly national organization, challenges to his authority would arise, but essentially from this point onward, Hitler maintained control.

No one except, perhaps, Hitler himself, could have envisaged the impact that this vote would have on world history. To Hitler, it marked the achievement of the first objective of his political struggle: to have a party of his own that embraced three basic principles. These included the requirements that the party must be *founded* on anti-Semitism; that Jewry be regarded as a race and not as a religion, and that the party's anti-Semitism must be "rational" and not "emotional." (My italics.) These were the pillars of Hitler's Nazi ideology that were to become much clearer to the world once they were put into action. "The National Socialist Movement," he would boast, "drove the Jewish question to the fore and succeeded in lifting this problem out of the narrow, limited circle of bourgeois and petit bourgeois strata, and transforming it into the driving impulse of a great people's movement."[8] Goebbels committed to his diary the observation that although the party was "subject to continuing changes and transformations, its one major constant was anti-Semitism."[9]

The party's twenty-five points contained compromises between Hitler's rabid anti-Semitism and nationalism, and those of the anticapitalist, socialist members of the party.

Hitler's demand for a pan-German state that would embrace all Germans, plus his insistence that the Versailles Treaty be scrapped, and that the Jews be stripped of all rights as citizens, were to be recurring themes that found expression in action, while the Drexler and more socialistic components fell by the wayside. Even before the crucial *Hofbrauhaus* meeting, the GWP had changed its name to the National Socialist German Workers' Party (NSDP, or Nazis). This reflected Hitler's desire for a mass party since the two great contemporary political currents were nationalism and socialism. The NSDP's socialism, however, was not what Drexler and others had envisioned. It bore no resemblance to leftist socialism, but was designed as a lure to increase the party's strength and broad-based support. As Hannah Arendt noted, "When public attention was equally focused on nationalism on one hand and socialism on the other; when the two were thought to be incompatible and actually constituted the ideological watershed between the right and the left, the National Socialist German Workers' Party offered a synthesis supposed to lead to national unity; a semantic solution whose double trademark of 'German' and 'Worker' connected the nationalism of the right with the internationalism of the left."[10] Franz Neumann has also shown how the Nazis shaped their phraseology in order to conquer the marxist masses to whom the terms would be familiar. Thus, Marxist "class struggle" would become the "proletarian war against capitalistic states;" the "labor theory of value," would be described as the "money fetish of the nation's productive power;" "classless society" would become the "people's community," and the "proletariat as the bearer of truth" was projected as the "German race" as the incarnation of morality.[11]

By the time Hitler assumed the party leadership, the membership was rapidly approaching the 10,000 mark, and had a distinct propaganda advantage by virtue of the acquisition in 1920 of the *Volkischer Beobachter*, a twice-weekly newspaper that became a daily and which benefited from party subscriptions. It became the party's official organ.

Lest anyone forget that the focus of Nazism was a world revolution aimed at supplanting what Hitler saw as the Jewish-dominated existing order in the world, with an "Aryan" new world order, Hitler chose the Swastika emblem for the party to symbolize "the struggle for victory of Aryan man... the victory of the idea of creative work which, as such, always has been and always will be anti-Semitic."[12] In its Nazi usage, the ancient Swastika symbol has been recognized as a symbolic twisting of the Christian cross, and was often referred to in Germany as the *Hakenkreuz* or crooked cross. As the German churches were to discover, it would be more than just a symbolic distortion of Christianity.

By 1922, the SA, whose members, with their Swastika armbands and brown shirts, constituted the formally recognized, uniformed party legion, became increasingly visible on the streets, and in halls where the party would hold demonstrations and rallies. By then, Hitler addressed crowds as large as fifty thousand; expanded party operations to other parts of Germany, and built the mass support that he felt was necessary to achieve a "national resurrection." He also attracted men who could be relied upon to do anything he ordered, including murder. Careers in the party were open to talents that could best devise methods for carrying out Hitler's intentions even, and often preferably, when those talents were criminal. "I do not look for people having clear ideas of their own," he said, "but rather people who are clever at finding ways and means of carrying out my ideas."[13]

Consequently, the party developed a bizarre egalitarianism in which criminals, murderers, army veterans, blue collar workers, wayward scholars, and intellectuals would rub shoulders with aristocrats, doctors, lawyers, and other professionals. Their common bond was a willingness to submerge their identities under the Führer's, and to dedicate their lives to obeying orders. And, just as in Vienna, Hitler felt he had rid himself of that Judeo-Christian "chimera" of conscience through what amounted to a moralectomy. His followers, too, became moral eunuchs whose distinctive feature was the cowardice of their amoral convictions. As he once told National Socialist President of the Danzig senate, Hermann Rauschning, his historical mission was to remove the "burden of conscience."[14]

Among the major willing subjects who were foremost in this experiment in overthrowing widely accepted human values were the likes of Heinrich Himmler, Hermann Goering, Joseph Goebbels, Reinhard Heydrich, Martin Bormann, Joachim von Ribbentrop, Alfred Rosenberg, Julius Streicher, Rudolph Hess, Hans Frank, Rudolph Hoess, and Adolph Eichmann. These, and lesser functionaries, each in his own way displayed a total absence of moral values and would, as Hitler had done in Vienna, and as Himmler was to say of Heydrich, that he had "overcome the Jew in himself."[15] All of these men contributed to the achievement of Hitler's *Weltanschaaung*, or world philosophy, and could say with Goering: "Adolph Hitler is my conscience."[16] Just as Hitler was their master, these men were bound by his amoral dogmatism not to serve the masses, but to become their masters. In this way, the so-called "Master Race" became, in fact, the mastered race. Auschwitz extermination camp commandant Rudolph Hoess expressed the quintessential Nazi attitude by saying, "Human emotions seemed to be a betrayal of the Führer."[17] In his wartime *Autumn Journal*, British poet Louis MacNiece offered a different perspective:

No wonder many would renounce their birthright,
The responsibility of moral choice,
And sit with a mess of potage taking orders
Out of a square box from a mad voice...

The Nazis, MacNiece wrote, "never sought more with their lives than permission to take orders."[18] In raising obedience to the highest virtue, the Nazis placed themselves in submission to Hitler, and demanded the same of others. Hitler's inflexible views on obedience were reflected in his attitude towards the unconditional responsibility of the military, but also by his choice of dogs. He preferred Alsatians because they were susceptible to obedience training, but despised dachshunds because of their reputed independence.

Hitler, the Mephistophelean leader that Himmler, Goering, and untold other Germans sold their souls to, was singularly lacking in those military habits he had been trained in, but which he demanded of others. Even after his release from the army, and when he was head of state and commander-in-chief of the armed forces, he retained something of his Bohemian would-be-artist habits by sleeping late in bed, and keeping a nocturnal schedule that included long, monotonous monologues directed at his staff.

He was essentially a person of the dark, not of the light, not only in his waking and sleeping habits, but also in his spiritual temper. Darkness, the time of night associated with fears, nightmares, murderous deeds, fantasies, dreams, and the realm of the subconscious, was the time that Hitler chose to mesmerize his followers. The Nazis became most infamous for their dark deeds that were carried out under the auspices of an elite group in black uniforms, and yet the Nazi ideology extolled the lightness of the ideal blond type. Sulla, a fair-haired, blue-eyed Roman featured in a popular German novel, was a favorite with Hitler and other Nazis. Indeed, Hitler was Germany's "Prince of Darkness"—a gargoyled philosopher-king who saw himself as called upon to serve his people and did so only out of a sense of duty. His idea of the "Volk" and "Aryanism" suggested a kind of ideal platonic realm of which the real world was but a mere shadow. This perverted platonism may have been the source of his strange voyeurism in which he did not take part in the murders he ordered, but took a necrophiliac's satisfaction in watching their execution on film.

As with the ancient Greeks, Hitler also saw the changes that time creates as being a disturbance of the timelessness of space and the world of organic nature. His distrust of time may have been linked to his anti-Semitism since it was Jewish influences that he insisted were disrupting the natural order of things. In Hebrew literature God created the world in a certain time, i.e., six days, and henceforth the Jews and God have become coworkers in history with certain tasks to perform. Because of its Jewish origins, this idea has become incorporated in the Christian tradition, thus, in both religious expressions, history is viewed as having a meaning that links past, present, and future. One consequence of such a linear view is the cultivation of time consciousness which has become the distinguishing feature between Western and all other civilizations, however rich their contributions have been to the human community.

Hitler's attitude towards time is significantly evident from the fact that he never wore a watch, the most ubiquitous modern symbol of time, and the one clock in his living quarters was not permitted to be wound. With his valet, Hitler would habitually play the game of "defeating time" by seeing how fast he could get dressed, and he had a penchant for racing against time as he was driven at high speeds along Germany's *Autobahnen*. He also set a four-year plan for the accomplishment of his first major goals, and regretted that the war did not start at least a year earlier (in 1938). He conducted that war like a man under great time pressure which, as will be suggested later, may have been one reason he did not invade England. His emphasis on the need for *Lebensraum*, which was linked to the extermination of the Jews, indicates that he may also have wanted to revert to a space-consciousness. In trying to exterminate Jewry, Hitler could be seen as trying to put an end to the eschatological dimension of history that the Jews gave to the world, and which envisions the realization of the identity of human origin and destiny. By "the Jew," as Ernst Nolte noted, Hitler meant the "historical process itself."[19]

By 1923, Hitler was like an impatient, nervous actor eagerly waiting to play his part on the world stage. Since the end of the war, events in Bavaria and throughout Germany became increasingly turbulent and were marked by economic and governmental crises, assassinations, post-war anxieties, astronomical inflation, and conflicts between the Reich and Bavarian governments. Bavaria provided a sort of dress rehearsal for the clash between nationalism and social democracy that was to involve the entire nation, and much of the world. In a bloodless revolution five years earlier, Social Democrats had established a Bavarian "People's State" under Kurt Eisner, a Jewish writer. But, within three months, Eisner was assassinated by a young right-wing officer. The workers then set up a Soviet republic, but this was soon crushed on May 1, 1919, in a bloody massacre by *Freikorps* and regular troops. Despite the restoration of a moderate social democratic government, Bavaria had made a definite move towards the right that was to favor Hitler's rise to power.

Bavaria provided a microcosm for what was to happen at the national level. On November 9, only two days before the armistice was signed, and two days after the social democratic republic was set up in Bavaria, a social democratic republic was proclaimed in Berlin. This signalled the abolition of the House of Hohenzollern and the numerous princedoms throughout Germany. Kaiser Wilhelm II abdicated and fled to Holland, and the Reich chancellor, Prince Max von Baden, resigned. The new republic's majority was led by social democrats Friedrich Ebert and Philipp Scheidemann. To the military and other rightists, even this moderate socialist government was anathema. Yet, while Hitler fumed at the 1918 social revolution, he was its most prominent beneficiary, for it was this social democratic event which broke the class barrier to politics and allowed Austrians of German descent to make Germany their home. The far left saw the revolution as a betrayal of the international socialist cause. Rosa Luxembourg and Karl Liebknecht, leaders of the Communist Sparticus League, were set on proclaiming a soviet republic, but they were no more successful than Communists in Bavaria. Even before they could carry out their plans, they were butchered by cavalry officers, but one more indication of the intense animosity the military felt towards socialism in any shape or form. On January 19, 1919, elections were held for a German national assembly. The governing social democrats won 13.8 million votes out of 30 million, and gained 185 of the 421 seats in the Reichstag. The Roman Catholic Center Party, the Democratic Party, and the National Liberals polled 11.5 million votes and picked up 166 seats. More than 3 million votes gave the conservative National People's Party

44 seats, and the right-wing German national People's Party had 19 deputies seated with a vote of 1.5 million.

The constitution of the new republic was thrashed out in a six-month debate, and then ratified on August 31, 1919. Borrowing from the best elements of the British and French cabinet-form governments, the American popular presidency, and Swiss referendum procedures, it contained one weakness that was later to prove fatal. In times of emergency, Article 48 granted dictatorial powers to the president. It was through this gap that Hitler would later create a national abyss.

From January to December, 1923, the value of the Mark had fallen from 18,000 to the dollar to worthless trillions to the dollar, and many Germans saw in this monetary crisis the great burden of reparations imposed by the Versailles Treaty. The truth is that a major contributing factor was that, as a device for escaping debt, the government let the mark decline. Meanwhile, some German industries were able to clear their debts by paying them off in highly inflated currency. Those who suffered most from inflation were the mass of Germans who were unable to buy basic food and clothing, and those whose savings were wiped out.

With a great degree of accuracy, even if it was self-serving, Hitler accused the state itself of becoming "the biggest swindler and crook." If, he asserted, "the horrified people notice that they can starve on billions (of Marks), they must arrive at this conclusion: We will no longer submit to a state which is built on the swindling idea of the majority. We want a dictatorship."[20]

With its consequent failure to meet reparations commitments, the German financial crisis triggered a move by the French and Belgians to take over Germany's rich industrial Ruhr region. This created a unifying spirit among Germans, many of whom for the first time rallied behind the Republican government. The dangers to his political future in such a development were not lost on Hitler, who recognized the expedient utility of having an enemy in order to unify the nation. But, at that particular time, France was the wrong enemy. He wanted the focus of blame and discord placed on the republican government which he associated with the "inner enemies" who must first be fought before taking on the external enemies among which France was certainly one. Hitler, therefore, took a singularly unpopular line by having his party oppose the government's passive resistance to the Ruhr takeover, but his party's stand was of no great consequence since it was then relatively unknown outside of Bavaria.

This changed, however, when the Bavarian and Reich governments clashed over the Ruhr issue. On September 26, 1923, Reich Chancellor Gustav Stresemann declared an end to passive resistance, and the resumption of reparations payments. The reaction from both right and left was furious. Stresemann and President Ebert invoked Article 48 to give precedent-setting emergency powers to Defense Minister Otto Gessler and Army Commander General von Seeckt. The emergency remained in effect until February 1924.

Bavaria's reaction was immediate. The cabinet declared its own emergency and granted Gustav Ritter von Kahr dictatorial powers as state commissioner. Kahr, a former Bavarian premier and right-wing monarchist, raised fears in Berlin that Bavaria might secede from the Reich and restore the Bavarian monarchy. Under the emergency powers, Bavaria was required to obey all Reich directives issued by General Otto von Lossow, Bavaria's *Reichswehr* commander; Colonel Hans von Seisser, state police chief, and Kahr.

Bavaria, however, refused to recognize the Reich state of emergency, and disobeyed Berlin's orders. As the Reich authorities prepared to act against Bavaria, Hitler weighed his chances of taking the biggest move yet in his political struggle—control, no less, of the Bavarian government as a prelude to forcibly moving on Berlin to seize the Reich government. In November 1923, he considered several plans before deciding on a course of action that had some of the aspects of a melodrama or comic opera. The locus of this event was Munich's large *Burgerbraukeller* on the evening of November 8. It was there that Commissioner Kahr was scheduled to outline Bavaria's stance in relation to the Reich. Colonel Seisser, Lossow, and other government officials were also to attend.

Fearing that Kahr might announce Bavaria's secession, and that a great political opportunity would have escaped him, Hitler alerted his Stormtroops. As Kahr launched into his speech, the Stormtroops surrounded the beer hall, and some of them mounted machine guns at the entrance. Pistol in hand, Hitler entered the hall, climbed dramatically onto a table, and called attention to himself by firing a shot into the ceiling. Then, accompanied by Rudolph Hess and a bodyguard, he walked to the platform, intimidating Kahr into letting him take over the podium. "The national revolution has begun,"[21] Hitler proclaimed, and he warned that six hundred armed men had the building surrounded; the Bavarian and Reich governments had been removed, a provisional government had been formed, and the army and police were marching on the city. Most of this was wish rather than fact.

At gunpoint, Hitler forced Kahr, Lossow, and Seisser into an adjacent room while Goering calmed the crowd by telling them that a new government was being formed. Having earlier sent an aide to fetch General Erich Ludendorff, Hitler informed the Bavarian government trio that they must join him in forming a new government in which they, and Ludendorff, would have high, though subordinate, positions to Hitler. None of the three would commit themselves and Hitler impulsively returned to the podium where he announced that the three had agreed to help him form a new national government. He then gave a brief speech unleashing his familiar tirades against the "November criminals" who had sold out their country, and the Versailles *Diktat*. Under his leadership, the new government would march on Berlin to save the German people—a march that, in his mind, had been inspired by Mussolini's "March on Rome" the previous year.

Meanwhile, Ludendorff, who had not been apprised of Hitler's plans beforehand, arrived and showed little initial enthusiasm for the *Putsch*, doubtless because he had no part in its planning, and also because he was to have a subordinate role to Hitler in the proposed new government. Reluctantly, however, he decided to go along with Hitler, and encouraged Kahr, Lossow, and Seisser to cooperate. They all returned to the platform with Hitler and made brief speeches before the gathering broke up. Hearing that Stormtroops had clashed with regular troops at a nearby army barracks, Hitler made the mistake of leaving the others in order to put an end to the trouble. Kahr, Lossow, and Seisser seized the opportunity of his absence to get away, and when Hitler returned later, expecting to find his new government subordinates hard at work and giving orders in preparation for the national revolution, they were gone and everything was at a standstill.

Kahr had actually moved his government to Regensburg, from which he ordered proclamations to be posted denouncing Hitler's actions, and reneging on their beerhall declarations of support which, because they were made under duress, were held to be null and void. For

Hitler, the worst aspect of Kahr's action was his outlawing of the NSDAP, and its associated fighting leagues, and the fear was also raised that, as an Austrian citizen, Hitler might be deported. For what Hitler regarded then as Kahr's treacherous act, he would pay for later with his life.

The next morning Ludendorff mustered more enthusiasm for the *Putsch*, which he thought could still be revived by marching into the city and taking over its central buildings. Because of his war hero status, he did not think the army and police would oppose him and so, shortly before 11 a.m. he, Hitler, Goering, and others led about three thousand Stormtroops from the *Burgerbrauer* area to the city center. On the Ludwig Bridge over the Isar River they were halted by armed police, who allowed them to pass only after Goering threatened to kill some hostages at the rear of the column. By noon, the marchers approached the War Ministry where, since the previous night, Stormtroop Commander Ernst Rohm and his men were surrounded by *Reichswehr* troops. As they traversed the narrow *Redenzstrasse* that leads to the broad *Odeonsplatz*, about a hundred police blocked the route, and during the consequent confusion a shot was fired that triggered volleys from both sides. No one knew where that first shot came from but, when the firing stopped a minute later, sixteen Nazis and three policemen lay dead, and many others were wounded, including Goering, who received a wound on his thigh.

Hitler flung himself to the ground and shortly thereafter sped away in a waiting car without any apparent concern for his wounded comrades, that years later he would inter in *Feldherrnhalle* vaults, solemnly commemorate in annual rituals, and to whom he would dedicate *Mein Kampf*. Nor did he display any signs of the heroism that earned him two Iron Crosses in the First World War. The true hero of the day was

Ludendorff. Accompanied only by his adjutant, he marched calmly through the armed police until he reached the *Odeonsplatz*. Hitler's other comrades fended for themselves. Goering and Hess fled to Austria. Rohm surrendered at the War Ministry and two days later Hitler was arrested in the country, where friends had given him refuge. This stage of his political struggle proved to be a debacle, yet Hitler did not commit suicide as he had threatened to do if the *Putsch* failed. He lived to struggle another day, and his trial, and subsequent political events, would work to his favor in unimagined ways.

The trial, which began on February 26, 1924, was held in Munich's Old Infantry School, and lasted twenty-four days. The little man whose distinctive physical feature was his small, dark mustache and forelock, suddenly became the center of national and some international attention. And despite the fame of Ludendorff, Hitler dominated the trial of what in later times would have been dubbed the "Munich Ten." The failure of key Bavarian officials to back Hitler's *Putsch* was reminiscent of Reich government leaders in Berlin to back Wolfgang Kapp, whose *Putsch* three years earlier in Berlin, also came to naught. Kapp, a founder of the Pan-German Fatherland Party, headed a contingent of troops and *Freikorps* members who seized control of Berlin, where Kapp was declared imperial chancellor. His *Putsch* failed through insufficient backing, but also because the incumbent Reich president and chancellor called a strike.

At their trial, the defendants denied all knowledge of the *Putsch* and, in this they differed from Hitler who boasted of his deeds. "I alone bear the responsibility," he told the court, and then in one of many speeches the court indulgently allowed him to make, and which sounded like those he had often given in beerhalls, he expressed the hope that one day his rough companies of men would "grow into battalions, the battalions into regiments, the regiments into divisions, that the old cockade (the imperial army hat despised by republicans) will be taken from the mud, (and) that the old flags will wave again..." The "eternal court of history," Hitler prophesied, would "acquit him and his comrades."[22]

He was dealt a five-year sentence, but was paroled on December 20, 1924, after serving only nine months in Landsberg Fortress. Except for Ludendorff, who was found not guilty, as he had been also for a minor part in the Kapp affair, Hitler's other eight comrades received prison terms. Thus, flophouse, barracks, beerhall, prison, and underground bunker would provide the varied asylums for Hitler's ideas that had first been cloistered inside his skull. In Landsberg, he had a room with a view, and was allowed many visitors who treated him as a national hero. It was there, too, that he began dictating *Mein Kampf* to Rudolph Hess, his willing amanuensis, and others. This turgid work spelled out with great frankness his ultimate aims. They were so audacious, in fact, that few persons in Germany, or throughout the world, took him seriously.

Upon his release from prison, Hitler turned his attention to patching up his party that, in some respects, had begun to disintegrate, and had experienced a number of defections. His first order of business was to get the party legally reinstated, which he did after meeting in 1924 with Bavaria's Prime Minister Heinrich Held. It was a brief respite, however, since the party's activities were again curtailed until 1927, and as late as 1928 in Prussia.

A major, yet necessary, and painful change in Hitler's tactics was the decision to abandon the direct road to power through the use of force (his preferred way), but to play, instead, the hated "Jewish game" of parliamentary democracy and electioneering. "Instead of working to achieve power by armed coup," as he told a party colleague who visited him in prison, "we shall have to hold our noses and enter the Reichstag against Catholic and Marxist deputies."[23]

But despite his belief that a "movement that wants to combat the parliamentary madness, must itself be free of it,"[24] Hitler temporarily foreswore the use of force, yet it was never far from his mind, and he always stood ready for the chance to use it whenever it was expedient to do so. Meanwhile, much of the party planning and organization was directed towards the day when he would no longer have to abide by democratic rules. Even so, he skirted these rules very effectively by deploying Stormtroops to combat opposition, particularly during the frequent election campaigns that were held between 1928 and 1933. His road to power was really a triadic combination of electioneering, strongarm tactics, and propaganda; the latter skillfully applied by modern technology.

With the certainty of a man who knew he would achieve his will, Hitler began building what amounted to a state within a state. He was greatly aided in this by Gregor Strasser, who, with his brother, Otto, had built up party strength in northern Germany. The Strassers would eventually part company with Hitler. Otto's break would come first when he saw that Hitler's idea of socialism was something quite different from his. When Hitler came to power, he found his way to Canada, but Gregor was less fortunate. After working tirelessly to build up the party and introducing innovative organizational programs, he clashed with Hitler over the issue of whether to join a coalition government, as well as on party policies. When they could no longer reconcile their differences, Strasser broke with Hitler and the party—an act that would cost him his life.

Even though Hitler dismantled much of Strasser's organizational setup, he retained its basic hierarchical structure. The party was divided into *Gaue*, or districts, that paralleled the Reichstag's thirty-four electoral districts, and each *Gau* was divided into *Kreise*, or circles, and even smaller units were the *Ostgruppe*, or local groups, and city cells. The party's two main divisions encompassed Hitler's all-embracing aim of destroying the existing social order and replacing it with his own. Political Organization 1 was assigned to undermine existing governmental authority, and Political Organization 2 was charged with laying the foundation of the new order. Consequently the party began laying the framework for its own departments of justice, economy, agriculture, race, culture, etc. Every activity in German life, from women to youth, doctors, teachers, and civil servants, was directed by organizations that came under party scrutiny or jurisdiction.

Hitler's organizational setup expediently allowed for contending viewpoints. In this way, he could gauge or flush out any potential troublemakers or challengers to his absolute authority. Petty jealousies and jockeyings for power among subordinates was a way of ensuring that authority. Hitler would intervene in party disputes only when it seemed they were getting out of hand, or their actions in any way obstructed his objectives. To minimize the need for his personal intervention, a party court was set up (the Committee for Investigation and Settlement). The numerous fiefdoms that developed within the Nazi system have led some historians to conclude that it was not totalitarian. This is true only if one overlooks the fact that all Nazi organizations served the aims of one man, and these were decidedly totalitarian in scope.

During the period when he was barred from speaking in public, Hitler found time to dictate more of *Mein Kampf* as well as for relaxation. On April 7, 1925, he renounced his Austrian citizenship, making him, in effect, a stateless person—a move designed to prevent the possibility of deportation should he clash again with authorities. He would not become a German citizen until 1932, the year before he became chancellor. In the summer of 1928, he rented a chalet above the village of Berchtesgaden that he would later purchase and expand when he became chancellor. This building, with its spectacular view of the Bavarian Alps, would come to symbolize the heights he had ascended in his political struggle just as his Reichschancellery bunker would signify the depths of his descent.

For a time, Hitler's half-sister, Angela Raubal, joined Hitler's Berchtesgaden entourage as house matron. She brought with her two daughters, Geli and Friedl, the former at the age of twenty becoming Hitler's frequent companion, and one of the few persons who apparently stimulated emotions in him that were other than scorn or hatred. In addition to taking her with him on mountain walks, and to important gatherings, Hitler installed her in a nine-room apartment on Munich's Prinzregenstrasse where, on September 18, 1931, she was found dead of a gunshot wound. Her death was ruled a suicide, but rumors circulated about Geli's unhappiness over her relationship with her uncle, and this gave rise to rumors that he had either shot her during a quarrel or had her shot. Hitler, however, may have had Geli Raubal in mind when, commenting on the surrender of three of his generals to the Russians, he told General Alfred Jodl: "When you think that a woman's got sufficient pride, just because someone's made a few insulting remarks, to go and lock herself in and shoot herself right off, then I've no respect for a soldier who's afraid to do that, but would rather be taken prisoner."[25] Since Hitler is reported to have quarreled with Raubel before her suicide, his remarks may indicate that she did, in fact, commit suicide. Several other women who became enamored of Hitler also committed suicide, and early in her relationship with Hitler, Eva Braun twice attempted suicide. In her diary, she revealed her dissatisfaction at his lack of attention to her except when he needed her for "special reasons," a possible allusion to his special sexual needs.[24]

From February 1919, until Hitler gained power in 1933, the Reich had a turnover of twenty-one governments and twelve chancellors—but one of many indications of the republic's instability. Depending on the state of the economy, the political compass swung from left to right and back again. In 1928, during a period when the economy appeared to be stabilizing, the Nazis polled 100,000 fewer votes than in 1924 when, under the banner of the National Socialist Freedom Movement, they fielded candidates for the first time, and won 32 Reichstag seats. The freedom movement was one of two discordant Volkischer groups that Hitler was to bring together, then purge the more troublesome members. The decline in Nazi support in 1928 proved to be temporary, and was due in part to the then improved state of the economy, but in December 1929, the year the Depression hit, the Nazis were heartened by results from communal and provincial elections. The NSDAP increased its rural support and in Berlin, where Goebbels was gauleiter (district leader), and worked hard on that city's urban vote, the Nazis showed a dramatic 400 per cent gain over the year before. This brought them renewed national attention. But more startling success came in 1930 when the votes were tallied in the new national elections. Even the Nazis were stunned to discover that they had won 6.4 million votes— a 90 per cent gain over 1928. The tally showed strong support among farmers and the middle class, the surest sign that the NSDAP was now a mass party. As a consequence, the Nazis saw 107 brownshirt party members seated in the Reichstag where they answered the roll call with outstretched arms and shouts of "Here! Heil Hitler!"

Two years later, in his one and only bid for public elective office, Hitler ran a strong race for the presidency against Hindenburg, and in the next Reich elections on July 31, 1932, the Nazis increased their showing by winning 14 million votes, and capturing 230 Reichstag seats, making the NSDAP the nation's largest party. It now seemed that the Nazis were getting closer to the power they so ardently sought. This belief was reinforced when the Reichstag convened in August, and the Catholic Center Party joined in voting for Hermann Goering as the Reichstag's first National Socialist president—an action that was much like welcoming the fox into the hen house. Then, on September 12, an event occurred that was crucial to Germany's invalid democracy. The Communist Party submitted a surprise motion of no confidence in the government headed by Franz von Papen, who tried to forestall the vote by presenting an order to dissolve the government. But, Goering chose to ignore Papen's order until after the vote was taken, and an infuriated Papen stalked out of the parliamentary chambers.

In an expedient move distasteful to him and the party, Hitler had instructed his rabid nationalist party to vote with the hated international "Jewish" Communists—an act that foreshadowed the Nazi-Soviet pact of 1939. Thus, was the government brought down by a vote of 513 to 32. In a cynical gesture, Goering picked up the dissolution order that Papen had planted on his desk, read it aloud, then ruled that since it had been signed by a chancellor (Papen) who had just been voted out of office, it was invalid. Goering's behavior was particularly irksome since, without the support of Papen's Catholic Center Party, he would not have been elected Reichstag president. Papen, who had the reputation of being one of the wiliest of parliamentary manipulators, may have been hurt most of all by the fact that for once he had been outsmarted.

Papen's own appointment as chancellor had been brought about by an aristocratic scheme aimed at undermining republicanism, and reinvigorating nationalism of the traditional kind in which the army and the civil service would provide the nation's bulwark. The Nazis were considered too extreme to be invited to take part in a government—even a coalition one. Now that Papen's government, as with that of his Center Party predecessor, Heinrich Bruning, had failed, new elections were set for November 6, 1932.

Bolstered by their impressive gains in the previous July elections, the Nazis confidently mounted an all-out campaign. Goebbels, who was not only Gauleiter of Berlin, but party propaganda minister, had refined, as no one in the modern era had done before him, the techniques of dissimulation, lying, and euphemism. And, with the aid of modern technology, he got across the Nazi message faster and to more people than had been done before in political campaigning. Hitler was flown from city to city, crisscrossing Germany, and millions heard his raucous, spellbinding voice over the radio that seemed to bestow on him the aspect of an omnipresent deity.

Despite these extraordinary efforts, however, the Nazis suffered heavy and widespread losses, indicating clearly that the party had passed its peak of public support. Their loss of two million votes was translated into a drop from 230 to 196 Reichstag seats. A month later in *landtag*, or provincial elections, they suffered more losses. Communist Party gains of eleven seats, which brought their total Reichstag seats to a hundred, worked to the Nazis' advantage, however, since it aroused in

Hindenburg, Papen, the military, and other traditionalists, renewed fears of a Communist takeover. Consequently, on November 19 a meeting was arranged between Hindenburg and Hitler, at which the possibility was explored of Hitler taking part in a coalition government. But, as he had done before when overtures were made to him, Hitler steadfastly demanded the chancellorship along with decree powers for his cabinet. It was a display of the "either or" principle that he had used so effectively in the showdown with his party in Munich that had gained him absolute control. Now he was trying it out on Hindenburg, but this time it did not work. Instead, Hindenburg called upon General Kurt von Schleicher to form a new government, the first militarist to head the government since 1890, and a harbinger of things to come.

Schleicher, however, was no more successful than Papen had been in creating a coalition, and his ministry lasted barely two months, from December 2, 1932 until January 28, 1933. Schleicher would go down in history as the last head of the democratic Weimar republic. The end of his government came amidst backroom machinations between Papen, the Nazis, and others. Upon Papen's recommendation, and despite Hindenburg's previous protestations that he could never appoint "that Austrian corporal" as chancellor, he did precisely that, and on January 30, 1933, Adolph Hitler became Germany's chancellor, fulfilling what Goebbels, in 1928, had spelled out in *Der Angriff*, his Berlin *Gau* newspaper. "We go into the Reichstag," he said, "in order to gather a supply of its own weapons in the arsenal of democracy. We will become Reichstag deputies in order to cripple the Weimar mentality with its own type of machinery. If democracy is so stupid as to provide us with free tickets and *per diem* payments for this injurious service, that is its own affair…

We come as enemies! We come like the wolf which breaks into the sheepfold!"[26] Since Hitler's nickname was Wolf, Goebbels' observation was particularly apt.

Having secured the chancellorship, Hitler must have been sorely tempted to consolidate his power by the full use of force. His army of Stormtroops could easily have commandeered key government centers, and arrested all officials who were likely to present a danger. But there was still Hindenburg and the army to contend with. As president, Hindenburg could impose martial law in case of an emergency, and Hitler dared not risk a confrontation either with the president or the army. He needed time to make sure he had the army behind him. The lessons of the 1920 Kapp *Putsch*, as well as his own 1923 botched coup attempt, had not been lost on him. It was not a time for an intuitive gamble; he had come too far, and too close to absolute power, for that.

Instead, he prevailed upon Hindenburg to dissolve the Reichstag, then set what was to be the last, ostensibly democratic, elections for March 5, 1933. His reason for this was obvious. Now that he had the prestige and authority of the chancellorship, he was better positioned than ever to achieve a near monopoly of electioneering that he hoped would give him an even greater voter mandate, as well as greater Nazi representation in the Reichstag.

In preparation for the election, the full energy and resources of the Nazi party were applied to giving the Hitler movement an overwhelming success. But, on February 27, a bizarre and unpredictable incident happened: the main hall of the Reichstag building was set on fire. A young Dutchman, Marinus van der Lubbe, was arrested in the burning building, and later confessed to having sole responsibility for setting it. It was widely believed that the Nazis planned the fire, and certainly it would have been in accord with their tactics. Besides, the timing could not have been better. Some historians now believe, however, that the Nazis were caught off guard, and this may have stimulated an overreaction which, if followed through, could have backfired. The most dramatic such reaction was Hitler's demand for immediate public hangings of all the Reichstag's Communist deputies and leaders. This was based on the Nazis' unsubstantiated allegation that the Communists were responsible for the fire. True or not, the Nazis used the occasion to build up a hysterical "Red scare" that they felt warranted raids on, and vandalization of, Communist Party headquarters, and the roundup of Communists and socialists. The fire would recall the great fire in Rome during Nero's reign which was believed to have been started on Nero's orders, but was blamed, instead, on the Christians who were subsequently tortured and murdered.

A fatal development for what was left of German democracy was the issuance of decrees the day after the Reichstag fire which, in effect, abrogated the bill of rights and the sovereignty of the federal states. These, and other measures taken during the fire's aftermath, had the effect of suspending personal liberties, exposing private properties to confiscation without compensation, silencing the Social Democratic press, and extending capital punishment to offenses that previously would have been regarded as misdemeanors, or no offenses at all. The outcome of the trial on December 23, 1933, did nothing to alleviate infringements on liberties, or to call a halt to terrorism. Based largely on his own confession, however it may have been obtained, Van der Lubbe was found guilty, but the other four defendants were acquitted, and Communist involvement was never established. Van der Lubbe testified that he set the fire to arouse German working classes into demonstrations against the National

Socialists—a motive that suspiciously seemed too well-tailored to Nazi political needs.

The fire controversy, and the near monopoly that Nazis had on electioneering, brought out a record 88.8 per cent, or 39.3 million voters. The Nazis won 43.9 per cent, or 17.2 million votes, which represented about a 10 percent increase in their showing of the previous November. However, considering the control they had over electioneering, this was not a dramatic increase, and it provided the Nazis with much less than the commanding lead they needed in the Reichstag. The Socialists dropped only about 2 per cent of their support from 20.4 to 18.3 per cent, and the Catholic parties (Center and Bavarian People's) dropped from 15 to 13.9 per cent; the Communists from 16.9 to 12.3 per cent. Out of 647 Reichstag seats, the Nazis won 288, the Center Party 73, the Nationalists 52, the Socialists 120, Communists 81, and the Bavarian People's Party 19. On the same day, Prussian Landtag, or state elections, gave the Nazis 44 per cent, or 10.3 million out of 23.5 million votes. Out of 476 seats, the Nazis won 211, the Socialists 80, the Center 68, Communists 63, and Nationalists 43. The remaining 11 seats were won by four smaller parties.

The Nazi election victories tended to overshadow the fact that 56 per cent of the electorate voted for parties other than the Nazis. Even so, they were now in a position, particularly with their leader as chancellor, to steer the wheels of government onto the autobahn of dictatorship. The Reichstag fire decrees made it possible to step up the campaign of terrorism whose initial targets were Communists, trade unionists, socialists, and Jews. The Communist deputies, who had helped the Nazis to power with their "no confidence" motion in the Papen government, were barred from taking their Reichstag seats. This meant that there would be 81 fewer votes cast; votes that most assuredly would have been registered against the Nazis.

Meanwhile, the Stormtroops and the SS fanned out in lightning moves to install party officials in key Reich, state, and local positions, and the Swastika flew ubiquitously over public buildings alongside the restored imperialist flag, but one more way of deceptively signifying that the new Hitlerian order was a fulfillment of the old. The implication was clear: Hitler was the messiah bearing the new testament of what had been merely foreshadowed in the old (imperial) testament.

In the month before the elections, and just after Hitler became chancellor, his conscripted Munich *Putsch* comrade, Ludendorff, sent a telegram to Hindenburg with the warning: "By appointing Hitler chancellor of the Reich you have handed over our sacred German fatherland to one of the greatest demagogues of all time. I prophesy to you that this evil man will plunge our Reich into the abyss and will inflict immeasurable woe on our nation. Future generations will curse you for your action."[27] It was a deadly accurate prophecy, and was perhaps the most prescient statement that Ludendorff ever uttered, even if it was ten years too late. Before he died, however, Ludendorff made his peace with Hitler, thus retroactively diluting the historical importance of his statement.

It is likely, however, that Ludendorff's telegram may have been prompted by spite at having been upstaged by "corporal" Hitler since Ludendorff also had Fuhrer-like aspirations. As with Hitler, he had developed a world theory in which freemasons, Catholics, Jews, and other internationalists were conspiring to dominate the world. In one of a series of pamphlets outlining his theory, Ludendorff warned that liberation of Germany, and all nations, depended on "the salvation from Jesus Christ," which happened to be the title of a book authored by his second wife. Ludendorff felt the wide dissemination of her book was essential.

Doubtless Ludendorff had come to realize that Hitler would use anything, or anybody, as he had tried to do with him, to achieve his will. The aura of tradition, and heroism that accompanied both Ludendorff and Hindenburg were useful to Hitler to show his continuity with the past. Privately, after he became chancellor, Hitler saw Hindenburg as an "old idiot," and an obstacle who would have to go at some point in time, hopefully through natural causes, so that Hitler could grasp power fully and irrevocably. Even the army that Hitler had always praised to the highest was cynically used from the start of his political struggle, and at the same time, the army mistakenly felt it was using Hitler. It provided his avenue to politics by supplying many of the stalwart followers who helped him gain control of the NSDAP, then the state, and he would use it to gain control over Europe. Despite his supposed reverence for the army, the old flag, and the cockade, Hitler used these devices to suggest a traditionalism he did not really possess, and which he did not intend to follow. This was particularly apparent when he got rid of some of the traditionalists in the military and replaced them with others who, eager for fame, promotion, or power, or who were hypnotized by his personality, became his lackeys and accomplices in genocide.

The only aspect of the army that Hitler truly admired was its authoritarianism, discipline, and unconditional obedience, and the army uniform which signified the one form he sought to impose on the German people. With the army and the civil service, two of the most revered of traditional German institutions on his side, Hitler would provide the Germans with symbols of conservative repose that concealed his party's infernal revolutionary movement of change that brought terror and extermination. Indeed, propaganda and terror were the real underpinnings of his movement. This could be seen on March 13, 1933, only eight days after the election, when Hindenburg was persuaded to authorize a ministry for public enlightenment and propaganda. Two days later, Himmler announced that a concentration camp to accommodate five thousand prisoners would soon be operating in Dachau in Munich. Just how soon Hitler had been thinking about these priorities was seen when he appointed Goebbels as party propaganda minister in 1929, the same year he made Himmler head of the dreaded SS. As early as 1923, in Landsberg Prison, however, he had already committed to *Mein Kampf* his estimate of the value of propaganda and terror in controlling the masses. Propaganda, he wrote, operates in advance of organization by providing the "human material to be worked on."[28] His own propaganda expertise had been gained in the army, and then in the German Workers' party where he used it in taking the first steps in his political struggle.

With the two Reichstag fire decrees reinforcing his power, Hitler had reason to be greatly satisfied when, on March 21, 1933, he came to Potsdam's Garrison Church for the inauguration of the new Reichstag. The ceremony involved the ritual passing of the reins of government from the old to the new regime. Surely, never in modern power transitions was there so little cause to believe that "God fulfills himself in many ways, lest one good custom should corrupt the world... "[29] No "shot heard 'round the world" from Concord Bridge or storming of the Bastille could match the insidious subtlety of the Nazi revolution that came in the guise of legality, and was accompanied by the full panoply of tradition.

As shown in innumerable photographs and newsreels, Hindenburg and Hitler, the two principals, were a study in contrasts. The venerable president-field marshal representing the old order that history had foredoomed to its dustheap because it was unwilling, or unable, to comprehend the true nature of the social forces being unleashed against it by the sorcerers' apprentices of both right and left. At 85, Hindenburg stood tall, stately and resplendent in his army uniform; his chest covered with rows of ribbons and medals that seemed as if they had been retrieved from a pawnshop for this special occasion; the victories they represented now but dimly perceived memories. Like some of the other dignitaries, Hindenburg appeared as an old actor persuaded to come out of retirement to act, for the last time, in the revival of a play originally intended as drama, but now an unmistakable farce. An empty seat had been set aside for the absentee Kaiser Wilhelm II, still safely in exile in Holland where he had fled to rather than remain to uphold traditions that he had so fervently espoused, and for which millions of his compatriots had suffered so much in which was to go down in history as the "Great War."

As Hindenburg bowed deferentially towards the Kaiser's empty chair, Hitler may have thought what he was later to express: "The injustice committed by the Kaiser at Bismarck's expense finally recoiled upon him. How could the Kaiser demand loyalty from his subjects when he had treated the founder of the Reich (Bismarck) with such ingratitude?"[30]—a reference to the Kaiser going to war to preserve the (in Hitler's mind) "foreign" Hapsburg dynasty when its Crown Prince Archduke Ferdinand of Austria was assassinated at Sarajevo. The Kaiser had also been responsible for removing Bismarck after he proposed a *coup d'etat* dissolution of the empire; an end to universal suffrage, and a drastic reduction of the Reichstag's powers. In many ways, Bismarck was Hitler's forerunner: the man of "blood and iron" preparing the way for the man of bloodshed.

As they stand side by side in the Potsdam church, Hindenburg towers over Hitler who is wearing a frock coat, striped pants, and holding a top hat in his hands. There is irony in this since Hitler sees frockcoats and top hats as the very symbol of the bourgeoisie. "When a monument was unveiled to the memory of Bismarck," he later reflected," or when a ship was launched, no delegation of workers was ever invited—only the frock coats and uniforms. For me, the top hat is the signature of the bourgeois..." At official functions, even after the (Social Democratic) revolution, he added, "there was nothing but top hats. The people were invited to such festivities only as extras."[31]

Both Hindenburg's uniform and Hitler's bourgeois apparel are like disguises, the former's concealing one power making its exit, and the other masking a demoniacal entrance. Hitler is the quintessence of the little man, the barrackroom and beerhall philosopher, not quite believing that his wildest fantasies have finally brought him to the corridors of the mighty. Hindenburg makes a brief speech calling on the Reichstag deputies to support the new government. Hitler follows with a longer speech in which he spews forth the familiar tirades he had perfected in Munich's beerhalls: the "Versailles *Diktat*," the "November Criminals," the "stab-in-the-back." When he finishes, he approaches Hindenburg, puts his bare hand into the president's gloved one, shakes it, then makes a deep bow that comes close to being obsequious—a gesture that is uncharacteristic, and will never be repeated. Surely, one thinks, the incongruity of the whole ceremony could not possibly have escaped him: he, a fallen-away Catholic who, as a child, reportedly spat out the host during mass, and who now intends to destroy the Jews and Judeo-Christianity, is here in this place—a Christian church—where, during a religious service that Hitler declined to attend, the organ had earlier played *Nun danket alle Gott* (Now Thank We All Our God). On this occasion Hitler resembles Nietzsche's mad man who frequented churches singing his *requiem aeternam deo*, and each time, when asked what he was doing, responded: "What are these churches now if they are not the tombs and sepulchers of God?"[32]

The hymn just played has long been associated with Frederick the Great's victory in 1757 at Leuthen. Frederick (and his father) entombed in this very church where Hitler now stands, is the new chancellor's great idol, and Hitler imagines himself as the reincarnation of his spirit. One can but guess what Frederick would have thought about the ex-corporal and now would-be dictator-emperor.

It is true that the two men had some parallels in their lives. Both had domineering fathers who opposed their artistic inclinations. Hitler's father would thrash him, and whistle for him to come to him as though to a dog; Frederick's father forced his son to kiss his boots. Frederick's first acts as king, however, were to abolish torture as a means of judicial interrogation, the quality of mercy became part of Prussian justice, and he abolished press censorship and religious discrimination. The Berlin Academy was revitalized by recalling exiled scholars and hiring foreign scientists. He wrote a treatise condemning political Machiavellianism, and encouraged the concepts of virtue, justice, and responsibility.

By contrast, Hitler was to start his dictatorship with terror, torture, extermination, press, religious, and thought control. Germany's once great universities saw the exodus, or the banishment, of great scholars and their replacement with political toadies. That Hitler could see his own demoniacal spirit as a reflection of Frederick's is but one measure of his capacity for self-delusion. Where Frederick was enriched by his friendship and intellectual discourse with Voltaire, Hitler had only his architect, Speer, and Mussolini.

The Nazi Brown House (party headquarters) in Munich had a portrait of Frederick in its main meeting room, and Hitler had another in his private quarters in Berlin. Some time after his inauguration Hitler returned to the Garrison Church, and placed a golden wreath on Frederick's tomb. About a century and a half before him, another aspirant to world empire, Napoleon, had also paid his respects at the same spot. And in yet another historical twist, Hitler, as conqueror, would stand over Napoleon's tomb in Paris. Unlike Napoleon, who sought to transform revolutionary change into the repose of permanent social patterns, and succeeded in transmitting a lasting legacy, Hitler's revolution was founded on nihilism, and was lost in nihilism.

Like a snake exuviating its skin, Hitler cast off his ceremonial attire, and put on his SA uniform to appear at the Kroll Opera House which, since the Reichstag fire, had been earmarked for the new Reichstag assemblies. His entire, self-satisfied manner had none of the kowtowing he displayed at the Garrison Church. No Communists were in attendance, most of them having been arrested under one of three decrees issued earlier in the day that allowed arbitrary arrests for "malicious" criticism of the government. Of the other two decrees, one had the effect of pardoning Nazi thugs who had been imprisoned for their efforts in bringing about the revolution, and the other set up special judge-only courts to try political offenders. At its brief meeting, the Reichstag reelected Goering its president, Thomas Esser of the Center Party as first vice president, and two other vice presidents, one a Nazi and the other a Nationalist.

In late evening, celebrations of Hitler's inauguration were marked by a massive parade of torch-bearing SA and

SS men along the *Unter den Linden*, a special performance of Wagner's *Die Meistersinger* was presented in Hitler's honor, and sometime during the performance, under cover of night, the first inmates, many of them Communists, were being transported by the Stormtroops to Oranienburg concentration camp on Berlin's outskirts.

On March 23, the depleted Reichstag met and voted on the Enabling Act—the *Law for Removing the Distress of People and Reich*, which transferred from the Reichstag to Hitler's Reich cabinet (which really meant to Hitler) essentially all legislative powers. The "Distress" referred to in the law's title was known to Hitler and his cohorts as the Jews, Communists, and others who must be "removed" from Germany—a euphemism, as it turned out, for extermination.

Ostensibly intended for four years, the Enabling Act lasted for twelve. It validated Hitler's dictatorship, allowing him to draft laws that could deviate from the constitution, and it contained supposed safeguards. Among these were the provision that the powers of the president would remain undisturbed, and another stipulated that the Reichstag's status would remain unaffected. Because of Hindenburg's age and declining health, the first was of no great significance, and the second would be treated with characteristic Nazi contempt. Indeed, even before the Act was passed, its provisions had been violated insofar as the Communists had been excluded from the Reichstag, bringing into question the very constitutionality of the vote.

Nevertheless, the Enabling Act was approved by 441 votes to 84. To its shame, the Catholic Center Party cast its 68 votes on the side of the Nazis. Only the Social Democrats cast all of their votes against the measure. Before the vote was taken, Otto Wells, the soft-speaking leader of the Social Democrats, provided the only light in the deepening darkness. "Never, since a German Reichstag has existed," he said, "has the control of public affairs, through the chosen representatives of the people, been eliminated to such an extent as is now the case, and will be still more so as a result of the new Enabling Act... The Weimar Constitution is not a socialist constitution. But we remain faithful to the principles incorporated in it, the principles of a state based on law, of equality, of social justice...No Enabling Act gives you the power to destroy ideas which are eternal and indestructible... "[33]

In all his fourteen years of political struggle, Hitler had never before held public office, but instead had remained in the wings, stage-managing all Nazi votes in the Reichstag. Now, as chancellor, he would make his first Reichstag address in response to Wells. It was the culmination of the battles that nationalists and socialists had been waging for years in public halls and on the streets throughout Germany. The Socialists' hour had struck, he pronounced, like the hour of everything "rotten, old and brittle" in German life. "I believe," he rasped, "that you do not support this act because your mentality makes the purpose which inspires us (and) in connection with it, incomprehensible to you...Nor do I wish that you support it! Germany will become free, but not through you!"[34] As a youth in Linz, Hitler had been transported after attending Wagner's opera, *Rienzi*, and it was then Hitler recalled when "it all began"—a reference to his sense of mission. Now, in the Kroll Opera House, he was an incarnation of Rienzi leading his people to a higher destiny. Democratic voting had made him dictator of his party, now the Enabling Act vote made him dictator of the nation.

By the end of March, and armed with the Reichstag decrees and the Enabling Act, the Nazis had dissolved all but one of the state governments. Prussia was the exception. Goering had already been installed there as minister of the interior, and through a program of terror he provided the prototype for Nazi policy throughout the nation. By April, Nazi governors were appointed in all states with powers to appoint or dismiss state officials, and to appoint or remove local governors. These governors had been chosen because they could be relied upon to execute Hitler's policies. They were all party members, and their actions had the effect of destroying Germany's federal system, and replacing it with dictatorial central authority. Despite Hitler's reassurances that the Enabling Act would be used with restraint, nearly 600 laws, or an average of 200 a year, were enacted between 1933 and 1935. Apart from a few rare occasions when it was required to formalize a law, the Reichstag had been rendered virtually obsolete. One by one the remaining non-Nazi parties dissolved so that by July 14, 1933, the Nazi Party decreed that it constituted the only political party in Germany. The decree also spelled out heavy penalties that would be imposed on anyone trying to form another party.

By means of his many decrees, Hitler brought under control nearly every organization in German society. His one great hesitation was the churches. He did not want to clash head-on with either the Protestant or Catholic churches (one notable exception being the Jehovah's Witnesses). Yet he could move with great freedom against the Jews notwithstanding his claim that they had great worldwide power and influence. He was prepared to bide his time until he could provide a final solution to Christianity as he was already poised to implement against the Jews.

His main tactic was to ensure that clergymen would confine themselves to purely spiritual matters and not engage in politics either by word or deed. In the case of evangelical Protestantism, he sought to have it under Nazi control, and he succeeded in getting a Nazi appointed as an overseer of "German Christians," a sizable body of Protestants whose official designation showed that Christianity was defined by its Germanness. This was what the Nazis termed "positive Christianity," and in which God was subordinated to Fuhrer. Some Protestant denominations saw themselves as Christians first and Germans second, and they balked at the Nazi proposals. But, except for a few valiant individual examples resulting in martyrdom, the Protestant complaints were largely doctrinal and jurisdictional. They were prepared to preach a true Christianity (whatever that might be) from their pulpits as long as they were not practicing it in opposition to Nazi crimes that were manifest violations of long-recognized Christian values. Most notable of Protestant, as well as Catholic derelictions, therefore, were in their omissive complicity in the persecution of Jews.

En route to power, Hitler had posed himself as a protector of Christianity, but when he felt he had solidified his hold on the state, he began to display his true attitudes. At a meeting with Protestant bishops on March 13, 1934, he was emboldened to tell them that Christianity would disappear from Germany as it had in Russia. Germans had lived without Christianity before its advent, and could do without it after it was gone, but until then the churches would have to adapt to the new order. "But for the coming of Christianity," Hitler was to say later, "who knows how the history of Europe would have developed? Rome would have conquered all Europe, and the onrush of the Huns would have been broken on the (Roman) legions. It was Christianity that brought about the fall of Rome—not the Germans or the Huns." And what Bolshevism had achieved at the materialist and technical level, Christianity had achieved on the metaphysical level.[35]

With the Catholic Church, Hitler had a special problem, for even though Catholicism takes on national
colorations, it is a universal church transcending national boundaries as signified by the ostensible spiritual
allegiance of all Catholics to Rome. Because the Vatican
is a state with emissaries throughout the world, the re-
percussions arising from actions taken against the church
were likely to be greater around the world than would
be the case against German Protestantism. Hitler recognized the expediency, therefore, in gaining an agreement
with the Vatican that might appear to the rest of the
world as a sanction.

Since the Vatican is noted for its cautious, reasoned,
and slow deliberations, Hitler applied pressure by sup-
pressing Catholic lay organizations, and other
intimidations that brought Vatican protests. These, however, were usually glossed over by Hitler, and his Vatican
representatives, or laid to the excessive zeal of Hitler's
followers. Empty promises were made to correct any infractions. The Nazi tactics succeeded in gaining a
concordat with the Vatican on September 10, 1933. But
even with this agreement, which served as a valuable propaganda device (how could the world believe the horror
stories seeping out of Germany if Christ's reputed vicar
on earth could sign an agreement with its Fuhrer?), the
Nazis conducted an increasingly vigorous anti-Catholic
program which resulted in deaths, persecutions, impris-
onments, and the dispatch to concentration camps of
many priests, and the closure of churches.

Now that he was in complete control in Germany, and
the war against his internal enemies was going according to
plan, the Concordat was a sign that Hitler was beginning to
turn his attention to his external enemies. Since part of his
plan was to gain as much as he could without going to war,
it was necessary, for diplomatic reasons, to momentarily

concern himself about world opinion (privately, he detested that opinion). The Concordat, therefore, notwithstanding the Vatican's sincere belief that it would provide a vehicle for the amelioration of wrongs, had the effect of pouring holy oil on the troubled waters of world opinion.

On October 14, 1933, two months after signing the Concordat, Hitler announced Germany's immediate withdrawal from the Geneva Disarmament Conference, and the League of Nations. The armed forces were alerted in case of League-imposed sanctions, but none came. Hitler capitalized on this by holding a plebiscite on November 12 that showed 95 out of 96 per cent of the electorate approved of his actions. A slate of Nazi Reichstag candidates was also approved by a 92 per cent vote.

Even allowing for intimidation, and doubtless this was a factor, the vote showed that a great majority of Germans approved of the Hitler regime. This, despite the fact that in the space of a year, Hitler had destroyed a democratic republic, and substituted a dictatorship, abolished all parties except the Nazi party, wrecked the federal system of government, ousted labor unions, put the churches in a nationalist straightjacket, drove Jews out of public and professional life, ended freedom of speech and press, imposed Nazi bias on the courts, and spread Nazi tentacles into every area of German life. The trade-off for Germans was more jobs, autobahns, Volkswagens, "Strength Through Job" vacations, national pride, and the arousal of the beast in the German bosom.

By January 1934, the Nazis had an iron grip on the state, and sources of potential problems had not materialized. The feared trouble from Communists after the Reichstag fire did not take place, and the Nazis quickly made the Communist Party a thing of the past. Hindenburg did not take any presidential actions that would have curbed Nazi power, but on the contrary signed decree after decree that entrenched it even more. As soon as Hitler was inaugurated, the army, with General Werner von Blomberg at its head, had thrown its support to Hitler. This support reflected the army's entrenched conservatism which, through secret propaganda activities and military preparedness, had kept alive a spirit of militarism in the face of postwar pacifism. Unwittingly, the army became a John-the-Baptist, preparing the way for the satanic messiah.

The first real trouble did not come from outside, but from inside the party: from the very SA that had played such a key role in the rise of the Nazi movement. But it was precisely because of this role that the SA contained the seeds of its own destruction—at least of its leadership. With the consolidation of power, which the SA helped him achieve, Hitler's political struggle against the "internal enemies" was nearing an end, and it would soon be time to turn attention to his military struggle beyond Germany, and for this he needed the army.

Even though the army was not politicized, it had a trained officer corps, and a nucleus of men who were battle-ready. Despite the fact that the Versailles Treaty had limited Germany's military to 100,000 men, the giant Krupp arms manufacturer, in cahoots with the military even before Hitler's advent, had been secretly developing weaponry for the day when Germany would rise again. The military, meanwhile, found a variety of ways to train men, and to avoid the scrutiny of the Inter-Allied Control Commission set up as a monitor. It is certainly true that Hitler would have preferred a politicized military, much like the Russians, with political commissars assigned to fighting units to make sure that warfare was conducted in line with ideological intentions. But, to Nazify the *Reichswehr* could have (although unlikely) met with some resistance, and it most certainly would have taken time, and that is something that Hitler felt he did not have. He decided, therefore, that the *Reichswehr* would become the Fatherland's "sole bearer of arms." It was a decision that was tantamount to throwing the gauntlet to Ernst Rohm, chief-of-staff of the SA, who had been expressing ever more openly his dissatisfaction with the SA's diminished role now that Nazi power had been consolidated. But Hitler's decision was also part of a larger tactic that would come later.

Even when he returned, at Hitler's request, from his soldier-of-fortune activities in Bolivia to take over command of the SA in January 1931, Rohm conceived of his task as building an army that ultimately would supplant the *Reichswehr* whose traditionalism he scorned. In his book, *The Story of a Traitor*, written during Hitler's struggle for power, Rohm noted that in his own political activities "I was and remained a soldier. In short, I demand primacy of the soldier over the politician. In particular, I demand this from those within the Nationalist movement."[36] This was completely at odds with Hitler's belief in the primacy of the political. Sooner or later, therefore, a clash between the two men was inevitable.

In 1934, Rohm also regarded the revolution as incomplete, believing it was time to move against the *Reichswehr* and industrialists who contained the traditionalist and aristocratic elements that he despised. He was partly right in this, not about the traditionalists, but about the status of the revolution. Hitler, despite many of his public pronouncements, shared Rohm's attitude about the military particularly in regards to its "Old Guard" general staff, and except for the fact that Hindenburg was still alive, and that the army had thrown its support behind him, Hitler did not have the absolute political control over the military that he wanted. As for Hindenburg, his age and health made it certain that his time was limited and so, that was a problem which likely would take care of itself. But somewhere down the line there would have to be a new relationship between Hitler and the armed forces. For now, however, he had to insist that the revolution—at least in its internal aspect—was over. With the army's help, the world revolution had still to come.

Rohm's public utterances, and the fact that he had built up the SA to a strength of four million men, both active and reserve, had given rise to great unease among the *Reichswehr* officer corps saw the SA as a very real threat. At stake was Hitler's relationship with the army which he planned to harness to his world revolution against the "international enemies" inspired by Jewry. Action, therefore, had to be taken.

Hitler resolved the matter on June 30, 1934, when he led an SS detachment to Rohm's temporary headquarters at Wiesee (near Munich). There, and at selected locations throughout the land, bloody and ruthless slaughters were carried out that should have shocked the German people, but did not, partly because of the confusion that official versions of the events had created, as well as to the wide public support that Hitler had built. To this day it is not known for certain how many murders were committed. Figures range from the official 61, given out by Hitler in a speech two weeks later, to 1,000 by non-government sources. It was reliably estimated that at least about eighty SA members were among the dead, including Rohm, who declined to exercise the choice of suicide, and was shot the next day in a Munich prison. The SA victims included most of its top officers, and many others were thrown out of the organization in a widespread purge.

Hitler chose the occasion to "settle accounts," a favorite expression that suggested double-entry bookkeeping. Gustav Ritter von Kahr, the 73-year-old former Bavarian prime minister and commissioner who had failed to support Hitler's *Putsch*, had his body hacked to pieces with pickaxes and tossed into a swamp. Gregor Strasser, who had challenged Hitler over the direction the party should take, was gunned down, as were General von Schleicher, Hitler's predecessor as chancellor, and his wife. Another victim was Father Bernhard Stempfle, an anti-Semitic priest of the Hieronymite Order. Stempfle had helped edit *Mein Kampf*, but may have been marked for death, certainly not for his anti-Semitism, but because he was privy to knowledge about a letter Hitler reportedly had written to Geli Raubal, and which had to be retrieved at considerable expense from a collector of rare documents. Stempfle's body was dumped in a forest near Munich with a broken neck and three shots in the heart.

The purge drew no significant outcry, and the Hitlerian cabinet quickly passed a *post facto* law spelling out the necessity and legality of the action that Hitler, in his speech, claimed was necessary to ward off a conspiracy to take control of the state. He also offered a "moral" justification by alluding to the homosexuality of Rohm and some of his cohorts; homosexuality, presumably, being a more serious offense than wholesale murder. Hindenburg sent telegrams of congratulation to Hitler, and to Goering who, along with Himmler, had directed the murder operations. Reflecting the *Reichswehr's* satisfaction with the way Hitler had dealt with the SA, Blomberg saw it as necessary to avert civil war. Even the rank and file of the SA seemed cowed by the purge, and soon settled down to a greatly-reduced role under Viktor Lutze, their new chief-of-staff.

Hitler's split with Rohm was more than just a difference of opinion on whether the SA should replace the *Reichswehr*, although that was undoubtedly an important factor. The SA had always been an emotional organization that had been used to displaying those emotions on the streets and in beerhalls. While it served its purpose in getting Hitler to power, this emotionalism was diametrically in opposition to Hitler's fundamental war against the Jews that he had always insisted must be "rational" and not "emotional." Many of Rohm's men were too steeped in beer-mug politics; Hitler needed a different breed of men who could guarantee that the "Final Solution" to the Jewish "problem" would be carried out in a "rational" way. By "rational," Hitler did not mean reasonable, but rather organized, systematic, and planned on a large scale in contrast to small "emotional" pogroms. And even though other ethnic groups would also be exterminated in large numbers, and their deaths were no less saddening, it was only the Jews that Hitler singled out for total destruction because of what he perceived to be their special historical role.

As early as 1924, when the Nazis gained their first seats in the Reichstag, under the banner of the Nationalist Socialist Freedom Movement, efforts were made to get legislation passed that would deprive Jews of basic rights. Under the Nuremberg Laws of September 15, 1935, the Jews were stripped of their German citizenship, forbidden to marry Aryans, and barred from hiring Aryan women under the age of thirty-five. These were but a few of the restrictions added to those already imposed in 1933 which excluded Jews from public office, the civil service, journalism, and many other areas of employment. By 1936, most Jews were forced into a condition of subsistence and after the Olympic Games in Berlin in that same year, the machinery began to grind that was to lead to the extermination of millions of Jews and make Germany *Judenrein* (free of Jews). The Games held a special significance for Hitler since he associated them with the antique world that he was about to resuscitate.

In 1938, Hitler allowed the SA but one significant departure from his rule of "rational" anti-Semitism. In what became known as *Kristallnacht*, or the "night of the broken glass," Jews were brutalized, synagogues were burned, and Jewish homes and stores were vandalized throughout Germany. This authorized terrorism, which was akin to historical pogroms, was ostensibly in retaliation for the shooting of a German diplomat in Paris by a Jewish youth who was distraught over the ill-treatment of his father by Nazis. But it also served as a temporary release for the pent up feelings of the SA which, since Rohm's death, had been assigned fewer roles because the party's political aims had been largely achieved in Germany.

In an article in *Deutschlands Erneurung* in April 1924, Hitler wrote: "The groundwork for the salvation of the Fatherland will be laid at the very hour in which the last Marxist has been either converted or annihilated. *Only after a domestic victory* will Germany break the iron chains of her foreign enemies."[37] (Original italics.) Now, more than a decade later, the domestic victory had been effectively won, and the new direction was towards a much larger terror. One indication of this was the promotion of former Dachau commandant Theodore Eicke to a new position as inspector of all concentration camps. Eicke, one of the SS officers who took part in the Rohm purge, and who had personally shot Rohm, received his promotion only three days later. The SS Death's Head units were also placed under his command; their principal assignment was to police the death camps, their black uniforms and skull-and-crossbones insignia indicating more than anything else the real nature of Nazism. Eicke came to his new job well-equipped. In addition to being commandant at Dachau, he had been assigned to coordinate all concentration camps that had previously been loosely organized. Until 1939, Eicke had put his particularly callous stamp on the concentration and genocidal camp system. His SS guards were specially trained not to show the slightest humanity towards inmates, either by look or gesture; they were to be hated as enemies and shown no mercy. Like Himmler, their chief, who had the reputation of being as cold as an "Icelandic codfish," the Death's Head guards became "inexorable specialists in brutality, henceforth insensible to any human emotion."[38] Eicke's appointment was one of a number of developments in 1934 that showed the growing emphasis being placed on terror. In April, Himmler added the Gestapo (the state police system) to his control, making him unassailable master of terror until the Allied armies brought the Third Reich tumbling down.

The establishment of concentration and genocidal camps paralleled the rise in importance of the SS, as well as the increasing attention that Hitler was giving to military preparations, and even if they seemed, at the time, to be very disparate activities, they were really closely connected. With his dictatorship sealed, Hitler was in a position to move at liberty against all internal enemies, and the swelling number of inmates in camps, as well as the number of killings, bore witness to who these enemies were. They included past, present, and potential enemies, communists, socialists, clergy, and most importantly Jews, who soon became the most numerous of victims. Paradoxically, the Jews, who had zero value in the eyes of the Nazis, assumed the negative status of being priority victims.

The concentration and extermination camps were the most evident sign that the "emotional" phase of terrorism as exhibited by the SA, and particularly in its anti-Semitic form, had given way to its "rational" counterpart, the SS with its central bureaucracy systematically employing terror. Under Himmler, the SS went from strength to strength. At all times, with its separate units, the SS was a special force at Hitler's exclusive disposition for whatever acts he ordered to be carried out. Unlike Rohm, who had shown potential for rebellion, Himmler sought nothing more than to serve Hitler, and thus became, in effect, his executive arm, ensuring that the core, demoniacal and atheistic aspects of his intentions were achieved. One need only turn to the great writers of literature—the true biographers of the human race—to see the Himmler type. Dostoyevsky, in *The Brothers Karamazov*, depicts Smerdyakov, the uneducated family servant, carrying out the murder of the dissolute Karamazov paterfamilias in accordance with the atheistic theories he has overheard from Ivan Karamazov, one of the three brothers. For the cold efficiency with which it carried out the Rohm purge, Himmler's SS earned from Hitler the status of an independent organization that was no longer subordinate to the SA. It was not only a reward for work well done, but for work yet to do.

On August 2, 1934, just one month after the last purge killings, Hindenburg died at Neudeck where he had been in a weakening condition for some time. He was approaching his eighty-seventh birthday. With his usual opportunism, Hitler had visited the dying man the day before, and saw that his end was near. That same night, in Berlin, Hitler met with his cohorts and planned his strategy for incorporating the powers of the presidency into the chancellorship. The upshot was a decision to hold a plebiscite on August 19. And, in a radio address on the night before the election, in a scene reminiscent of Richard III's feigned reluctance to accept the British crown he had so murderously worked to grasp, Hitler declaimed: "I must emphatically decline to derive, from a plenitude of power already bestowed, the right to take this most tremendous step in the reconstruction of the German Reich. No! The people themselves shall decide the matter!"[39] Of 42.5 million valid votes, the merger of the nation's two highest offices was approved by 38.2 million votes, or nearly 90 per cent—an awful indictment of German political and human sensibilities.

Even before this further demonstration of public sanction of Hitler's dictatorship, one other event occurred that was loaded with tremendous consequences for Germany and the world. On August 2, the very day of Hindenburg's death, General Blomberg ordered all members of the armed forces to swear a personal oath of allegiance to Hitler. Doubtless Blomberg's order was issued at Hitler's bidding, and significantly it was issued on the 20th anniversary of the start of the First World War which Hitler had so joyfully welcomed in Munich's *Odeonsplatz*. Despite its break with tradition, the oath was dutifully sworn by all members of the armed services without dissent. It went as follows: "I swear this sacred oath, by God, that I will render unconditional obedience to Adolph Hitler, the Fuhrer of the German Reich and people, the Supreme Commander of the Armed Forces, and will be ready as a brave soldier (sailor and airman) to risk my life at any time for this oath."[40] The day after the plebiscite, Germany's other traditional and highly respected bastion, the civil service, also swore fealty to Hitler.

Henceforth, Hitler's state fitted Thucydides' description of Corcyra which he saw as typical of many Greek cities. "Fanatical enthusiasm was the mark of a real man, and to plot against an enemy behind his back was perfectly legitimate self-defense. Anyone who held violent opinions could always be trusted, and anyone who objected to them became a suspect...Family relations were a weaker tie than party membership, since party members were more ready to go to any extreme for any reason whatever. These parties were not formed to enjoy the benefits of the established laws, but to acquire power by overthrowing the existing regime; and the members of these parties felt confidence in each other not because of any fellowship in a religious communion, but because they were partners in crime."[41]

With the powers of the presidency and the chancellorship firmly in his grasp, the military forces and the civil service bound to him by oath, and the people, as indicated in the plebiscite results, almost solidly behind him, Hitler was now an absolute dictator. What had only been expressed as a wish in his Hepp letter nearly thirty years before, had now been fulfilled. He had come a long way towards carrying out the other wishes expressed in that letter: of getting rid of Jews, Communists, parliamentary democracy, etc., and had consequently made the nation a "purer place," rid of "foreign influences," and "inner internationalism." And some of his army comrades, like Rohm and others, who had been "lucky enough" to return to the Fatherland, and helped Hitler carry out his aims, were not so lucky once those aims were achieved. They were slaughtered instead on the orders of the little corporal who had first identified himself with Germany, but now identified Germany with himself.

CHAPTER TWO: BIBLIOGRAPHY

1 Hitler, *Mein Kampf* 220.

2 Hitler, *Mein Kampf* 223.

3 T.L. Jarman, *The Rise and Fall of Nazi Germany* (New York: Signet Books, 1961) 71.

4 Hitler, *Mein Kampf* 373.

5 Hitler, *Mein Kampf* 373.

6 Hitler, *Mein Kampf* 370.

7 Eliot Barculo Wheaton, *The Nazi Revolution 1933-1935* (New York: Doubleday & Co., Inc., 1961) 52-53.

8 Hitler, *Mein Kampf* 561.

9 Joachim C. Fest, *The Face of the Third Reich*, tr. Michael Bullock (New York: Pantheon Books, 1970) 164.

10 Hannah Arendt, *Totalitarianism* (New York: Harcourt, Brace and Jovanovich, 1968) 55.

11 Franz Neumann, *Behemoth* (New York: Harper Torchbooks, 1966) 170.

12 Hitler, *Mein Kampf* 497.

13 Heinrich Hoffmann, *Hitler, wie ihn keiner kennt* (Berlin, 1932) x-iv.

14 Hermann Rauschning, *The Voice of Destruction* (London: Appleton-Century Co., 1939) 109.

15 Fest 107.

16 Fest 75.

17 Fest 302.

18 Louis MacNeice, *Collected Poems* (London: Faber & Faber, 1966) 139.

19 Ernst Nolte, *The Three Faces of Fascism* (New York: Mentor Books, 1969) 511.

20 Heiden 131-133.

21 Heiden 187.

22 Shirer 75-78.

23 Jarman, T. L. *The Rise and Fall of Nazi Germany* (New York: Signet Books, 1961) 111.

24 Jarman 111.

25 Nerin E. Gun, *Hitler's Mistress Eva Braun* (New York: Bantam Books, 1969) 72.

26 Wheaton 97.

27 Payne 251-252.

28 Hitler, *Mein Kampf* 579.

29 Vol 2. *The Norton Anthology of English Literature* (New York: W.W. Norton, Inc., 1968) 840.

30 Roper 62.

31 Roper 48.

32 *The Gay Science* from the Nietzsche Reader (New York: Penguin Books, 1977) 125.

33 Wheaton 291.

34 Wheaton 292.

35 Roper 254.

36 Hans Ernest Fried, *The Guilt of the German Army* (New York: Macmillan Co., 1942) 42.

37 *Warum Musste ein 9 November Kommen?* (Why was a November 9—the Day of the Munich Putsch— bound to come?), Hitler article in the Deutschlands Erneuerung, April 1924.

38 Wheaton 498.

39 Wheaton 508.

40 Shirer 227.

41 Thucydides, *The Peloponnesian War*, tr. Rex Warner, (Harmondsworth, Middlesex: Penguin Books, 1959) 209.

CHAPTER 3

❧❀❧

MILITARY STRUGGLE:
PART I—THE TESTING PERIOD

At a meeting in Berlin on December 27, 1936, a bare three years after Hitler came to power, Hermann Goering told a group of industrialists that "We (Germany) are at war. All that is lacking is the actual shooting." Goering spoke bluntly about an approaching military struggle that would demand a "colossal measure of production capacity and unlimited rearmament."[1]

Since Goering was head of Germany's Four-Year Plan as well as temporary plenipotentiary for war economics, his speech underscored the end of Hitler's political struggle, and the increasing concentration on his upcoming military struggle. As early as March 16, 1935, two years after Hitler became chancellor, he announced a buildup in the armed forces and the introduction of military conscription, both clear violations of the Versailles Treaty. This mobilization came two years after the boycott of Jewish businesses, and preceded by only seven months the passage of the anti-Jewish Nuremberg Laws—but two of many indications of how closely the military struggle and anti-Semitism were entwined in Hitler's mind as they would become on Europe's battlefields, for just as National Socialism became the host to Hitler's anti-Semitic political struggle, the Army would become host to the SS's execution of the "Final Solution" to the Jewish "problem." And these political and military hosts were but the outward manifestations of Hitler's mind which had hosted anti-Semitism in the first place.

In contrast to Hitler's militarization program, which drew condemnatory resolutions from British, French, and Italian diplomats meeting in Stresa in Italy on April 11, 1935, and by the League of Nations at Geneva, no great official clamor was made against Germany's anti-Semitic measures even though unofficial voices were raised in many parts of the world. And just as the omissive complicity of Germans in Hitler's frequent anti-Semitic diatribes, and the passage of the Nuremberg Laws had enabled him to gauge German responses to his anti-Semitism, so the League's mild reaction to his illegal rearmament policy gave him the first clear sign of the timidity of the European nations. It emboldened him to gain as much as he could by increments and without resort to war which, as his arms buildup testified, he knew was ultimately inevitable; more than that, desirable. By his own peculiar "logic," Hitler believed that all his demands and actions were based on an infallible right which he alone determined, so that when this right was denied, not he, but those who denied it could be blamed for starting war. That "right" was predicated on his belief that Germany, the leader of the so-called Aryans, was involved in a life or death struggle with world Jewry.

Nevertheless, in a speech on May 21, 1935, only months after giving his rearmament orders, Hitler postured himself as the great peacemaker, denouncing war as horrible, senseless, and useless. "The bloodshed on the European continent in the course of the last three-hundred years," he asserted, "bears no proportion to the national result of the events. In the end, France remained France; Germany, Germany; Poland, Poland; and Italy, Italy." Only dynastic egotism, political passion and patriotic blindness, he added, had attained apparently far-reaching political changes by shedding rivers of blood. "If these states," said Hitler, "had applied a mere fraction of their sacrifices to wiser purposes, the success would certainly have been greater and more permanent." Hitler went on to say that Germany's racial theory "regards every war for the subjection and domination of an alien people as a proceeding which sooner or later changes and weakens the victor internally, and eventually brings about defeat." Germany "needs and desires peace," Hitler continued, "and recognizes Poland as the home of a great nationally conscious people." As for Austria, Germany neither intended nor wanted to interfere in its affairs or to annex it to the Reich. If the Versailles Treaty were scrapped, Germany would return to the League of Nations, and would abide by all provisions of the Locarno Treaty which, among other things, had rendered Germany's Rhineland demilitarized.[2] This speech made it seem as though the evil Mr. Hyde had suddenly reverted to the good Dr. Jekyll, and it succeeded in disarming much of the world's opinion even as Hitler was rearming with the intended objective of building thirty-six army divisions from the hundred-thousand-man army prescribed by the treaty.

Unaccustomed to the working of Hitler's mind, however, and ignoring his program of conquest in *Mein Kampf*, as well as the murders, persecutions, and the dismantling of democracy in Germany, many newspapers lavished praise on his speech as an augur of world peace. *The Times* of London was a typical example, praising the speech for being "reasonable, straightforward and comprehensive." It was to be hoped, *The Times* wrote, that the speech would be taken everywhere as "a sincere and well-considered utterance meaning precisely what it says."[3]

Such laudatory editorials proved the effectiveness of Hitler's propaganda which was aimed at luring Europe into a false sense of security even as he was arming to the teeth. Later, the world would come to understand that when Hitler spoke benignly about a country, as was the case with Poland and Austria, it was a sure bet that it would become his most certain victim, or when he proclaimed that he had no further territorial demands to make, he was assuredly preparing to make them. That Hitler "needed and desired peace" at that particular time was certainly true since he was, in effect, buying time. As it turned out, everything he did was calculated to further his purpose. The lessons of Germany's 1918 defeat, as well as his own failed *Putsch* of 1923, which almost ended his political struggle, remained factors in Hitler's decisions, and caused him to move cautiously so as not to similarly jeopardize his military struggle.

It would be premature to use force to achieve his aims so long as he could still use other means, and while his military strength could not yet guarantee success. There would be war, but only when he determined that the time was right, and the enemy was of his choosing. Meanwhile, he would expediently have to resort to diplomacy—the approximate international equivalent to the hated parliamentarianism he had to engage in during his political struggle. Cunningly, however, he employed threats and intimidations of force, both as a means for testing the will of potential opponents, as well as a device for winning concessions without resort to arms. And, when concessions were made, it was his *modus operandi* to up the ante so as to achieve the maximum gains short of war. In a world of shattered nerves, whoever had the strongest nerves stood the best chance of winning.

The political, economic, and moral climate of post-First World War Europe was most suited to such tactics, for it was, indeed, a world of shattered nerves. Under the influence of Marxism and the Russian Revolution, socialist ideas and politics were infiltrating monarchist, conservative, and capitalist states. The transformation of society from the few aristocrats with firm opinions to the masses with no opinions, left the masses wide open to tyrants imposing their opinions. Movements for change were threatening desires for repose. The economies of European countries had been thrown into disarray by the Great Depression—a factor that provided fertile soil for both socialism and nationalism. In addition, there was the trauma of the war which ended its blood orgy with the hope that it was *the* war to end wars. The torn corpses of soldiers, strung out on Flanders' barbed-wire to be pecked by vultures and gnawed by rats, were ghastly symbols of the doom that seemed to hang over the civilization the soldiers had ostensibly died to defend, and which the political carrion on the left and right were poised to devour.

Moral values, too, fell with the soldierly victims, giving rise to deep questionings of the Judeo-Christian civilization in which such horrors could occur. This moral uncertainty and ambiguity was reflected in the writings of poets and novelists, and was evident in the judgments of statesmen who found themselves caught in a dilemma created by moral principles they no longer firmly held, and the realities of a world falling apart, and which they seemed powerless to hold together.

This world of moral uncertainties left itself exposed to amoral certainties derived from chiliastic ideologies on the one hand, and resurrections of presumed classical and Teutonic glories on the other. In Italy, Mussolini sought to ward off Communism, the major expression of the former, by reviving his version of the Roman Empire. What a poor imitation it turned out to be. His savage attack on Abyssinia succeeded only in proving that Abyssinia was no Carthage, and Mussolini was no Caesar. In Spain, and with the aid of Hitler and Mussolini, Franco destroyed his country's fledgling republic, but at least he had no grandiose visions of becoming a big Caesar, but settled for being a little one. He confined his fascistic activities within his own borders, and remained aloof from the cauldron of general conflict. While the world had come to fight in Spain's civil war, he was not about to take his country into the world's great civil war even though he was ready to act as a vulture if the German and Italian eagles were successful in capturing their prey.

In a Europe of shattered nerves, Hitler emerged with the strongest nerves of all. He had, as well, a much stronger will, and a more realistic appraisal of the cadaverous condition of European morality. Before establishing a distorted Greco-Roman empire laminated with pseudo-Teutonic mythology and social Darwinism, which he labeled a "New World Order", Hitler saw the necessity of destroying the Jewish-inspired civilization which had supplanted the classical world. And since Jewry was the visible evidence and original carrier of this "poison", corporate Jewry must first be eliminated within Germany, then throughout as much of the world as he had time to conquer through a combination of political machinations and armed conflict.

Just as his Stormtroops were strategically used in his political struggle against his "internal enemies", Hitler would use the army to threaten and intimidate, and then to conquer the "international world of enemies". Hence, his military struggle took on two forms: the first was a testing period during which, through combined political and military threats, he achieved his aims without resorting to arms, and the second involved the actual use of force which he initially hoped to use in a limited way until he was ready for the war against Bolshevik Russia that in 1924 he had projected in *Mein Kampf* as part of his war against world Jewry.

During the testing period, Hitler made the most of the Versailles Treaty, condemning it over and over again, and vowing to see it abolished. Signed on June 28, 1919, the treaty was one of several resulting from the postwar Peace Conference whose main objectives were to prevent a revival of pan-German power, and the creation of a European system which recognized the rights of self-determination among peoples in dismantled empires. As a companion to this it was felt that nation states should be as ethnically complete as possible—a requirement made difficult by the polyglot of cultures in what remained of the former Austro-Hungarian Empire.

The Versailles and St. Germain Treaties blocked Austria's inclusion in the new German Reich even though it was a greatly reduced Austria, and a predominantly German-speaking state. Treaty drafters thought that a German-Austrian union would present a potential threat to the politically-sculptured Czechoslovakian state that was intended as a barrier against any future German designs on Central Europe. Czechoslovakia's three million Germans, outnumbering all other ethnic groups except the Czechs with four million, presented the potential for future problems. Other peoples such as the Slovaks, Magyars, Ruthenians, and Poles totaled nearly five million.

The former German territories of Posen and West Prussia had been assigned to Poland, constituting what became known as the Polish Corridor. Linked to Danzig, the German Baltic port that the League had declared a free city under Polish customs' jurisdiction, the corridor's population of three million comprised two-thirds Poles and one-third Germans—the latter having Polish citizenship imposed upon them.

On the Eastern side of East Prussia, a smaller corridor was created which included the Baltic city of Memel. This city was ceded to the Allied and Associated Powers in order to weaken any future German threat in that area. Several years later, however, Memel was incorporated into Lithuania. Other Peace Conference decisions resulted in the return of the northern part of Schleswig-Holstein to Denmark following a plebiscite, and the coal-rich Saar region of West Germany was placed under the League-of-Nations control pending a plebiscite in 1935.

As a result of Versailles impositions, German territory was cut by about an eighth, and its population was reduced by 6.5 million. All of this was added to severe restrictions on military strength as well as harsh reparations requirements. The army was limited to 100,000 men and confined to German territory; the Navy was fixed at 15,000 men, and neither submarines nor naval aircraft could be built. Reparations included the confiscation of a sizable part of Germany's railroad stock, and the payment of about five billion dollars in gold, ships, and other commodities. Annual deliveries of these materials were to be made to France, Belgium, and Italy over a ten-year period.

Only the Brest-Litovsk Treaty, inflicted by Germany on Russia, and later abrogated after Germany's defeat, was a match for the severity of the Versailles Treaty's demands. It is worth noting, however, that peace treaties have much in common with the punishment of criminals. There is a need to mollify public anger by imposing harsh sentences on those who are deemed to be criminally responsible—a judgment that the victors reserve the right to make. Only later when public anger has subsided, and the criminal has shown signs of improved conduct, is it possible to consider a reduction in sentence or the granting of parole. The severity of the Versailles Treaty was due, in part, to the climate of anger built up against Germany, as well as a need to block future German ambitions. These factors made it well-nigh impossible to produce a reasonable, non-punitive treaty. Among the consequences were a slower economic recovery that was further aggravated by the worldwide Depression, as well as German guilt and anger at having lost the war.

Hitler made the most of these conditions by excoriating the treaty, and vowing to abolish its provisions as well as "settling accounts" with those he blamed for Germany's defeat. But even before Hitler's advent, there had been a growing consensus in Europe that something would have to be done to alleviate Germany's plight. In 1922, for example, after Germany defaulted on its reparations payments, the Allied Reparations Commission proposed the appointment of a committee of experts to see what could be done. Under American banker Charles G. Dawes, the Dawes' Plan approved a loan of 800 million Marks in gold as a way of stabilizing German currency, increasing production, and improving Germany's ability to meet its financial commitments.

Inaugurated on August 20, 1924, the Dawes' Plan was widely regarded as evidence that the major European powers were moving to correct some of the damage done by the Versailles Treaty as well as preparing Germany for rehabilitation within the European community. Germany's improved behavior alone, however, was not the only spur to ameliorative action. The Western capitalist nations were also concerned that if some action was not taken to soften the Versailles Treaty, then Germany would end up in the Soviet camp. These Western nations found themselves between a rock and a hard place. Too much rectification would enhance Germany's potential to revive its European ambitions; too little might push it into an unhealthy alliance with Communist Russia.

Nearly thirty years after signing, the lessons learned from the Versailles Treaty would contribute to West Germany's rapid recovery following the much more devastating Second World War. The anger and demand for retribution found then among the Western Allies, became focused on the war criminals who were tried at Nuremberg. This judicial revenge, along with a Western fear of Communism, made it possible to implement the Marshall Plan for West Germany's recovery which, though broader in scope and more rapidly implemented, owed much in its conception to the precursor Dawes' Plan. In addition, it ensured West Germany's alliance with those Western nations forming the postwar North Atlantic Treaty Organization, and also facilitated the reunification of Germany forty-five years after the war.

Early in 1925 under the new climate created by the Dawes' Plan, Germany's Chancellor Gustav Stresemann proposed a treaty between Britain, France, Germany, and Italy which would guarantee the 1919 Rhineland frontier while promising to arbitrate all future disputes. Then, in October 1925, at Locarno in Switzerland, Belgium joined the other four powers in signing seven treaties. Four of these called for arbitration conventions between Germany on the one hand, and France, Belgium, Poland, and Czechoslovakia, on the other. Two other pacts augmented relations between France and Czechoslovakia, and these two countries and Poland, and yet another called for a mutually guaranteed pact between Britain, France, Belgium, and Italy. Russia's absence from participation in these treaties was conspicuous, and was a sure sign that Germany was being wooed back into the Western European political club from which Communist Russia was excluded—a cold-shouldering that prefigured the Cold War.

Encouraged by these developments, the League's Assembly on September 8, 1926, unanimously elected Germany to membership, and two days later the German delegates took their seats. But when Hitler came to power seven years later, he quickly showed that he was not about to wait around for arbitration conventions or additional treaties to dismantle the Versailles Treaty. Indeed, these diplomatic moves to dismantle the Versailles Treaty might, if they had been implemented fast enough, have frustrated Hitler's bid for dictatorial power by obviating the need for his fanatical nationalism. As Nazi party defector Hermann Rauschning would later observe, "the great danger for National Socialism was an early ripening of moderate nationalist ambitions. That would have made National Socialism a superfluity. Its leaders were forced to launch the nation on an incalculable wave of revolutionism in order to maintain their own power."[4]

Thus, during his first year in power, there was plenty of evidence that Hitler was hell-bent on scrapping the treaty as soon as possible. He would soon show his contempt for it as well as the League. The Saar, the Rhineland, Austria, Czechoslovakia, Memel, and Danzig, all of which had figured large in the League's remapping of Europe, would become stepping stones in Hitler's eager territorial aggrandizement. In the immediate months after achieving power, these place names would become familiar to the world through constant Nazi agitations and subversion which were a prelude to takeover, either by political or military pressures, or a combination of both.

In light of the relative ease with which Hitler was to gain the Saar, the Rhineland, Austria, Czechoslovakia, and Memel, it is likely that he could have redressed most of the Versailles Treaty's wrongs through negotiation, but this would have blocked his move to gain *Tötungsraum* for the annihilation of Europe's Jews. Indeed, from 1925 until his rise to power, moves were already being aimed at dismantling the Versailles Treaty. In addition to the Dawes' Plan, the Allied Control Commission had been withdrawn, the Rhineland had been demilitarized by the evacuation of Allied troops, the Young Plan greatly alleviated reparations payments far beyond the Dawes' Plan's provisions, and international control over the Reichsbank and German railroads was abolished. But what the Allies perceived as ways of bringing Germany back into the Western European community was viewed by Hitler as efforts by world Jewry to keep Germany in its clutches. The Versailles Treaty, the Locarno Pact, the Dawes' and Young Plans were all anathema to Hitler, whose ultimate aim went far beyond the rectification of the Versailles Treaty. He wanted to destroy the "existing order" throughout Europe which encompassed all forms of parliamentary democracy, Communism, etc. In effect, he wanted to roll back the carpet of history to a pre-Judeo-Christian era.

For the most part, however, Europe's statesmen thought that Hitler merely wanted to restore Germany to its prewar position. After Russia went to war against Germany, even Stalin was to comment: "As long as Hitler occupied himself with the rectification of the injustices of Versailles, we could and did support Germany. Now Hitler is striving for world domination. This we cannot tolerate."[5] Britain's Prime Minister Neville Chamberlain, too, had belatedly reached the same conclusion when

Hitler, having digested Austria and Czechoslovakia, began to show his aggressive interest in Poland. Reluctantly for Britain, as well as for France, Poland became the Rubicon that Hitler dare not cross. Neither Britain, France, Poland, Russia, nor any other country, however, could see that Hitler was not just intent upon conquest of territory or world domination for the sake of power and domination, even though these were necessary to his aims. Everything he did followed from his *Weltanschaaung*, or world philosophy, which he had spelled out in *Mein Kampf*. The bedrock of this philosophy was that for centuries international Jewry had been engaged in an attempt at world domination, and this was reflected in various movements such as social democracy, parliamentarianism, Christianity, freemasonry, and Communism. All of these and more, Hitler believed, were marked by their international character as well as their tendency to band the weak together as a way of overcoming the strong, particularly the "Aryan" races, founded on blood and soil. Hitler, therefore, reduced his philosophy to its simplest terms: a life or death struggle between "us" (the Aryans) and "them" (world Jewry).

Since Hitler's Nazi political movement was *founded* on Anti-Semitism, it followed that his political and military struggles would be directed against Jewry, and particularly against Europe's Jews who were, in his mind, the physical carriers of the social democratic, parliamentary, Communistic, and other "poisons" that were threatening the very life of the "Aryans," of whom the Germans were the prime representatives. Hitler's military struggle was necessary, therefore, to the conquest of those lands with the most Jews, and where expressions of international Jewry were most evident, as in the USSR since, in addition to being the home of nearly five million Jews, it was also the standard-bearer of what Hitler saw as Jewish-inspired

Bolshevism, and the final form of the Jewish bid for world domination.

Under the justification that his military struggle was designed to gain *Lebensraum* (living space) for a greater Germany, Hitler's priority motive was really to win *Tötungsraum* (killing space) for the extermination, or "Final Solution", to the Jewish "problem". Hence the Army would act as a bulldozer, clearing land so that the SS, with its *Eintzsatsgruppen* or killing units, could round up Jews and other "poisoners" for annihilation. The space acquired in this vast pursuit of Jews would later be used to perpetuate an evil empire in which the elite of Nazidom would dominate, in Spartan fashion, millions of lesser breeds of Helots.

Preparations for this two-pronged approach of gaining ground on the one hand, and killing Jews on the other, were already evident from the time Hitler achieved power in 1933 until the Second World War began in 1939. During this period, Hitler's politico-military tactics were aimed at retrieving as much territory as he could before risking a general conflict. Parallel with these tactics, he took steps to strip Germany's Jews of all rights as a prelude to their removal from Germany, and their ultimate destruction—a pattern that would be sedulously followed wherever the German army and the SS went.

In 1933, for example, Germany withdrew from the League of Nations, and the Disarmament Conference, both of which Hitler considered to be restraints he preferred to cast off before pursuing his military struggle. In the same year, his anti-Semitic actions were marked by the boycotting of Jewish businesses, and the banning of Communism that Hitler saw as the final stage of a worldwide Jewish conspiracy inaugurated by Judeo-Christianity—the "first Bolshevism".

In 1934 there was a relative lull in anti-Semitic activity, probably due to Hitler's absorption with the problem presented by SA leader Ernst Rohm's clamor for a second revolution that would rid Germany of its old guard aristocrats, and make the SA, instead of the traditionalist army, the main instrument of National Socialism's military struggle. Hitler chose that year to purge the SA's top leadership, including Rohm, as well as others on his hate list. And with an eye to his future machinations, he also rejected the Locarno Treaty while the Nazi Party in Austria succeeded in assassinating Chancellor Dollfuss after botching an earlier attempt. Also in that year, Himmler was assigned as deputy chief of Prussia's *Geheime Staatspolizei* (Gestapo) or secret police, and systematically began expanding it as a branch of the SS. The Gestapo had been organized by Goering as an instrument of terror by which thousands were arrested, tortured, and murdered as political heretics.

The beginning of 1935 saw the Saar plebiscite delivering a resounding victory for Nazism with the return of this territory to Germany. Perhaps bolstered by its recovery, Hitler gave veiled warnings against Jewry during a speech at Nuremberg in the fall. His warnings acquired greater menace in light of the passage of the Nuremberg Laws (Hitler's "gift" to the Nazi party for winning Germany's freedom from its enemies) spelling out special conditions for full German citizenship that excluded Jews. Another law prohibited the marriage or sexual relations between Jews and Germans, and forbade German girls from working as domestic servants in Jewish households.

Since 1936 was the year that Germany hosted the Olympic Games, overt anti-Semitic activities were held in abeyance as Germany presented the facade of being a perfect host even to the extent of stomaching the participation of such "subhumans" as Jews and blacks who, it so happened, were among the most-honored athletes. The German army's occupation of the demilitarized Rhineland in that year, however, showed that Hitler was looking ahead to his military struggle. In addition, a law enacted on February 10, 1936, placed Himmler's Gestapo beyond the law; it became untouchable, and no court could interfere in its operation no matter how inhuman its actions. Since Hitler had become Germany's "supreme judge", the Gestapo's activities were deemed to be legal as long as it was carrying out Hitler's will. After the success of the Olympics, the tyrannical nature of Hitler's Germany became apparent again in 1937 as one thousand Catholic monks were put on trial, and the state assumed financial regulation of the Protestant Church.

More than the enactment of anti-Semitic legislation or the acquisition of the Saar and Rhineland territories, Hitler's actions in 1938 showed unmistakably the real nature of his intentions which combined territorial expansion with his desire to exterminate the Jews. On March 12 the German army entered Austria, and annexed it the following day—a move that was approved the next month by a majority of voters in a Nazi-manipulated plebiscite. Achieved without firing a shot, this territorial gain was followed on October 1, by the German occupation of Czechoslovakia's Sudetenland. Meanwhile, on November 9-10 in Germany, the Nazis murdered 100 Jews, arrested thousands of others, burned synagogues, destroyed other Jewish property, and fined Germany's Jews one billion dollars to cover the damages the Nazis themselves had caused. All of this purportedly was in retaliation for the assassination on November 7 in Paris of German diplomat Ernst von Rath. His assailant was a 17-year-old Jewish youth distraught over the deportation of his father to Poland, as well as other Nazi actions against Germany's

Jews. The Nazi attack on Jews and their property became known as *Kristallnacht* or "Night of the broken glass." Although the attack supposedly was unplanned, there are indications that some such event was already in the works as a way of testing public reaction to harsh anti-Semitic measures; the Rath assassination conveniently provided a justification. The timing of the event was particularly significant since it came on the 20th anniversary of the socialist revolution and the end of the First World War that Hitler believed was part of a Jewish conspiracy.

Kristallnacht bore some of the characteristics of the emotional pogroms that East European Jewry had been long familiar with, but in a Reichstag speech on January 30, 1939, Hitler drew wild and sustained applause from his followers by prophesying the destruction of the Jewish race in Europe. A few months later, in March, his troops would complete the takeover of Czechoslovakia begun the year before, and Memel would be annexed to the Reich. But his major move, which promised to fulfill his prophecy of the destruction of European Jewry, came with the invasion of Poland on September 1, 1939, and two days later this forced Britain and France to declare war on Germany, thus igniting the Second World War in just twenty-one years.

Hitler's military service in the First World War was fundamental to the reinforcement of the world view he had developed in Vienna. He hailed that war as the first hopeful sign of a resurgence of nationalism against the encroachments of Jewish internationalism in its many forms. The response to the Fatherland's call by the German working class, of which he counted himself as one, was an indication to Hitler that the working class was awakening to the dangers of "Jewish" internationalism. "Marxism," he wrote, "whose goal is and remains the destruction of all non-Jewish national states, was forced to look on in horror as, in the July days of 1914, the German working class it had ensnared, awakened and, from hour to hour, began to enter the service of the Fatherland with ever-increasing rapidity." "Suddenly," Hitler added, "the gang of Jewish leaders stood there lonely and forsaken, as though not a trace remained of the nonsense and madness which for sixty years they had been funneling into the masses."[6]

In *Mein Kampf*, Hitler also wrote that "If we pass all the causes of the German collapse in review, the ultimate and most decisive remains the failure to recognize the racial problem and especially the Jewish menace." Without the clearest knowledge of the racial problem and hence of the Jewish "problem" there never would be a resurrection of the German nation. "The racial question gives the key not only to world history, but to all human culture."[7]

Hitler had hoped then that the "Jewish poisoners" of the people would have been exterminated. His multiple references to extermination show that this was not a belated notion, but signified a long-standing intention whose execution required the right time, methods, and circumstances. Since the German working class had found its way back to the nation during the First World War, Hitler believed it would have been "the duty of a serious government to *exterminate* mercilessly the agitators of the nation. If the best men were dying at the front, the least we could do was to wipe out the vermin. All the implements of military power should have been ruthlessly used for the *extermination* of this pestilence."[8] In 1918, Hitler had reflected, "there could be no question of a systematic anti-Semitism," and he could remember the difficulties that one would encounter then in uttering the word "Jew". But by the winter of 1918- 19 "something like anti-Semitism began slowly to take root. Later, to be sure, the National Socialist Movement drove the Jewish question to the fore in quite a different way. Above all, it succeeded in lifting this problem out of the narrow, limited circle of bourgeois and petit bourgeois strata and transforming it into the *driving impulse* of a great people's movement."[9] (My italics.)

In giving expression to his anti-Semitism, Hitler used numerous synonyms for world Jewry such as "pestilence," "poison," "vermin," "bacilli," "international world of enemies," "social democracy," and "Marxism." In light of the exterminations which were ultimately carried out under his orders, it is unmistakable that when he wrote or spoke of "extermination," he meant it. This, in fact, is what distinguished his anti-Semitism from all of its prior German and Austrian expressions, and his aim for a systematic and final solution to the "Jewish Problem," constituted a departure from all antecedent historical exhibitions of anti-Semitism which were merely partial solutions. Hitler believed that ideas, in themselves, achieved nothing unless they were translated into action. He often scoffed at what he called "antiquated theoreticians," and wrote that "If any man wants to put into practical effect a bold idea whose realization seems useful in the interests of his fellow men, he will first of all have to seek supporters who are ready to fight for his intentions."[10]

Hitler's hopes that the German working class had found its way back to the path of national righteousness were dashed by Germany's military defeat, and the social democratic revolution, both of which came almost simultaneously in November 1918. The reason for the defeat, and the revolution, lay, according to Hitler, in the machinations of Jewry in politics, in international capitalism, in control of the press, and in other areas—all accusations which were without foundation. They (the Jews and those under Jewish influence) had stabbed the German army in the back, and this was possible not because a certain section of Germany's leaders were "bad or malevolent," but only because "their activity was condemned to sterility since the best of them saw, at most, the forms of our general disease and tried to combat them, but blindly ignored the virus."[11]

The war, therefore taught Hitler an indelible lesson: it would require a world philosophy to counter what he saw as Jewish-inspired ideologies and political movements which pitted the "proletarian voting cattle" against the race-based aristocratic principle of leadership. Since Hitler believed that the Jews were at the heart of Germany's *and* the world's problems, he concluded that "historically it is just not conceivable that the German people could recover its former position without settling accounts with those who were the cause and occasion of the unprecedented collapse which struck our state." ("Settling Accounts" was included in a cumbersome first title for his book, and would be included in the subtitle to the first volume of *Mein Kampf*). In this work, Hitler stressed over and over again that the *extermination* of the Jewish "virus" was *necessary* to Germany's survival. "The nationalization of our masses will succeed," he wrote, "only when, aside from all the positive struggle for the soul of our people, their international poisoners are *exterminated*."[12] (My italics.)

In these and other statements can be seen the roots of Hitler's political and military struggles, and notwithstanding the irrationality of his beliefs, they were held with fanatical intensity. His political struggle, therefore, was not only designed to achieve power, and least of all for power's sake, but in order to root out all influences in German society which he believed worked against the survival of the German race. Once this was achieved, he would be free to eradicate these influences beyond Germany's borders. This would involve him in a military struggle which would make sure that "all the implements of military power" would be used "ruthlessly," as he felt they should have been used in the First World War in order to "*exterminate* this (Jewish) pestilence."[13] (My italics.) And since the German state was under his absolute control, there would be no "Jewish press," social democracy, or parliamentarianism to stab the army in the back, and while he was engaged in his military struggle, the Nazi party—through the SA, the SS, and the Gestapo—would make sure that the morale at home was not disrupted by dissenters.

Hitler would resume the military struggle against the "Jewish international world of enemies" which had blocked Germany from winning the war of 1914-18. Since Germany's generals in that war did not have a unified political philosophy to back them, ex-corporal Hitler would make sure that the two would go together in the next military struggle. Then, he would be the supreme commander of the armed forces as well as absolute dictator. In addition, he would put an end to the long-standing, closed, snobbish system of the Junker class in the army by opening the higher levels of command to a new breed of officers more sympathetic to Nazi ideology.

Apart from the Second World War's great advances in technology, the one factor that distinguished it from the First World War was the extermination of the Jews and other carriers of their "poison". To Hitler, it was this missing component that led to Germany's First World War defeat. It is doubtful, however, that anti-Semitism alone would have enabled Hitler to win his political struggle, and to nearly succeed with his military struggle, for even though anti-Semitism was the foundation of his political movement and the glue that held the Nazi party together, other factors came into play, and Hitler used them like a battering ram to gain power. Not the least of these was the humiliating military defeat of 1914-18, the attendant penalties imposed by the Versailles Treaty, and the deplorable state of Germany's postwar economy. All of these factors, as well as anti-Semitism, were hammered home to the German electorate, and yet they were insufficient to give the Nazi party an overall majority in elections, but only the highest number of votes of any single party. Together, the other parties, in the second election of 1932 which entrenched Hitler's power, received 56 per cent of the vote to the Nazi Party's 44 per cent. Nevertheless, and allowing for the element of fear in a dictatorial system, the German people soon rallied to fanatical support of their Fuhrer. The long history of anti-Semitism in Germany that was being vigorously expressed even by Martin Luther in the 17th Century, cannot be ignored, and it was likely a potent undercurrent in the minds of German voters. But whether that anti-Semitism was strong enough to sanction the wholesale extermination of European Jewry will never be known with any degree of certainty. In Hitler's mind, however, anti-Semitism had been brought to full consciousness with a consequent willingness to carry it to what he believed to be its logical and final conclusion with the extermination of the Jews.

The secrecy of the extermination program, along with Hitler's reluctance to put into writing his extermination orders, however, suggests he might have felt that the public would not support his genocidal program, or even if he did, he may not have thought it worth the risk to put his feelings to the test. There is much to suggest, however, that his murderous plans already had been inadvertently, or perhaps even intentionally, tested by the *Kristallnacht* persecution of Germany's Jews in 1938, as well as by the euthanasia program directed at the mentally deficient and incurably insane. Hitler signed a decree in late October 1939 launching the program, but back-dated it to September 1, 1939—the date of his attack on Poland—possibly as a whimsical gesture signifying the beginning of his war against world Jewry which was to involve similar methods of first gassing the victims, then burning their bodies in crematoria. The euthanasia program became a virtual prototype for the much vaster extermination program to come under the cover of Hitler's military struggle.

Because of the widespread public outcry they initiated, both the *Kristallnacht* pogrom and the euthanasia program were important bellweathers for the Nazis. They were made even more significant by the fact that *Kristallnacht* was an overt exhibition of ferocity against the Jews while the euthanasia program was conducted secretly against mentally defective Germans who were possibly "guinea pigs" for the ultimate extermination of the Jews and other victims. Hitler no doubt learned that even absolute dictators can neither ignore domestic nor world opinion, particularly while international aims still required the exercise of diplomacy however duplicitous it might be. *Kristallnacht* showed him that while Germans might not oppose the denial of civil rights to the Jews, it was not certain that they would support their wholesale destruction. Nevertheless, public concern for the euthanasia program greatly exceeded that displayed over the attacks against Jews.

When word of the euthanasia program leaked out, it was also evident that the Christian churches contained the seeds for potential trouble. The program drew fire from both Protestant and Catholic clergy, and this the Nazis at first ignored. But on August 3, 1941, Munster's Catholic Bishop (later Cardinal) Graf von Galen delivered a sermon in St. Lamberti Church describing in detail how the mentally sick were being put to death. While protests had been registered as early as 1939 when the euthanasia program began, it was Galen's sermon that had a decisive effect. Distributed throughout Germany, it prompted some of Hitler's paladins to call for the bishop's execution. Recognizing the danger of such an action, Goebbels prevailed upon Hitler not to take such a drastic step that both he and Hitler doubtless would have relished. Instead, he ordered the euthanasia program abandoned. He could always "settle accounts" with Galen and the Catholic Church later as he hoped to do with all churches once Europe was in his hands.

It seems safe to infer that the outcry of the clergy over euthanasia, as well as the public reaction to *Kristallnacht*, helped Hitler decide to install major death factories in conquered territories. He also learned that while he could still spew hatred at the Jews in his speeches, and even refer to their ultimate annihilation, it was expedient to maintain secrecy about their actual extermination. For this reason, the euthanasia program that resulted in the deaths of some 70,000 Germans provided a valuable political lesson. In addition, the format of gassing, followed by incineration, served as a model for Himmler's staff as they scoured conquered territories for secluded sites to exterminate millions of Jews, and others, from all over Europe. Thus, Hitler could derive satisfaction at having developed his *Lebensraum* policy which provided an expedient justification for the *Tötungsraum* that, for political reasons, had been denied to him in Germany. Testimony at Nuremberg disclosed that in 1935 Hitler had told Nazi medical leader, Dr. Gerhardt Wagner, that "if war came, he would pick up and carry out this question of euthanasia" since "the Fuhrer was of the opinion that such a program could be put into effect more smoothly and readily in time of war." In addition, during the general upheaval of war, the anticipated resistance from the churches would not have had such a great impact. Hitler's attempt to inaugurate euthanasia before the war started supposedly came in response to a father's direct appeal to the Fuhrer that his malformed child be given a mercy death.[14] If Hitler felt that war would provide a smokescreen for euthanasia, it is reasonable to assume that he saw it also serving as a cover for his larger genocidal program. *Lebensraum*, therefore, became a cynical euphemism for *Tötungsraum*, as well as the rationale for the military struggle that served as a valuable cover for mass murder.

In a secret speech on April 5, 1940, for example, before Germany's invasion of Norway and Denmark, Goebbels told selected German media representatives: "Today we say *Lebensraum*! Everyone can interpret it however he wants...Until now we have succeeded in leaving the enemy unclear about the real objectives of Germany, just as our domestic opponents until 1932 did not know what we were aiming at..."[15] The wording of Goebbels' remarks makes it evident that *Lebensraum* was a deception to conceal Germany's "real objectives". The conduct of Hitler's military struggle, and the extermination program of the Nazis, show that *Lebensraum* was really an excuse for gaining access to Europe's Jews as well as to Russia which had one of the largest Jewish populations in Europe, as well as being the bastion of "Jewish" Bolshevism. His ultimate aim of having the German "master race" lording it over "lesser" breeds in conquered territories was secondary, therefore, to his program of annihilation in which the Jews were the priority target followed by communists and a list of other "subhumans".

The idea of *Lebensraum* was the one important addition to the world philosophy that Hitler had begun formulating during his Vienna days, and *Lebensraum* was a logical extension of this philosophy which, since it was founded on anti-Semitism, required that not only must the Jews be cleared from Germany, but also from as much of the world as Germany could win by force of arms. Sporadic emotional pogroms, carried out against Jews throughout history, had reinforced Hitler's view that the Jews were a world "problem". His recognition of the limitations of these "emotional" assaults on the Jews led to his development of the idea of "rational anti-Semitism" which would be systematically exhibited in action as the "Final Solution" to the Jewish "problem". *Lebensraum* then became a fitting companion theory to "rational anti-Semitism", ensuring that it would be translated into action both in Germany and far beyond Germany's borders.

German historian Werner Maser records that while the notes that Hitler wrote in 1921-23 leave no doubt as to what he meant by such familiar and frequent utterances as "Germany will be liberated", and "settling accounts with the brood of despoilers", at the time he jotted them down he had not yet developed his *Lebensraum* theory in which anti-Semitism would be enmeshed with his military struggle. During the night of February 3, 1932, Maser points out, Hitler told some old comrades it was only towards the end of his detention in Landsberg Fortress that he realized Germany's territorial ambitions must go hand-in-hand with the eradication of the Jews both in Germany and the conquered territories. "The policies he pursued as Fuhrer and Reich chancellor", Maser wrote, "culminating in his declarations of war on Poland and the Soviet Union, and the extermination decrees, were thus so many consequences of the concepts he had clarified during his detention."[16]

Despite all of Hitler's idealistic talk about noble peasants working in the new living space of a Greater Reich, he was clearly a man who was fascinated by modern technology in which he invested a last-minute hope of developing a "miracle" weapon. It is highly unlikely that he would have gone against the modern trend of industrialization which is accompanied not by the need for more space, but less. One of the most significant developments of the modern age has been the great migration of peoples from the land to the cities. Indeed, Hitler himself grew up in rural Austria, and displayed no signs of being a true tiller of the soil, but migrated instead to urban Vienna, then to Munich and Berlin. During the war, when his aides chose a country house as his military headquarters, Hitler rejected it because he did not want "cowsheds, horses, and farm noises all around him."[17] Besides, the resettlement of large numbers of Germany's 70 million people over Poland and the vast reaches of Russia would have tended to make Germany more vulnerable to invasion from without. Indeed, it would have taken many generations of breeding to produce sufficient numbers of Germans in conquered lands to act as Spartans governing millions of Helot-like subhumans. There is additional irony in the fact that Hitler, the originator of this wild idea, never procreated, and was probably incapable of doing so.

An even more telling argument against the seriousness of Hitler's *Lebensraum* policy is that there was very little real planning for what Hitler projected as a vast resettlement program. By contrast, the planning for the "Final Solution" was meticulous, all-encompassing, and carried out with great efficiency and dispatch. Whereas experts in extermination moved rapidly with the army to begin their killing operations, none were sent in to similarly execute a *Lebensraum* policy. There was no vast bureaucracy assigned to develop the conquered living space as there was for killing space, nor were experts called to conferences to coordinate a resettlement program as they were at Lake

Wannsee to coordinate the "Final Solution". The sheer scope of the roundup of victims for the extermination program, extending from Norway to the Greek Islands, and from France to Russia, shows that *Tötungsraum*, not *Lebensraum*, was Hitler's priority consideration. There is also no indication that Hitler was personally involved in seeing that a resettlement policy was carried out, whereas there is much evidence that he was eagerly interested in the acceleration of the "Final Solution", especially when his armies showed signs that they were losing the military struggle.

Had there been planning and execution of resettlement policies with the same speed as there had been for extermination, there might have been something that the conquered nations would have had to contend with. But, as Pieter Geyl, the Dutch historian, points out, there was "no planning, no large-scale political or social reconstruction...nothing that might be termed a policy for the occupied territories. Nothing but subjugation, oppression, exploitation. And as soon as the occupied nations gave signs of having discovered that the occupation meant, indeed, no more than the advancement of the interests of the occupying power, all they got was worse subjugation, worse oppression, and worse exploitation".[18] Or, as Franz Neumann noted during the Second World War, Hitler had advocated the consolidation of the European Empire especially by "acquiring eastern territories; and rejection of colonial expansion. But it is precisely in the east and southeast that Jews form compact minorities. Were there no racial theory, the incorporation of these territories would have meant giving the Jews, who have a much closer affinity to German culture than have Poles, Czechs, Slovaks, Croats, Rumanians, and Bulgars, a status equal to or even superior to the non-Jewish inhabitants..."[19]

Considered separately from his extermination program, therefore, Hitler's *Lebensraum* policy just does not make sense solely as a living space policy. Germany was not, as Hitler claimed, overpopulated when compared to other European countries, and rather than trying to curb the birthrate, as is widely advocated today in light of the world "population explosion", Hitler encouraged more births. Hitler's Germany was also not short of raw materials or markets. There was no empty space anywhere in Europe which Germany could have colonized. Yet, despite British offers of concessions on former German colonies, Hitler turned his face away from colonial expansion, insisting that Germany's future must lie eastward, and specifically at Russia's expense irrespective of how the Russians felt about it. Had Hitler's prime objective really been living space, he would not have allowed the extermination program to obstruct it or to permit the use of valuable personnel, material, and transportation facilities in the pursuit of genocide which had the further damaging effect of stirring the determination of the Soviet Army as well as partisans throughout Europe.

Not only was Hitler's war against Jewry the major *differentia* from the First World War, it also occasioned the ruthless disregard of internationally recognized rules of warfare. Had there been no extermination policy, Hitler, at war's end, could possibly have fulfilled his often-expressed wish to live out his life in Linz pursuing his interests in art, architecture, and music. But while Kaiser Wilhelm was able to retire to Holland after the First World War, Hitler's genocidal program ensured that had he lived he would have had to face trial and quite certain execution.

Although the idea of *Lebensraum* had been bandied about in Germany for a very long time, Hitler used this shopworn concept in an entirely innovative way to carry out a horrendous mass extermination program that no previous purveyor of the idea would have thought possible. In the 18th Century, Friedrich Ludwig Jahn ("Father" Jahn), a Prussian school teacher and lecturer, was espousing the need for *Lebensraum*, linking it to concepts of race, blood, soil, anti-Semitism, bookburning, and the longing for a Fuhrer. For these reasons, he has been labeled the "first Stormtrooper". Johann Gottlieb Fichte, the German thinker, was another expounder of similar notions in the 19th Century, as were others, and in 1926 the *Lebensraum* idea gained wide currency with the publication of *Volk ohne Raum* (Nation Without Space), a bestselling political book by Hans Grimm.

For Hitler, who was then reviving his slumped political fortunes, Grimm's book must have seemed very timely, as were the anti-Semitic and geopolitical ideas being fed to him by the Nazi Party's "philosopher", Alfred Rosenberg, his deputy during his time in prison, and Karl Haushofer, the geopolitician who imbibed the ideas of Sir Halford Mackinder, the Scotsman whose thesis in political geography was presented to the Royal Geographical Society in 1904. In it, Mackinder expressed the view that, with the decline in the importance of seapower, Asia and Eastern Europe would constitute the "heartland" or strategic center of what he called the "world island".

There can be little doubt that Hitler's geopolitical ambitions were far-reaching. The conquest of Europe would be but a prelude to reaching out to India and Africa from which he would take on the American giant in a fight for world domination. But such domination was always linked to his world philosophy which called for ridding the world of Jews and Jewish influence. "Before foreign enemies are conquered, the enemy within must be annihilated."[20] How then, it must be asked, could Hitler free Germany and Europe of Jews except by extermination? Besides, the very idea of the "Final Solution" to the

Jewish "problem" meant that to be *final* there must be no Jews left in the world. The zeal with which Jews were rounded up from Europe's far-flung corners makes it certain that had Hitler conquered Britain, Ireland, or any other country, then the Jews in those countries would have met the same fate as did those Jews throughout Germany and the rest of Europe. Indeed, if the war was designed only to gain living space in the East, why did those attending the Wannsee Conference include Britain, Ireland, Turkey, and other countries, in their plans for the extermination of Jews?

The idea of *Lebensraum* was clearly linked with the military struggle when, on November 5, 1937, Hitler opened a secret conference in Berlin of his top military chiefs. From a number of standpoints, the conference is of the utmost significance. It was the occasion when, except among close associates, Hitler for the first time confided the specifics of his war aims, and made it clear that, in the event of his death, his remarks were to be considered as his last will and testament. Subsequent events also indicate that the meeting was something of a Hamlet-like "mousetrap" devised by Hitler to "catch the conscience" of those whose enthusiasm for his objectives, he may have suspected, was much less than he demanded. Even if this was not his overriding concern, at least it fitted in with his intention to put himself in unfettered command of the military, as well as to supplant the top echelons of the traditionalist militarists with more pliable men. Three years earlier Hitler had purged the SA in order to appease the army; now he was preparing to purge the army in order to satisfy his own aims.

Set on a major military struggle, which would serve his anti-Semitic purpose, Hitler needed to be certain that he had absolute military power. And where the brutal slaughter of SA leader Rohm and others had been welcomed by the army, and drew little public reaction, more devious and less bloody methods would have to be used to put the prestigious army in its place and the ex-corporal uncontestably in control of it. If the army was to become the bulldozer clearing space for the SS killing units to fulfill their murderous tasks, then Hitler needed to be the driver. He had not struggled his way to political power only to have the military retain a measure of independence which might contain the seeds for his overthrow or to block his ideological aims. To have done so would have been uncharacteristic as his meteoric rise to power had shown.

He had become leader of the Nazi Party by abolishing parliamentarianism; he had ended democracy after becoming Germany's dictator and, following Hindenburg's death, he quickly added the presidency to his chancellorship, and then the supreme command of the *Wehrmacht*. Yet, while the *Luftwaffe*, with the committed Nazi, Goering, at its head, could be counted on to wholeheartedly support Hitler's military struggle, the hidebound traditionalists in the army could not be relied upon to conduct warfare in the brutal fashion that Hitler had in mind. He would have preferred that the military be totally Nazified, but there was not time for that. In the future, that could be achieved by creating special *Waffen* (combat) SS divisions, and filling the ranks with young men thoroughly indoctrinated by the Hitler *Jugend* (Hitler Youth). In the meantime, the army constituted the "last freemasonry" which had to be overcome. As with the Luftwaffe, on the other hand, the Navy did not present a great problem; it did not have the long and aristocratic "Junker" tradition of the army which tended to close its doors to men from the lower social orders. This had been one of the factors in the army's defeat in the First World

War. As previously noted, the general staff then did not want to create additional army divisions because there were not enough of the "right kind" of aristocratic officers to fill the new commands, and they were unwilling to open up such commands to social inferiors—a strange class bias that found its odd counterpart in the Nazi race doctrine.

As the Berlin conference showed, the army would have to be brought to heel, particularly before international political poultices lost their salving effect on Hitler's festering militancy. During this conference, it was clear from the reactions of General Werner von Blomberg, Reich war minister and the *Wehrmacht's* commander-in-chief, also General Freiherr von Fritsch, *Reichsheer* (army) commander-in-chief, and Constantin von Neurath, foreign minister, that they were not in accord with Hitler's analysis of Europe's political, economic, and military realities, nor did they appear to sense the urgency of the Fuhrer's war aims which were justified on the familiar grounds of Germany's need for *Lebensraum*. None of these men seemed to exhibit the concern for added space or were fearful that Germany would not survive without it, and particularly since they believed that Germany was ill-prepared for a major military struggle. No such reservations were held by Goering, head of the *Luftwaffe*, nor by naval chief Admiral Erich Reader, two Hitler enthusiasts who were also present.

Blomberg, Fritsch, and Neurath, however, were clearly at odds with Hitler, whose war mentality was reflected in small ways. He had, for example, changed Blomberg's title of Reich Defense Minister—a hangover from the hated Weimar Republic—to Reich War minister. The term, *Reichswehr*, which originally had denoted all of the Reich's armed forces, but had become ignominiously associated only with the greatly limited 100,000-man *Reichsheer* (army) imposed by the Versailles Treaty, was changed to the more aggressive *Wehrmacht*—a title that also covered all three services, but whose appendage "macht" (power), more accurately reflected what the Fuhrer had in mind.

Hitler had, indeed, made it clear to all present that he had already charted a course that would lead to war. As subsequently recounted by Oberstleutnant Friedrich Hossbach, a general staff officer assigned to Hitler as personal military adjutant, the Fuhrer said it was his "irrevocable decision to solve the German space problem (*Lebensraum*) no later than 1943-45" although the opportunity might present itself much sooner—even as early as 1938, which was then only months away. As he had spelled it out in *Mein Kampf* and elsewhere, Hitler again stressed that additional living space must be won by pushing east to Russia, and this would involve the initial conquests of Austria and Czechoslovakia. Hence, it was likely that Germany would be confronted by Britain and France. Nevertheless, because of Germany's dire need for raw materials, foodstuffs, and living space, "the only way out...is the securing of greater living space." Thus, the German problem could only be "solved by force".

For the improvement of Germany's military and political situation, Hitler said, it must be the first aim "to conquer Czechoslovakia and Austria...in order to remove any threat from the flanks...The annexation of the two states to Germany...would constitute a considerable relief, owing to shorter and better frontiers, the freeing of fighting personnel for other purposes, and the possibility of constituting new armies up to a strength of twelve divisions". While Hitler's opening remarks were focused on *Lebensraum* as the broad justification for this military struggle, when it came to specifics, such as the conquests of Austria and Czechoslovakia, he spoke only of their strategic importance in the larger struggle. He made no mention of resettlement in these two countries or, as in countless public speeches, the necessity of bringing their German populations into a greater Reich. Instead, Austria and Czechoslovakia would provide "shorter and better frontiers", and also free fighting personnel for "other purposes."[21]

That Hitler wanted his remarks to be regarded as his last will and testament in the event of his death is indicative of the importance he attached to his warlike utterances, and are inexplicable apart from the context of *Lebensraum*. This *provisional* "last will and testament", given before embarking on war, had one theme in common with his *actual* last will and testament at life's end. (My italics.) In the first instance, he asserted that the aim of German policy "was to secure and preserve the racial community and to enlarge it. It was, therefore, a question of *Lebensraum*." As became known later, and was well-known in the inner Nazi circles, "preserving the racial community" and *Lebensraum* would involve the extermination of Jews and other "poisoners" of the German race. In the second instance, Hitler enjoined the "government and the people to uphold the racial laws to the limit, and to resist mercilessly the poisoners of all nations, international Jewry."[22]

In 1937, therefore, the year before he made his move to acquire Austria, Hitler obviously could not countenance less than full support from those around him. While he was intent on war, Blomberg spoke of the lack of preparedness and raised the specter of defeat if Britain and France chose to check German ambitions. Blomberg had already shown less than a steady nerve the year before, after he ordered three army battalions to reoccupy the demilitarized Rhineland. A few days after the March 7, 1936 takeover, Blomberg's fears that the British and French might intervene prompted him to recommend a withdrawal east of the Rhine. But Hitler rejected the proposal and, as it transpired, neither the British nor the French used their forces to challenge the Rhineland move, even though it violated the Versailles Treaty.

While Blomberg's behavior in this crisis was unlikely to endear him to Hitler, neither that behavior alone, nor the unwarlike attitude of Neurath and others, was sufficient to bring about the developments that grew out of the "crisis of 1938." This crisis found its focus on what became known as the "Blomberg-Fritsch affair", and resulted in the removal of both men from their high military positions. But it actually involved a complex of problems which Hitler had to resolve before embarking on his larger and more dangerous conquests. Among these problems was the future relationship between the Fuhrer and the traditionalists in the officer corps, interservice rivalries, and the status of the SS, particularly in its relationship to the army—the latter being essential to Hitler's mass extermination plans.

As Fuhrer, who had won a personal oath of loyalty from every individual in the armed services, Hitler could not tolerate any intermediary group whose task was more than merely carrying out his orders. As an artist turned dictator, he was set on becoming the artist as supreme commander. In Wagnerian terms, therefore, what he had accomplished between 1933 and 1938 was but the overture to the grand military "opera" he was soon to conduct. This called for using the military and all those around him as human material for achievement of his objectives. After all, Hitler had observed that scientific experiments had made it possible for "one to wonder what distinguishes live bodies from inanimate matter".[23] His own apparent answer was that live (human) bodies could follow orders whereas inanimate matter could not. But, as Hitler came to discover, while humans can follow orders, they can also refuse to follow them, or to carry them out with less than great zeal, particularly when those orders are ideologically motivated and breach the officer corps' traditional military ethics. But what the army regarded as military ethics Hitler saw as a kind of freemasonry that kept the army aloof from revolutionary politics. The relationship between the Fuhrer and the army, therefore, would have to change, and change drastically. Hitler, the politician who had climbed from flophouse to Reichstag screaming that the Jew-ridden press and politicians had stabbed the venerable army in the back, was himself preparing to stab the army in the back, and Blomberg and Fritsch were the chosen vehicles for so doing.

Like the spider welcoming the fly into its "parlor" before making its deadly strike, Hitler began his relationship with Blomberg, Fritsch, and the army in a most auspicious manner. From 1933 until 1938 the army and Hitler worked hand-in-glove. Hitler had reinvigorated the army and, just as he had put millions of Germans back to work, he lifted the army out of its Versailles-imposed doldrums of virtual military unemployment. In addition, massive public works projects, including the *Autobahnen*, were engaging German labor and holding out prospects of transporting armies to new military ventures. National pride had been restored, and it seemed as though the army and the Nazi Party were fulfilling their often-described complementary roles as the "two pillars of the state". Hitler reinforced this idea when, marking his forty-seventh birthday on April 20, 1936, he promoted Blomberg to *Generalfeldsmarschall*—the first officer to attain this rank since the First World War, and the first to hold this rank in the Third Reich. Fritsch and Goering were also promoted to *Generaloberst* while Raeder became *Generaladmiral*.

Blomberg and Fritsch would not enjoy the preroga-
tives of their new rank for long. Within two years they
were removed from their posts and relegated to the lists
of inactive officers. Both men were toppled by morals
charges which would not even move the scales when
weighed against the gross amorality which had brought
about the end of democracy, and ushered in a regime of
terror, murder, and unspeakable horrors. Nevertheless,
such words as "decency" and "honor" would frequently
trip off Nazi tongues even as they directed millions of
victims through human abattoirs.

Blomberg was dismissed when it became known,
through a conveniently produced SS dossier, that the secretary he had married was a former prostitute. Fritsch
was brought down on trumped up charges of homosexuality which, even when proven false, did not result in his
reinstatement. In light of Hitler's own illicit affairs, first
with his niece, Geli Raubal, and then with Eva Braun, the
Blomberg charges were preposterous. The charge against
Fritsch was of particular interest since complaints of
homosexuality among the SA had been made to Hitler by
Ludendorff and others as early as 1926. Hitler's reaction
then was one of total indifference. "I don't care," he said,
"whether they (the SA members) f... through the front or
the back."[24] Ironically, Blomberg retired to Bad Wiesee,
the very same town where the SA's Rohm was staying
when Hitler and the SS came two years earlier to initiate
the bloody purge which Blomberg had been among the
first to welcome.

There can be little doubt that Goering and Himmler
had a hand in the Blomberg-Fritsch downfall. Goering had
always exhibited, in extreme form, the rivalries between
the army, navy, and air force. He was given to petulance
and irrational anger whenever the army, particularly, received preferential treatment over his *Luftwaffe*. He was

naturally jealous, therefore, not only of Blomberg's position as war minister and head of the *Reichswehr*, but also of his promotion to *Feldsmarschall*. Himmler, on the other hand, directed his attention upon Fritsch who stubbornly resisted SS incursions into the army. In addition to protecting their own fiefdoms, however, Goering and Himmler were more importantly serving Hitler's interests which found their focus in both Blomberg and Fritsch. Blomberg's removal cleared the way for Hitler's control of all three services, and together with the ouster of Fritsch, made possible greater SS access to army Nazification.

Looking ahead to his military struggle, in which the Army would acquire *Tötungsraum* for the SS, Hitler had to position himself so that a military revolt against the horrors to come would be difficult, if not impossible. With the fall of Blomberg, Fritsch, and other top generals, the solidarity of the Officer Corps had effectively been broken. Years later Blomberg found the reason for his removal in the totalitarian principles which governed the state. "Hitler and his party," he reflected, "wanted total power in their hands; no secondary powers, no independence of action, no centrifugal expression or diversionary tendencies would be tolerated, only the totalitarian, indivisible, untrammeled power could prevail. This had been accomplished everywhere except in the armed forces. Direct command functions were in the hands of a soldier, myself; the Fuhrer held only indirect command powers. This created distrust."[25] Blomberg, for example, had issued the order for the military occupation of the Rhineland, albeit in accordance with Hitler's wishes. But if, as war minister and head of the *Wehrmacht*, he had exercised his power to withdraw the army from the Rhineland as he had wanted to, Hitler could have faced a major and damaging confrontation with the army. The missed opportunity for Blomberg and the army was also a missed opportunity for Britain and France. Had they challenged Hitler in the Rhineland, they might well have handed him an unrecoverable political and military setback.

Now, two years after the Rhineland venture, Blomberg was out of the way and, on February 4, 1938, a decree was issued giving Hitler supreme command of the *Wehrmacht*. Announced on the radio, it quoted Hitler as saying: "From now on I take over, personally, the command of the whole armed forces."[26] This meant that henceforth the army, navy, and the air force, which previously had reported to Hitler indirectly through the war minister, would come under his direct command. The war minister position was abolished, and Hitler seemed at last able to do what he felt should have been done in the First World War, i.e., to "use all the implements of military power" for the extermination of this (Jewish) pestilence."[27]

Blomberg and Fritsch's tumble from power was followed by a shake-up in other areas of government. Neurath was forced to hand over his post as foreign minister to Joachim von Ribbentrop, a former champagne salesman. Walter Funk became economics minister—a position vacated the previous year (1937) when Horace Greeley Schacht retired under duress. The appointments of Ribbentrop and Funk, two ardent Nazis, were clear evidence that the posts of economics and foreign affairs would be fully integrated with Hitler's politico-military struggle. As events would show, Ribbentrop and his staff, in addition to "normal" diplomacy, became involved in facilitating the extermination program, particularly as it related to the Nazi roundup of Jews in collaborator countries. Funk's department helped German industrialists acquire slave labor which was often a prelude to extermination through deprivation, killing, or both. In taking over Schacht's ministry, Funk was stepping into very large shoes, for it was really Schacht who masterminded it, and introduced such public works projects as the *Autobahnen*, for which Hitler gained the major credit.

A former Reichsbank president, Schacht was a haughty individual who, while attracted to National Socialism, never became a Nazi. Despite his economic and financial wizardry, however, his "New Plan" for Germany's economy brought him into conflict with Hitler. The main point in their divergence was Schacht's unwillingness to totally surrender his "plan" to the requirements of Hitler's military struggle. He believed that Germany should pay its way in international trade by making sure that German exports were balanced with the importation of raw materials, nor would he countenance the printing of currency to inflationary levels. And while supportive of rearmament, Schacht viewed it as a part of his overall plan, but he was not prepared to see his carefully devised plan sacrificed on the altar of rearmament. This did not comport with Hitler's idea of the objectives of the Plenipotentiary-General for War Economy—a title that was bestowed on Schacht in May 1936, on top of the economic portfolio he was given in August 1934.

Schacht also upset Hitler and his coterie when he angrily complained about the Nazi Party's purchase of foreign exchange to pay for its international propaganda. Consequently, his authority over foreign exchange was taken from him, and Goering was appointed Coordinator for Raw Materials and Foreign Exchange—a position that was bound to intrude on Schacht's domain. Goering's appointment, therefore, exacerbated the growing antagonism between Schacht and the Hitler regime. Where Schacht saw the vital need for the promotion of German exports, Hitler announced the Four-Year Plan aimed at achieving German economic self-sufficiency—a plan that was as pleasing to the I.G. Farben (chemical) industry as it was upsetting to Schacht. (Farben was to greatly profit from the plan by producing synthetics, most notably gasoline and rubber.)

Schacht was certainly not attuned to Hitler's ideological aims that were designed to forswear international finance and trade which he associated with world Jewry. In its initial stage, Hitler's military struggle would depend on economic self-sufficiency until territorial conquests ensured Germany's raw material needs. In 1937, Schacht's days were clearly numbered when he not only warned that the *Wehrmacht* budget would have to be limited to ten billion Reichsmarks, but also sent Goering a lengthy note "tutoring" him on the necessity to postpone rearmament under the Four-Year Plan. And so, in mid-November 1937, after clashing with Goering, he submitted his resignation to Hitler (he had earlier given up his Plenipotentiary-General for War Economy post), and on December 8 it was accepted; Goering being temporarily appointed to fill Schacht's positions. It was precisely at a secret meeting in this same month that Goering was emboldened to tell industrialists of the need for unlimited rearmament and colossal production because: "We (Germany) are already at war. All that is lacking is the shooting."[28]

The shooting, however, could not begin until Hitler was sufficiently assured that there would be no challenge to his authority, particularly from the army. As a practitioner of the art of the "stab-in-the-back," it was natural that he would expect the same from others, and would do his utmost to prevent it. More importantly, he needed to make certain that the direction of his military operations would conform to his ideological intentions. Since these operations, among other things, would make it possible to conduct mass exterminations, it was necessary that they be carried on without army interference and preferably with army cooperation. So, even the military oath of loyalty to the Führer, and the removal of Blomberg, Fritsch, and other generals, were not sufficient guarantees that Hitler would have the kind of control over the army that he wanted, for in line with its traditional role as *the* senior service, the army officer corps naturally expected that this would be its continued role in any future military engagements, as it had been in the First World War. But, as president and chancellor, carrying the titular role of commander-in-chief of the armed forces, Hitler forestalled such expectations by making himself *de facto* commander-in-chief of the armed forces, or *Oberkommando der Wehrmacht* (OKW) which, in effect, made the army's commander-in-chief, *Oberkommando des Herres* (OKH), but one among equals with the heads of the air force and navy, i.e., the *Oberkommando der Luftwaffe* (OKL) and *Oberkommando der Kriegsmarine* (OKM). This meant that the commanders of these individual services would be subordinate to Hitler. Supposedly masters in their own "houses," they would be subject to his direct commands. Not only that, as head of the OKW, Hitler would be the only person with an overview of war strategy and aims which he could share or withhold, as he pleased, with the individual service commanders. As will be seen, this would prove essential when the military gained *Tötungsraum* so that SS units could round up victims for shooting, as they did initially, as well as transporting them later to murder factories. The SS and its *Sicherheitsdienst* (Security Police), were not part of the *Wehrmacht* but, through Himmler and his staff, were at the exclusive disposition of Hitler for whatever special tasks he decreed. The army, therefore, had to reach a working agreement with these special detachments which came yapping at its heels like long-starved bloodhounds eager to get at their prey.

Of the three services, only in the case of Goering, the *Luftwaffe* chief, was Hitler likely to confide his intentions, since Goering was part of the Nazi inner circle. Before Goering's fall from grace toward war's end, Hitler could say of him: "... you can't have a better adviser in a crisis than Goering. In a crisis he's forceful and ice cold. I've always noticed that when it's a case of break or bend he's ruthless and as hard as iron... a better man can't be found. He's been through all the crises with me, the worst crises, and that's why he's ice cold."[29]

Goering, who had blazed a trail of Nazi terror in Prussia, met Hitler's prescription for his commanders that they not be just military men, but political as well. When he first learned of Mussolini's assassination in 1943, Hitler blamed it on the Italian generals around *Il Duce* who were not thoroughly politicized.[30] And, throughout the war, this was to be his incessant complaint against his own generals, noting shortly before his death: "I want my epitaph to be 'He was the victim of his generals.'"[31] Both the *Luftwaffe*, under Goering, and the navy, under Raeder, and later under Admiral Dönitz, were suitably nazified, but the army was not, and this would prove to be the Achilles heel in Hitler's power structure, pitting his "intuitive" approach to military strategy against the professional, rational methods of the generals.

Hitler may have regretted that he did not carry out the "second revolution" that SA leader Rohm had advocated, and in which the "old guard" army officers' corps would have been violently purged, much as Stalin had purged the Red Army, and installed watchdog commissars to ensure adherence to his aims. Had Hitler achieved a similar purge, then the SA, instead of the *Reichswehr*, would have become Germany's "sole bearer of arms." But since Hitler did not risk such a move, he was forced to gain personal and direct control over the army in a less drastic manner and, at the same time, pave the way for SS killing operations in territories newly-won by the army. Several tactics were employed, however, that were aimed at the ultimate Nazification of the army. Despite army opposition, for example, Goering's air force reserved its jurisdiction over anti-aircraft artillery which, in other countries, had become the responsibility of the army. Through this, and other methods, Goering was able to build up a surplus of some twenty divisions which, though they would fight under army command, were still part of the *Luftwaffe*.

Thirty Waffen SS divisions were also created by Himmler, raising to fifty the number of Nazified divisions out of a total of about 200 regular divisions engaged in the final stage of Hitler's military struggle. In addition, the army's ranks were being renewed by the influx of graduates from the Hitler Youth, whose members were thoroughly indoctrinated in Nazi ideology. Indeed, Hitler used the same tactics for the Nazification of the army as he had done in his political struggle, except on a much vaster scale. He had swollen the ranks of the German Workers' Party with *Freikorps* members, and others, in order to gain control of the party which he then directed in accordance with his ideological intentions. It is clear that had he been successful in conquering Russia, he would not only have achieved the "Final Solution" to the Jewish "problem" in Europe, but also the final solution to his remaining problem with the army, for just as he had used the war as a cover for his extermination program, he was also using it to nazify the army, which in the prewar days of Rohm's SA, it might have been politically fatal to attempt. In his political struggle, Hitler did not want to be part of one of the mainline political parties; he wanted a party of his own. He also wanted an army of his own, but that was more difficult to achieve.

For a time, at least, until he had used the army to win major victories, he would have to wait.

In 1938, however, as Hitler was maneuvering to get control over the army so that he could open it to SS influence, he still felt constrained to select for top army positions, men who were not identified with the Nazi Party. As a replacement for Fritsch, therefore, he chose Colonel-General Walter von Brauchitsch, whose position as *Oberkommando der Reichsheer* (OKH) was greatly weakened by virtue of Hitler's supreme command of the *Wehrmacht*. Consequently, Brauchitsch was kept in the dark about Hitler's overall strategies, and was put in a position where his protests and complaints were rendered ineffectual. Two other appointments, those of Generals Wilhelm Keitel and Alfred Jodl, reflected Hitler's deftness in making selections. While neither man was a Nazi member—a point in their favor among the officer corps—neither did they show much backbone in challenging Hitler's decisions. Keitel's appointment as chief of *Oberkommando der wehrmacht* (OKW) was of little consequence since Hitler had assumed active command of the armed forces and, so, Keitel became a sort of amanuensis with no authority to initiate orders, but only to relay them. Jodl became chief of operations and planning for OKW—a job that entailed making sure that Hitler's decisions would be implemented, no matter how much these contravened recognized professional military operations. Indeed, throughout the war, both Keitel and Jodl were little more than "yes" men who often barred the way to generals with reports which attempted to introduce realities where Hitler chose to weave only fantasies.

And so it was that in addition to having tightened his grip on the army by February 4, 1938, Hitler could look back with satisfaction on his testing period in which he had recovered the Saar through the ballot box, and the Rhineland by an unresisted march by his army. He had built up his military strength, stripped the Jews of their rights, and begun subversion and agitation in those countries which were earmarked for conquest. He was now getting to the point where the hazards of testing wills with other nations, particularly Britain and France, had become greater. Yet, within weeks of the dismissals of Blomberg and Fritsch and the reshuffling of the German army's high command, Hitler was ready for his greatest gamble thus far—the annexation of Austria.

In *Mein Kampf* and speeches, he had made it clear that Austria's German population belonged in a greater Germany. "The destiny of this state (Austria)," Hitler had written, "is so much bound up with the life and development of all Germans that a separation of history into German and Austrian does not seem conceivable." And, as though expressing his own feelings as an Austrian who had become a German, Hitler wrote: "The elemental cry of the German-Austrian people for union with the German mother country... was the result of a longing that slumbered in the heart of the entire people—a longing to return to the never-forgotten ancestral home."[32]

But just as Hitler, the Austrian, had come to Germany and attempted to take power through a *Putsch* that almost ended his political struggle, he had also put his military struggle in jeopardy by a near disastrous *Putsch* aimed at the overthrow of the Austrian government. On that occasion at noon on July 25, 1934, more than 150 members of the SS Standarte 89, disguised in Austrian army uniforms, barged into the austrian Chancellery and, at close range, shot Chancellor Engelbert Dollfuss in the throat, then watched him bleed to death. Other Nazis seized the radio station and falsely reported that Dollfuss had resigned. At Bayreuth's annual Wagner festival, Hitler was attending a performance of *Das Rheingold* as a guest of Friedelind Wagner, granddaughter of Hitler's favorite composer. An aide, who had been in telephonic communication with the Austrian Nazis from a room adjoining the Wagner family box, whispered to Hitler the news of the failed *Putsch*.

Even before Dollfuss's assassination, Austria's Nazis had been active in blowing up vital installations and government buildings while a Hitler-approved Austrian legion of several thousand men were at the ready in Bavaria to cross the border into Austria. Such an act was forestalled, however, when Austrian government troops, led by Kurt von Schuschnigg, arrested Dollfuss's assassins, thirteen of whom were hanged. In an official statement, Germany denied responsibility for the attempted *Putsch*, but had it succeeded, another statement was at hand in which Hitler would have proclaimed the inevitability of Austria becoming part of the greater German Reich.

The attempt showed that Hitler had succumbed to his ever-present urge to achieve his aims by violence. But when it did not turn out as expected, he must have experienced a sense of *deja vu* in light of his failed Munich venture eleven years earlier. "We are faced with another Sarajevo!" he was fearfully heard to exclaim after learning of the botched Austrian affair—a reference to the Austrian Archduke Ferdinand's assassination at Sarajevo that triggered the First World War. His fears, however, were groundless since neither Britain, France, nor Italy intervened, but merely issued a joint statement affirming the importance of Austria's continued sovereignty.

Now, four years later, in 1938, Hitler was ready to try again, but this time, instead of a *Putsch*, he would use his own brand of bullying "diplomacy" to achieve his aims. A number of factors would work in his favor. Among these were the signing in October 1936, of a pact between Germany and Italy that created the Berlin-Rome Axis, and presented a united front against the other European nations. The following month, Germany and Japan signed an anti-Comintern agreement and, ironically, earlier in the year, Germany and Austria had also signed an agreement affirming Austria's independence and containing a German promise not to interfere in Austria's internal affairs. The Berlin-Rome Axis was, in part, designed to give pause to France and Britain against any move to forestall Axis ambitions, and the German-Japanese agreement was intended to achieve much the same effect on the Soviets. Mussolini's conquest of Abyssinia in 1936, along with the start of Franco's fascist rebellion against the Spanish Republic, also drew British attention to its vital interests in the Mediterranean. Austria itself, however, had greased the path for its own takeover. It had become a hotbed of the Nazi ideology that had been formulated by Hitler in his Vienna flophouse. Many of Hitler's most virulent followers were to come from Austria and, not infrequently like Hitler, they were also Catholics. Even politicians who were not Nazis nevertheless practiced a politics that had many of the hallmarks of Nazism even as they professed their Catholic-Christian faith. Such was the case with Chancellor Kurt von Schuschnigg, the man who would meet with Hitler in an effort to save Austria from German envelopment. Schuschnigg, the successor to the murdered Chancellor Dollfuss, had been a party to the Dollfuss government's brutal slaughter of Social Democrats on February 12, 1934—an act that had many parallels with Hitler's roundup of German Social Democrats and Communists after he gained power. Schuschnigg had been a member of the Dollfuss government when it turned seventeen thousand government troops and fascist militia on Vienna's workers' flats, leaving a thousand women, children, and men dead, and another four thousand wounded from artillery, rifle, and machine-gun fire. Political freedom was stamped out, and a fascist-like regime was installed. All of this was designed to strengthen the Austrian government's hand so that it could better stand up to Hitler.

Thus, when Schuschnigg met with Hitler at the Fuhrer's mountaintop retreat near Berchtesgaden on February 12, 1938, his own hands were not exactly clean, however mild-mannered, intellectual, and Catholic he seemed to be. Schuschnigg preferred to cloak the brutalities of realpolitik in refined language, whereas Hitler chose, when it suited him, to be brutally frank. Their meeting had been suggested and arranged by the wily Papen, who had been rewarded for his efforts with reinstatement to the ambassador-to-Austria post from which he had been recalled a short time before.

The meeting was like the rumblings of the first boulder that would trigger the oncoming European avalanche. Schuschnigg was met on the steps of the Berghof by Hitler, clad appropriately in a Stormtroop uniform. It was, indeed, a most unusual meeting. The Austrian-born Hitler, who only seven years earlier had become a German citizen, was meeting with the Austrian chancellor in what amounted to a demand that Austria surrender its sovereignty to Germany. From the huge window of the Berghof, Hitler and his guest could look across the border to Austria from whence Hitler had come to Germany as a young man from his flophouse room in Vienna. Significantly, he had opened *Mein Kampf* with the reflection: "Today it seems to me providential that fate should have chosen Braunau-on-the-Inn as my birthplace. For this little town lies on the boundary between two German states which we of the younger generation at least have made it our life work to reunite by every means at our disposal."[33]

Now, from his much higher perch near the German-Austrian border, Hitler interrupted Schuschnigg's polite comments about the spectacular scenery from the Berghof's window. "Yes, but we have not met to talk about the lovely view or the weather," Hitler remarked, then launched into a tirade against Austria which he asserted had "never done anything to help the German Reich. Her whole history is one uninterrupted act of treason to the race...But this historical contradiction must now be brought to an end. And I can tell you this Herr Schuschnigg, I am resolutely determined to make an end to all this business..."

In trying to defend Austria's contributions to German culture, Schuschnigg even introduced the name of Beethoven who, though born in Germany, spent the latter part of his life in Austria. "... there are many Austrian achievements," said Schuschnigg, "which cannot be separated from the German cultural scene. I'm thinking among others of Beethoven, for example... "

"Indeed," said Hitler, "I regard Beethoven as a lower Rhinelander."

"He was an Austrian by choice, like many others," said Schuschnigg. "It would never occur to anybody, for example, to describe Metternich (the great Austrian-born European statesman) as a Rhinelander."[34]

This was certainly an odd way to begin diplomatic talks of such ominous import. And while Schuschnigg's ambivalence reflected a perception among many Austrians of the interchangeability of Austrian and German culture, it did not necessarily indicate a willingness to merge Austria with Nazi Germany. At the moment when Schuschnigg became defensive about Austria's contributions to German culture, Hitler must have sensed that Austria would land in his hip pocket. This became even clearer when Schuschnigg bowed to Hitler's verbal bullying, and agreed in principal to the appointment of Austrian Nazi sympathizer Seyss-Inquart as minister of the interior with control of Austria's police. In addition, the foreign and economic policies of Germany and Austria would be coordinated. With German generals called in to intimidate him, Schuschnigg signed Hitler's draft proposals with the proviso that they would require the confirmation of Austria's government. In what appeared to be a concession, Hitler agreed to disavow the illegal activities of Austrian Nazis who would be required to move to the Reich. This was as if an assassin had been persuaded to fire one bullet less than the six he had intended.

After initial opposition to the agreement from Austria's President Wilhelm Miklas, Schuschnigg had it ratified, and on February 16 he duly reshuffled his cabinet in accordance with Hitler's demands. But just as Hitler was feeling comfortable with his "negotiated" intrusion into Austria's affairs, Schuschnigg decided to ask the Austrian people to resolve for themselves the question of independence. On March 9 he announced that a plebiscite on the question would be held on March 13. But Schuschnigg's belated attempt to undo the effects of his own weakness hastened instead the Nazi acquisition of his country. The plebiscite was never held. Instead, the Schuschnigg government received three ultimata on March 11 demanding that it be called off. The last of these set a deadline of 7:30 p.m., after which German troops would be ordered to march if the plebiscite was not scrapped. Schuschnigg's momentary act of courage soon evaporated. He rescinded the plebiscite, and resigned from office—a move that opened the way for Seyss-Inquart to invite German troops to enter Austria under the pretext of restoring order.

On March 12 they did just that, and Hitler, wallowing in his success, crossed the border into Austria at his birthplace, Braunau-am-Inn, from whence he rode in his open Mercedes to Linz. There, in the city where Wagner's operas had first inspired visions of future glory, he received a tumultuous welcome from the townsfolk, and met with his old history teacher, Dr. Leopold Potsch who, upon shaking the Führer's hand, may well have wondered at the phenomenal metamorphosis of his once scrawny pupil into powerful dictator. In his speech, Hitler saw the hand of Providence at work in his accomplishments. "If Providence once called me forth from this town to be the leader of the Reich," he said, "it must, in so doing, have given me a commission, and that commission could be only to restore my dear homeland to the German Reich..."[35] In Vienna, the Linz welcome was repeated on a vaster scale, and Hitler's beaming face could not conceal his glee at returning to the city that rejected him as an artist, and he had loathed for its "mongrel mixture of races" that he intended to purify.

The *Anschluss* (union) of Austria and Germany, now a *fait accompli*, won overwhelming approval in Nazi-conducted plebiscites in Austria and Germany. On April 10, German voters approved the union by a vote of 99.1 per cent. And even allowing for Nazi orchestration of the voting, it nevertheless reflected a high level of approval for the Nazis and their leader, as subsequent responses from the German and Austrian masses were to show.

As they were to do in every country they occupied, the Nazis turned their attention to the Jews—a clear sign of Hitler's anti-Semitic priority. Thousands of Jews were quickly rounded up and dispatched to concentration camps from which most never returned. Many were subjected to humiliation by leering Stormtroops and SS men who had them scrub Vienna's streets and latrines. Hundreds of onlookers, who might have been expected to show sympathy, instead hurled insults and taunts at these hapless people. In what may, in part, have been calculated to gauge international receptivity (or lack of it) to accepting Jewish refugees, a relatively small percentage of Jews was allowed to buy rights to immigrate to freedom. Many of these were shunted from country to country before finding a safe haven—a situation that doubtless gave the Nazis much satisfaction. In New York harbor, within sight of the Statue of Liberty with its welcoming inscription to the world's "tired and huddled masses yearning to be free" which, ironically, had been authored by a Jew, one ship carrying Jewish refugees was turned around and sent back to Germany. These Jews later lost their lives in concentration camps.

The Office of Jewish Emigration, set up by the SS, and administered by Adolph Eichmann, another product of Linz, may have been organized initially as a cynical test of world attitudes toward Jewry, for in a speech to the Reichstag in January 1939, Hitler noted: "It is a shameful spectacle to see how the whole democratic world is oozing sympathy for the poor, tormented Jewish people, but remains hard-hearted and obdurate when it comes to helping them, which is surely, in view of its attitude, an obvious duty..."[36] In any case, it was not long before this short-lived Jewish emigration office was converted into the vehicle for the organized round up, transportation, and extermination of millions of European Jews. Indeed, it was in Austria that the Nazis refined the organizational process for what became known as the "Final Solution" to the Jewish "problem". And it was in Austria's major city, Vienna, that Hitler had honed his anti-Semitism. In fact, the terror and brutality unleashed on Austria's Jews foreshadowed not only the *Kristallnacht* horror that was visited on Germany's Jews nine months later, but also the Holocaust itself. For those who had eyes to see and ears to hear, both expressions of terrorism exposed the true anti-Semitic face of Nazism.

Now that Austria had been brought into his orbit, Hitler turned his attention to Czechoslovakia, the other country whose possession would, as he had expressed it at his secret conference the year before, provide "shorter and better frontiers". Of all the incongruous diplomatic creations following the First World War, Czechoslovakia was a veritable geopolitical ugly duckling. Alternatively, it gave the appearance of a jigsaw puzzle whose pieces had been forced together in disregard of their contours or whether the end result would produce an integral picture. And yet, out of this mishmash, the country's first leaders, Jan Masaryk and Edouard Benes, worked tirelessly to shape the only truly liberal democracy in central Europe.

Created from parts of what had been the Austro-Hungarian empire, Czechoslovakia comprised the Sudetenland, Bohemia-Moravia, Slovakia, and Ruthenia. The predominantly German-populated Sudetenland (named after the Sudetes Mountains) plus Bohemia-Moravia, formed the Western or predominantly Czech half of the country, and Slovakia and Ruthenia constituted the Eastern or mostly Slovakian portion. With a total population of nearly 12 million, Czechoslovakia had 4 million Czechs, 3 million Germans, under 3 million Slovaks, 700,000 Poles, 60,000 Magyars, and 500,000 Ruthenians. Hitler first focused his attention on the largely German-populated Sudetenland that formed a collar-like territory almost surrounding Bohemia-Moravia. With what had been German Austria, the Sudeten Germans had once dominated the Hapsburg Empire. But, with the creation of Czechoslovakia after the First World War, the Sudeten

Germans had never felt at ease in what amounted to their reverse status in the Czech-dominated state that was administered from Prague in Bohemia-Moravia.

Soon after Hitler achieved power in 1933, the Nazi Party, backed by Berlin, actively fomented violence in the Sudetenland, but due to its subversive activities and bullying tactics, the Czech government banned the party in 1934. Under Konrad Henlein, however, the Sudeten German Party was formed as a Nazi front organization with Berlin's covert (later overt) support in order to pressure the Prague government into granting Sudetenland autonomy. When Prague responded by offering to give ethnic areas throughout Czechoslovakia some measure of local control on the condition that national unity would be maintained, Henlein, at Berlin's urging, resorted to the familiar Nazi tactic of demanding more.

Taking advantage of the Nazi-orchestrated troubles, Poland and Hungary soon asserted their interests in those parts of Czechoslovakia having populations with ethnic links to their respective countries. Meanwhile, at the beginning of September 1938, German troops massed along the Czechoslovakian border in a move clearly intended to intimidate Prague into handing over the Sudetenland, and raising fears of a general war throughout Europe.

On September 15, therefore, Britain's Prime Minister Neville Chamberlain met with Hitler at Berchtesgaden in the first of what would become several fateful meetings which, while intended to prevent war, went a long way toward ensuring its inevitability. At his first meeting with Hitler, Chamberlain became convinced that unless the Sudetenland was conceded to Germany, a general war would erupt. A day later, when he returned to London, Chamberlain conferred with French Premier Edouard Daladier and others in the French cabinet. The outcome was an agreement on a joint policy that called for the incremental cession of the Sudetenland to Germany. It was proposed that an international body with Czech representation would supervise the cessions, and Britain would join in an international guarantee of the new boundaries provided that Czechoslovakia's existing military alliances be scrapped, most notably the Soviet-Czechoslovakia Mutual Assistance Pact which the Germans found particularly unpalatable because of their own prospective political intrigues and military designs.

On September 21, despite frustrating and bitter opposition, the Czechoslovakian government bowed to British and French pressure by accepting the proposed plan. At Godesberg the next day, Chamberlain had his second meeting with Hitler, and was confident that the proposals would meet with the Fuhrer's approval. But once again Hitler rejected what he previously had indicated would have been acceptable. Germany, he asserted, must be allowed to immediately occupy the area at issue, and there would be no international guarantee on the remainder of Czechoslovakia until the problem of all ethnic minorities was resolved. Specifically, Hitler wanted the Sudetenland ceded immediately, and occupied by German troops no later than October 1. These areas would be left with all civilian and military establishments intact. In other areas not ceded, plebiscites would be held before November 25, but only persons who had lived in these areas prior to October 1918, would be allowed to vote.

Hitler's new demands sent shock waves throughout Europe, and were roundly rejected by Britain and France. War now loomed imminent as Germany repeated its threats against Czechoslovakia, and military preparedness became the order of the day in Britain, France, and other countries. Meanwhile, a British suggestion for a five-power conference between Britain, France, Germany, Italy and

Czechoslovakia, found favor with Mussolini who, having consulted with Hitler, thought the idea should be explored. Hitler, however, insisted that any such conference should exclude representatives from Czechoslovakia—the very country whose fate would be decided.

At Munich on September 29-30, a four-power pact was worked out which, among other things, allowed German occupation of the Sudetenland in successive stages. International groups were to occupy disputed areas, and an international commission was to determine the final frontiers of the dismembered state. The agreement, which became known as the Munich Agreement, was rammed down Czech throats, and was to go down in history as a synonym for appeasement. It henceforth also served as a universal warning against bowing to the demands of dictators. Indeed, following Iraq's invasion of Kuwait in 1991, Munich appeasement was frequently invoked as a justification for the U.S.-led war against Iraq's Saddam Hussein even though Kuwait and Czechoslovakia were far from being exact parallels.

In accordance with the Munich pact, German troops moved into the Sudetenland on October 1, triggering a land grab by neighboring states. In the Teschen area, the Poles seized 650 square miles of land with a population of about 361,000, comprising about two-thirds Poles and about one-third Czechs. Hungary snatched about 7,500 square miles with a population of about 500,000, which included about two-thirds Magyars, and one-third Slovaks. These acquisitions were sanctions by the two Axis partners, Germany and Italy. In addition, Germany benefited from a reshuffling of the Prague government. Prime Minister Benes, the doughty defender of liberal democracy, resigned when he became sickened by the complicity of Britain and France in the carving of his country. He was replaced by an aging jurist, Emil Hacha, who, with his Prime Minister Rudolph Beran, failed to demonstrate the kind of courage and political skill their country needed, although it is doubtful, given the British and French stance, that any Czech politician could have blocked Nazi ambitions.

As would be seen, the aggressive beast, which was ever present within Hitler, was becoming increasingly impatient with the testing period of his territorial aggrandizement. While the Munich agreement had gained him the Sudetenland, it had not given him control over Czechoslovakia, which he had often confided to his inner circle was his ultimate aim. Upon returning to Berlin after signing the Munich pact, Hitler was heard to say that Chamberlain had "spoiled my entry into Prague"— an indication that a forceful takeover was something that he would have relished.[37] It soon became evident, however, that the Sudetenland was merely a beachhead from which Hitler would launch his bid to control all of Czechoslovakia. In its turn, this country would provide the springboard for the invasion of Poland and signal the end of Hitler's amazingly successful testing period.

Even as the year 1938 was coming to a close, and the fateful year of 1939 had not yet begun, the Prague government was to see evidence of the Jew-hatred which Hitler had already exhibited in Germany and Austria, and which had been exacerbated years before during his mental struggle as a Vienna flophouse resident. Indeed, with its mixture of races, Czechoslovakia doubtless reminded Hitler of the racial mixture he abhorred in Vienna, and had recorded in *Mein Kampf*. In December 1938, the month after Jews were subjected to terror throughout Germany, Prague bowed to Hitler's pressure by suspending all Jewish teachers in German schools, and dissolving the Communist Party.

The Jews were also the focus of a meeting in Berlin on January 21, 1939, between Hitler and the Czech Foreign Minister, Frantisek Chvalkovsky. Hitler listed a string of demands, including the imposition of laws to outlaw Jews as had been done in Germany with the Nuremberg Laws. "With us (the Germans)," Hitler made it clear, "the Jews will be destroyed."[38] In a Reichstag speech little more than a week later, Hitler gave the world a glimpse of where his territorial conquests were leading with remarks that foreshadowed the Holocaust in store for Europe's Jews. "The world," he said, "has sufficient space for settlement, but we must once and for all get rid of the opinion that the Jewish race was only created by God for the purpose of being in a certain percentage a parasite living on the body and the productive work of other nations. *The Jewish race will have to adapt to sound constructive activity as other nations do, or sooner or later it will succumb to a crisis of an inconceivable magnitude.*"

"... In the course of my life I have very often been a prophet and have usually been ridiculed for it. During the time of my struggle for power, it was in the first instance the Jewish race that only received my prophecies with laughter when I said that I would one day take over leadership of the State and with it that of the whole nation and that I would then, among many other things, settle the Jewish problem. Their laughter was uproarious, but I think that for some time now they have been laughing on the other side of their faces. *Today I will once more be a prophet. If the international Jewish financiers in and outside Europe should succeed in plunging the nations once more into a world war, then the result will not be the bolshevization of the earth, and thus the victory of Jewry, but the annihilation of the Jewish race in Europe!*"[39] (Italics in the original.)

In *Mein Kampf*, Hitler had often expressed the necessity of exterminating the Jews but, in this speech, it was the first time, as a world leader, that he had prophesied their destruction throughout Europe, and it is significant that Hitler' speech linked "sufficient space (*Lebensraum*)" in the context of Jewish annihilation. Filmed records of the speech show the Fuhrer's glazed eyes and vigorously gesturing arms as he worked himself to fever pitch to emphasize the "annihilation of the Jewish race in Europe"—a prospect that drew rousing approval from the packed Reichstag audience. Hitler's prophecy of Jewish annihilation gains added menace from the fact that it was coupled in the same speech with the reference to the Jewish race succumbing sooner or later to "a crisis of inconceivable magnitude."

Hitler's pressures on Prague to implement anti-Semitic measures can be seen then as further steps toward fulfilling his own prophecy. Parallel with these pressures, separatist movements were being encouraged by Nazi elements in Slovakia, and by the Nazis and Hungarians in Ruthenia. In the wake of these agitations, President Hacha, in a belatedly courageous move reminiscent of Schuschnigg's attempts to hold a plebiscite in Austria as a way of forestalling the Nazis, dismissed Ruthenia's autonomous government on March 6 and, on the night of March 9-10, similarly disposed of the Slovak government, proclaimed martial law, and ordered the arrest of Slovak Premier Monsignor Tiso and other Slovak leaders sympathetic to the Nazis. A new Slovak government was named under President Karol Sido, who had been the Slovak representative in Prague.

Sidor's first cabinet meeting in Bratislava on March 11, however, was rudely interrupted by Seyss-Inquart, Austria's Nazi governor, Josef Buerckel, Austria's gauleiter, and a bevy of German generals. Unless the Slovaks declared their independence, Seyss-Inquart warned the cabinet members, Hitler would settle Slovakia's future with little regard for its ultimate fate. Sidor was able to put off the intruders on the grounds that the cabinet needed time to consider the Nazi demands, but in the interim, his predecessor, Tiso, escaped from the monastery where he was under house arrest and, in response to an invitation, met with Hitler at the Reichschancellery on March 13. There, he was directed that, upon his return to Bratislava, he was to send a Nazi-authored telegram to Berlin declaring Slovakian independence, and requesting Hitler to take the new state under his protection.

The next day, and through Berlin pressure on Hacha, a declaration of Slovakian independence, prepared by the German foreign office, was read by Tiso to the Slovak parliament. After feeble attempts were made to debate the declaration and, faced with the threat of German army intervention, the document was approved, and Sidor was voted in as prime minister of a new government. Ruthenia followed suit by declaring its independence as the Carpatho-Ukrainian Republic which lasted for only a day before Hungary, with Germany's blessing, moved to annex it.

With Germany's acquisition of the Sudetenland, its "protection" of Slovakia, and Hungary's annexation of Ruthenia, the predominantly Czech Bohemia-Moravia was all that was left of the Czechoslovakian state. But even this remnant would soon come under Nazi control as became clear during a meeting in Berlin on March 14-15 between Hitler and Hacha. It bore striking resemblance to the meeting a year before between Hitler and Austria's Chancellor Schuschnigg.

As with Schuschnigg, Hacha was subjected to the Führer's virulent and arrogant verbal lashings, and stunned by his demands. The German army, Hitler warned, had already received orders to invade Bohemia-Moravia, and to forcibly annex it to the Reich unless assurances could be given that there would be no resistance. In other words, the last part of Czechoslovakia was being asked to surrender. Documents of surrender had already been prepared for Hacha, and his foreign secretary, Chvalkovsky, to sign. They did so after a night of relentless pressure in which Goering and Ribbentrop circled the two Czechs seated at a table, frequently thrusting papers at them with demands to sign. If they did not sign, they were warned, Prague would be left in ruins. Hacha fainted from the ordeal and had to be revived by injections administered by Hitler's doctor. A few minutes before four on the morning of March 15, Hacha and Chvalkovsky applied their signatures alongside Hitler's—an unwilling acknowledgement that the threatening sword can be much mightier than the pen.

Within hours of the signing, German troops marched into Bohemia-Moravia and by the same evening, as he had done the year before in Vienna, Hitler made his triumphal entry into Prague. From the historical Hradschin Castle, where he spent the night, he proclaimed the Protectorate of Bohemia. Neurath, his one time foreign minister, was brought out of retirement to serve in the nominal post of Protector. Henlein, who had done so much to facilitate the Nazi takeover, was made head of the civil administration, and Karl Hermann Frank, the Sudeten deputy leader, became secretary of state. The real control over the "protectorate," however, was exercised by the SS under the arch-Nazi Reinhard Heydrich, who would later be handed the order to coordinate the "Final Solution" which, until his assassination, he did with particular zest, possibly to wipe out that "damned spot" of Jewish blood that was believed to be coursing his veins.

Not until March 18 did the British and French protest the German domination of Czechoslovakia. British and French public outrage at Germany's actions, however, had the effect of jolting the leaders of the two governments out of their appeasement paralysis. In Britain, particularly, Chamberlain was faced with a revolt from at least half of his cabinet and other supporters who now wanted his appeasement policy ended. In a speech he had hurriedly drafted on March 17 as a substitute for one he had planned to give on domestic affairs in his constituent city of Birmingham, Chamberlain would say that "No greater mistake could be made than to suppose that because one believes war to be a senseless and cruel thing, this nation has so lost its fiber that it will not take part to the utmost of its power in resisting such a challenge if it ever were made."[40]

Within a week of Chamberlain's speech, Hitler made another of his triumphant entrances into Memel which, following the familiar pattern of Nazi machinations in Austria and Czechoslovakia, had been softened up by SS-created disturbances. Threats of force had been used to make Lithuania's government agree to the occupation of this Baltic port with its 40,000 inhabitants, mostly Germans. Significantly, Hitler travelled to Memel in the battleship *Deutschland*—an experience that made the Austrian-born landlubber seasick.

Coupled with increased German agitations in the Danzig corridor, Memel's takeover made it apparent that just as the Sudetenland had been used to gain a toehold in Czechoslovakia, Danzig would provide the excuse for aggression against Poland. Although Hitler had hoped that, through pressure, he could gain his objectives in Poland, as he had done in Austria and Czechoslovakia, without resorting to war, he was realistic enough to see that bloodless conquests were no longer possible. Henceforth, his military struggle would have to resort to nude force instead of a combination of political pressures and military intimidation.

Hitler's assessment of his declining options were spelled out on May 23, five months before his attack on Poland. At a secret meeting of his military chiefs at the Reichschancellery, he asserted that further successes could no longer be gained without bloodshed, and it was clear from his remarks that his objectives were not limited to Danzig for, as he noted, "Danzig is not the subject of the dispute at all. It is a question of expanding our living space in the East...There is no other possibility in Europe." Germany, Hitler added, could not expect "a repetition of the Czech affair. There will be war. Our task is to isolate Poland...

"If it is not certain that a German-Polish conflict will not lead to war with the West, then the fight must be primarily against England and France. Fundamentally, therefore, conflict with Poland—beginning with an attack on Poland—will be successful if the West keeps out of it. If that is not possible, it is better to fall upon the West and to finish off Poland at the same time."[41]

For Hitler, the ideal scenario would have been to reach some agreement with Britain, as he had done with Italy, so that he could have swallowed Poland without any interference. Absent Britain on its side, France could be expected not to intervene. Then, after digesting Poland, he could have pursued his main objective: the conquest of Russia with its attendant extermination of Jews, Communists, and others. Britain, however, imposed a stumbling block in the path of his intended aggressions. Responding to mounting public anger over his appeasement policy, Chamberlain, on March 31, told the House of Commons that if Poland was attacked, "His Majesty's government would feel themselves bound at once to lend the Polish government all support in their power." He had been authorized, Chamberlain noted, to say that the French government "stood in the same position."[42] His speech showed that belatedly Chamberlain was about to awaken the slumbering British Lion, but it would be left to his successor, Winston Churchill, to provide the "lion's" roar.

Before that point could be reached, however, European diplomats scurried to and from this country and that in the quest of treaties which were best felt to be in their respective countries' national interests. They were like compulsive gamblers placing their bets at a Monte Carlo casino just seconds before the roulette wheel has been spun. Chamberlain was too late in placing Britain's "bet" on the "red" (Russia). But, having more experience at political gambling, Hitler beat him to it by signing a Nazi-Soviet pact on August 23, which, on the one hand, was meant to intimidate Britain and France so that they might not keep their commitment to Poland when Hitler made his conquistador move on that country. On the other hand, he hoped to avoid conflict with his targeted enemy, Russia, until he had successfully defeated Poland. Germany was a much more persuasive suitor than the British whose reticence in wooing the Russians stemmed from Chamberlain's stubborn anti-Communism mingled with disdain for the Russians—an ironic attitude in light of Hitler's willingness to submerge his purple hatred of Communism long enough to achieve his more immediate aims which he knew would better position him for his ultimate objective of conquering Russia.

In the House of Commons, on May 19, only a few months before the Nazi-Soviet pact was signed, Chamberlain explained his own failure to negotiate an Anglo-Soviet pact by observing how a "sort of veil, a sort of wall" existed between the two governments which "it is extremely difficult to penetrate."[43] But this veil, this wall, was largely Chamberlain's own doing, and at that point in time, it worked against Britain's security interests. In the postwar years, Chamberlain's "veil" and "wall" metaphors would find echo in Churchill's speech at Fulton, Missouri, when he dramatically announced that an "iron curtain" had descended across Europe, separating the Communist world from the Western democracies—a curtain that would become symbolized by the quite literal wall the Russians had built in East Berlin.

In 1939, however, Chamberlain chose not to bet on the Russian "red," but instead made the quixotic gamble of committing Britain to the defense of a Poland that not only was a great deal less than democratic, but also was so removed by distance that there was no immediate way in which Britain's commitment could be made with military force. France could only come to Poland's aid by clashing first with contiguous Germany which, as a counter to France's "impregnable" Maginot Line, had feverishly constructed the Siegfried Line running the length of France's northern boundary. While the British and the French made their commitment to Poland in trepidation, the Poles received it like a shot of adrenalin that encouraged them to rebuff every Nazi attempt to make of Poland another Austria and Czechoslovakia. In addition, the Poles were familiar with dictatorial methods; they had a dictatorship in their own country, and had quickly shared in the Nazi spoils by grabbing Czechoslovakia's Teschen area. When Berlin, therefore, suggested that Danzig be restored to Germany, and that Germany be given a motor road and railway across the corridor, the Poles promptly rejected the proposal or any change in the *status quo*. No threats, no sweet talk, no promises, no warnings, would make the Poles give in or surrender their sovereignty or any part of it. Clearly Hitler's testing period had ended, his only option now was force, which he had been planning as an alternative all along.

PART II—WAR BEGINS

In a Reichstag speech on September 1, 1939, just twenty years after joining the obscure German Workers' Party, Hitler told his people how, on the previous night, Polish regular soldiers had crossed the border into Germany and attacked at several points, including the radio station at Gleiwitz. As a consequence, Hitler said, "we (Germany) have been returning the fire, and from now on bombs will be met with bombs, whoever fights with poison gas will be fought with poison gas. Whoever departs from the rules of humane warfare can only expect that we shall do the same..."[44] Hitler's reference to the use of bombs, poison gas, and inhumane warfare were part of his familiar technique of transposing to others the brutal actions he himself planned to commit. As a soldier in the First World War he had written a letter to an acquaintance expressing the view that thousands of "those (Jewish) poisoners of the (German) race" should have been gassed, and now, embarked on war, he once again made reference to poison gas which, as events would show, would be the precise method of exterminating his most hated enemy, the Jews.

Hitler's Reichstag speech signaled the end of the testing phase of his military struggle that began with the Rhineland takeover in 1936. He had now moved away from the pseudo-diplomacy that had served him so well, and had brought Austria, Czechoslovakia, and Memel within his despotic maw. At a meeting in Berchtesgaden Hitler is reported to have said that the "occupation of Austria and the Sudeten territory were semi-diplomatic, semi-military operations; a mixture of war and propaganda, diplomacy, and subversive revolutionism."[45] Now that mixture was no longer possible. The dice had been rolled. Germany and Poland were at war, and within two days of his invasion of Poland, Britain and France honored their commitments to Poland by declaring war on Germany.

But contrary to Hitler's version of how the war began, it was not Polish soldiers who had fired the first shots, but SS men disguised in Polish army uniforms. Having commandeered the Gleiwitz radio station, the SS made a brief inflammatory announcement, then fled, but not before leaving an unidentified concentration camp victim in civilian clothing to serve as a supposed fatal victim of Polish aggression. More than 100 concentration camp inmates were similarly dumped at selected locations to serve the same purpose. These unscrupulous actions were designed to preserve Hitler's fiction that it was not he, the ardent striver for peace, but the Poles who had unleashed the dogs of war.

As described by Hitler, however, the events did not conform to the facts, nor did they square with Nazi activities leading up to the war. Within months of his ascension to power in 1933, for example, the Nazi Party was already hyperactive in Danzig where, in the summer of that year, it had gained control of the free city's government. Soon Danzig would become a microcosm of Hitler's Germany. Its Senate passed an enabling act modeled on the one passed in Germany, allowing purges of the courts, police, and all key institutions. By banning all non-Nazi political and social organizations, the Nazi Party also became the city's sole political organization. This suppression of rival parties, along with the arrests of Catholic priests, and the disenfranchisement of Jews, followed the pattern already set in Germany, and would be copied throughout Europe.

A disillusioned Hermann Rauschning, the Danzig Senate's first Nazi president, appealed in vain to Hitler against these persecutions, then resigned and subsequently went into exile. "(National) Socialism," Rauschning would later reflect, "ceases to be a regulative idea of justice and equity when it sheds the Western principles of legality and of the liberty of the person."[46] The Nazis, however, were quick to select a successor to Rauschning. He was Arthur Greiser, a fanatical and violent Nazi, who could be depended upon to follow the Party line as dictated from Berlin. He would serve the Nazi cause in Danzig as Seyss-Inquart had done in Austria with such good effect, and as Henlein had so slavishly done in Czechoslovakia.

Even though Danzig's Constitution came under League of Nations jurisdiction, Greiser and Albert Forster, Danzig's Gauleiter, would emulate Hitler's contempt for the League. When the League's conscientious high commissioner Sean Lester ruled that many of the Danzig Nazi's oppressive decrees were in violation of the Constitution, the Nazis countered with fierce attacks against him. At a meeting of the League's Council in Geneva, Greiser unleashed a tirade worthy of Hitler in which he asserted that either the commissioner should stop interfering in Danzig's internal affairs, or that his position should be abolished. Back in Danzig, Greiser ignored further contacts from the commissioner, and displayed the kind of contempt for the League that Hitler had shown before him. The League had exhibited its ineffectiveness when Hitler marched into the Rhineland, Austria, Czechoslovakia, and Memel. It had also taken no action against Mussolini's invasion of Abyssinia, Franco's revolt against the Spanish Republic, or Japan's invasion of Manchuria, and similarly showed its lack of spunk in the face of the contemptuous actions of Danzig's Nazis. Following up on a misguided Polish suggestion, the League appointed a University of Zurich professor, Karl Burckhardt, to succeed Lester as Danzig's high commissioner. Since he had a strong affinity for Germany, Burckhardt's appointment was warmly received by the Nazis, who continued their now untrammeled campaign against political and other enemies in what became an arrogant prelude to Germany's invasion of Poland.

With the attack on Poland, Hitler reverted, on the international level, to the "straight course" of violence that he had been forced to abandon after his failed 1923 *Putsch*. He had achieved absolute power in Germany by resorting to a mix of democratic electioneering, harassment, and bullying tactics. And he had gained the Rhineland, Austria, Czechoslovakia, and Memel by a combination of diplomacy, subversion, and military intimidation, but with Poland, he was thrown back on the naked use of force. Now that the war was underway, he could devote his entire energies to the military struggle that had always been his aim, and he would do so with all the unrestrained demonism of his brutal personality. No treaty, no state, no people, no person, no morality, no rules, no laws, no feelings could restrain his satanic will. And while historians would point to many parallels in the careers of Hitler and Napoleon, it had to be said that wherever Napoleon's armies had gone, Jews had been liberated, but wherever Hitler's armies went, Jews were exterminated.

In starting the war, it seemed that the Germans were taking on more than they could handle. Their 98 divisions in various stages of readiness would ostensibly be pitted against 130 divisions of Polish and French troops. The British, whenever and however they brought their troops into action, would total about a half dozen regular divisions, 26 territorial divisions, with another 29 being readied at the outbreak of war. Neither the British, French, nor the Poles, however, had kept abreast of modern military weaponry or tactics. The Poles would pit their cavalry against German tanks, the French placed a too heavy reliance on their "impregnable" Maginot Line, and the British failed to develop a large mobile army with new tanks despite the fact that the first experimental armored force in the world had been formed in Britain as early as 1929.

The potential of mobile warfare had been first seen by General Alfred von Schlieffen, chief of the German army general staff (1891-1905), who proposed the deployment of cavalry to pierce enemy lines to reach long-range objectives. His idea was not enthusiastically received, but with the advent of tanks his idea was revived to become a major technique in modern mechanized warfare. Among those influenced by Schlieffen's idea were British military thinkers such as Basil Liddell Hart. Yet, his book, *The Defense of Britain*, and other articles, had little effect on British, French, or Polish war planning. A few young German officers, however, became captivated by Hart's writings, and were to demonstrate to the world the stunning effectiveness of armed mobility that the Britisher had described. But, like their British, French, and Polish counterparts, the German general staff, in the main, was afflicted with the static, defensive mentality associated with the 1914-18 war. Perhaps due, in part, to his antipathy towards the old guard military staff, Hitler was more receptive to the novel ideas of some of the younger officers who were enthused about the potential of mobile warfare. And, if only belatedly, Churchill, too, would come to recognize the tactical importance of mobile armory. After the war, he reflected: "Neither in France nor in Britain had there been any effective comprehension of the consequences of the new fact that armored vehicles could be made capable of withstanding artillery fire, and could advance a hundred miles a day."[47]

German tanks, supported by an aggressive air force, brought the Poles effectively to their knees by September 28 when Warsaw capitulated. Confident of victory, Hitler already had made a triumphal entry into Danzig on September 19. By October 5, all but a few pockets of resistance had collapsed. About 80,000 Polish soldiers escaped to neutral countries, and many of these found their way to Britain where they formed the Free Polish Army. The Germans, however, were not to gain all the fruits of their lightning victory. Under the pretense of protecting Eastern Poland's White Russians and Ukrainians, the Soviet army moved into this region and met with the German army on the line running south from East Prussia past Bialystok, Brest-Litovsk, and Lwow to the Carpathians. Poland was then divided along lines agreed to by Berlin and Moscow.

It was not until September 17 that the French first engaged the Germans, by which time the Poles were well on the way to defeat. The slowness of the French to enter the conflict was due largely to the 1918 military syndrome which required careful preparation, particularly by the prior use of heavy artillery as a softening up tactic before the commitment of ground forces. The Germans, in turn, showed that modern warfare would no longer be dependent upon massive numbers of infantry but in the adroit, flexible, and speedy deployment of mechanized vehicles in conjunction with air support. The Maginot Line, as the word "line" implied, was developed in accordance with a defensive rather than an offensive mentality. The deficiencies of this archaic attitude were fatally exposed by the highly mobile German panzer divisions which, instead of conveniently confronting the Maginot Line defenses, skipped rapidly around them. In so doing, the Germans showed that the days of infantry-artillery dependency would give way to tank-plane ascendancy—an evolution which had begun on a limited scale in the First World War, but was accelerated in the Second. The U.S.-led war against Iraq in 1991 showed that, under certain circumstances, massive air power alone could greatly reduce the need for land forces.

The German invasion of Poland, therefore, could be said to have provided the first demonstration of the refinement of tank-plane warfare; it also revealed to the world the unfettered fury of the Hitler regime. Warsaw was ravaged far beyond any military necessity. The cream of Poland's military, its intellectuals, and nobility, were quickly and brutally liquidated and, as in Germany, Austria, and Czechoslovakia, the Jews were rounded up as part of an increasingly systematic process that would lead to the destruction of a large part of European Jewry. Indeed, Poland would become the major center for implementing the Final Solution. With his mental and political struggles behind him, Hitler's military struggle would show that his priority aim was the extermination of Jewry along with all those he considered to be carriers of Jewry's "poisonous" spirit.

The invasion of Poland also marked the midpoint in Hitler's ruthless career. He had been in power for a little more than six years, and no one, at the time, could have foreseen that within another six years the empire he boasted would last for a thousand years would come crashing down upon him. And while the Polish invasion was an astounding military success that would lead to others, it also placed Hitler's dictatorship in the path of jeopardy. He would learn what many despots before him had learned, that once conflict is provoked with countries not under one's control, then all the carefully crafted devices of dictatorship within a closed system become fatally exposed to the outside world, and particularly to those nations dedicated, even if imperfectly, to the proposition that the greatest human legacy is freedom, not slavery. Like all absolutists, Hitler had a limited perspective of the world beyond absolutism.

From the end of September 1939, when Poland was defeated, until May 10, the war was much less than full scale, and did not involve any large land offensives. While the armies behind the Maginot and Siegfried Lines would sporadically lob shells at each other, and probe respective defenses, there were no large offensive campaigns. During this period, the Second World War was variously labeled the "phony war", the *Sitzkrieg* (sitting war), and the *Blumenkrieg* or flower war. Hoping to avoid a war in the West long enough to digest Poland, then to conquer Russia, Hitler would make overtures to the British and French. In a speech at Danzig on September 19, he asserted, "I have neither toward England nor France any war claims...You know of my offers to England. I had only in mind the great goal of attaining the sincere friendship of the British people..."[48] On October 10 in Berlin's Sportspalast, he said, "I have given expression to our readiness for peace. Germany has no cause for war against the Western Powers..."[49] Hitler even tried to split the British-French alliance. In the Munich speech on November 8, 1939, he accused the British of wanting war, and noted:

"We regret that France has allowed herself to be taken into the services of these British warmongers."[50]

Ignoring Hitler's diatribes, and efforts to weaken their resolve, the British and French continued preparations for the inevitable conflict. Thousands of British troops were dispatched to France in what seemed like a reprise of the British Expeditionary Force's shipment to France in 1914. Indeed, the military mindset of the British and French was very much of the 1914-18 vintage. The prevailing thought was that the "invincible" Royal Navy of Britain's insular seafarers, combined with the "impregnable" Maginot Line of continental France, could effectively wear down the enemy's will to resist. The focus of the war's first stage, therefore, fell upon the Royal Navy. Assigned to impose a blockade on Germany, the Navy's ships engaged the Germans in a number of momentous sea battles, the most dramatic being the British chase of the battleship Admiral Graf Spee into Argentina's Montevideo Harbor. There, before thousands of Argentine spectators seated in bleachers to watch the epic encounter, the Germans scuttled their ship, and the crew offered themselves up for internment to the neutral Argentinians, whose sympathies then, and after the war, lay largely with Germany, some of whose worst Nazis, including Adolph Eichmann, found a haven in Argentina.

While the Germans were engaged in naval battles with the British, the Russians, in October 1939, sought to improve their strategic position by setting up military installations in Latvia, Lithuania, and Estonia—the three small Baltic republics which were not in a position to resist these impositions. Russian demands for territory on the strategic Karelian Isthmus, as well as several small islands in the Gulf of Finland, met with Finnish opposition, and triggered a Russian invasion on November 30. By March 12, 1940, the Finns capitulated, and were compelled to grant even more territorial rights than the Russians had first demanded. This Russian impatience to improve its defensive position was an obvious sign that the Russians had little confidence in the longevity of Nazi-Soviet relations, notwithstanding the nonaggression pact the two countries had signed the year before.

The Russians were not alone in their need to secure strategic positions. On April 5, 1940, both Britain and France had notified Norway and Sweden that the neutrality of their territorial waters would no longer be respected when it was felt necessary to intercept ships carrying materials to Germany. Since the war began, the two countries had allowed German ships to breach their neutrality, consequently creating a serious gap in the Allied blockade. A particular sore point was the shipment of high-grade ore which was vital to German steel production.

On April 9, however, four days after the Allied note to the Scandinavian countries, the Germans showed that their strategic planning was much farther advanced than that of the Allies. At dawn, German troops marched into Denmark while others landed from merchant ships at Norway's major ports. By early afternoon, tiny Denmark came under what the Nazis, with their penchant for euphemism, called "protection". Norway was a more difficult proposition. Norwegian troops offered valiant resistance, which was reinforced when the Allies sent naval and army forces. The British Navy was able to strike successful blows at German shipping, but with the Luftwaffe dominating the skies, the Allies withdrew by May 3, leaving Norway effectively under German control. The conquest of the two countries not only added appreciably to Germany's much needed supplies of vital resources, but gave the Germans the opportunity to round up more Jews for deportation.

But the German victories had momentous consequences, particularly in Britain. There, on May 10, in the face of public anger over the Norwegian defeat, Prime Minister Chamberlain—the man who had given the Germans so much through appeasement—was forced to resign. He was succeeded by Churchill who, at 65, had begun to believe that history would not assign him a high vocation. His ascension to leadership came on the same day that the Germans launched simultaneous attacks on Holland, Belgium, and Luxembourg. Once again the pretext for the invasion was that these small neutral countries needed protection from possible Anglo-French aggression.

The German offensive against the low countries, however, signaled the prelude to the full-scale invasion of France. German infantry divisions swept across the Rhine, thrusting towards Rotterdam while others headed for the Hague—the center of Dutch government and communications. Simultaneously, Panzer attacks were launched across the Meuse and through the Ardennes Forest. Not expecting this latter mechanized thrust into such a heavily-wooded area, and in an effort to help the Belgians and the Dutch, the Allies sent their main forces northward along the coastal regions and to the west of the Maginot Line. Luxembourg was taken on the first day; Holland on May 17, and by May 20, Panzer units had already swept towards the coast at Abbeville, cutting off the Allies. Then Belgium capitulated on May 28, but as the Panzers veered north from Abbeville to attack the Allies in the rear, a personal order from Hitler halted them about ten miles south of Dunkirk, the small French port that forever after would be associated with British and Allied salvation. Between May 28 and June 4, 338,000 British and Allied troops were evacuated from Dunkirk, enabling them to live to fight another day. Thousands of fishermen, weekend sailors, and other volunteers, crossed the English Channel in their small boats to aid the Royal Navy in the evacuation effort—an expression of British grit that would be dramatically repeated by Royal Air Force fighter pilots during the Battle of Britain.

The reasons for Hitler's halt order to his troops remains uncertain and stands in strong contrast to his "stand fast" orders in Russia. One reason may be that he remembered Ypres in which his regiment lost half of its 3,500 men when the German high command made a bid to reach the English Channel, but were blocked by the British who routed them in a four-day battle. It was also during this battle that Hitler was temporarily blinded. The probable major factor, however, is that he did not want to effect a rout of the British because he still hoped he could prevail upon them to withdraw from the war, thus allowing him to concentrate his efforts against Russia. This seems to be borne out by Hitler's remarks during a visit to Field Marshal von Rundstedt's Charleville headquarters on May 24, the day after the halt order had been given. After the war, Rundstedt's operational chief, General G. Blumentritt, told Liddell Hart that Hitler was in an exultant mood, and was high in praise and admiration of the British and their empire. Blumentritt reported Hitler as saying that "his aim was to make peace with Britain on a basis that she would regard as compatible with her honor to accept." By letting the British forces escape at Dunkirk, Blumentritt believed Hitler was trying to conciliate the British as an insurance that they would not pursue the war.[51] This is but one more example of Hitler's obsessive intention to pursue his extermination plans against the Jews and Communists.

His often expressed praise of the British, therefore, has to be viewed in the light of his long-range intention. In *Mein Kampf*, as well as in speeches and conversations before and after the war began, he had also spoken highly of Britain, suggesting that even in the 1920s when he wrote *Mein Kampf*, he could foresee the need to appease the British, at least until he had finished his extermination program throughout Europe. He had similarly lavished praise on France and Poland when it suited his purpose. But his real attitude towards Britain can be seen in the program of terror he envisioned for the British if he had proceeded with Operation Sealion—the code name for his planned invasion of Britain.

Captured German documents show that Brauchitsch had signed a Hitler-initiated directive that all able-bodied British males between the ages of seventeen and forty-five would, with few exceptions, be rounded up and transported to the continent. In addition, all but normal household stocks would be confiscated, hostages would be taken, executions would be carried out for such minor infractions as the posting of placards found unsuitable, or the failure to surrender firearms and radio sets within twenty-four hours.[52] That this directive was signed by Brauchitsch shows that in 1940—one year before the onslaught on Russia, the German army was prepared to collaborate with Nazi terror in violation of the Geneva Convention's rules governing warfare, and particularly in the treatment of civilians.

The army's actions in England, however, would have been but a supplement to what the SS had in store for the British. Himmler had assigned Heydrich, as head of the Reich Central Security Office (*Reichssicherheitshauptamt*), or RSHA, to organize *Einsatzgruppen* (killing units) which, operating from Britain's largest cities, would round up Jews, freemasons, and numerous others considered to be enemies. Since the *Einsatzgruppen* in Russia followed on the heels of the army to round up Jews and others for extermination, it is certain that a similar fate would have met the British if their country had been taken over by the Nazis.

Indeed, an SS hate list makes it clear that some of the more prominent Britishers who most likely would have been executed included Churchill, Aldous Huxley, H.G. Wells, Virginia Woolf, E.M. Forster, and many others.

Just as the Rohm purge in 1934 had given Hitler the opportunity to order the execution of those like General von Schleicher and Gustav von Kahr who had stood in his way on the road to power, he also planned to wreak vengeance on exiles in Britain, such as Edouard Benes and Jan Masaryk, the two Czech leaders who had attempted to frustrate his designs on their country, and Hermann Raushchning, the Danzig Senate president who had renounced his Nazi membership, and denounced all that Nazism stood for. Zionist leader Chaim Weizmann was also on the death list, along with psychoanalyst Freud who had, however, died in England in 1939.

In light of these and other brutal plans if Britain had been invaded, it would seem that too much has been made of Hitler's professed admiration for the British whose leaders, after all, were to Hitler part of a worldwide Jewish conspiracy which included international capitalism as well as Communism. When it suited him, Hitler had been extravagant in his praise of other countries which later became his victims. When his honeyed words failed to produce his desired political objectives, he would revert to form by castigating those countries which had failed to accommodate his aims. And, since Eastern Europe contained a preponderance of the world's Jews, and Russia was the standard-bearer of what Hitler believed to be Jewish-inspired Communism, his priority objective lay in the East where he planned to exterminate European Jewry and the Russian Communists. Politically as well as militarily, therefore, it was expedient to try to remove Britain (and France) from the war so that he would have a free hand in the East, and avoid a second front in the West. In

January 1934, probably with his future squeezeplay on Austria and Czechoslovakia in mind, Hitler persuaded Poland to sign a nonaggression pact as a way of keeping Poland as a bystander. But, on April 28, 1939, in anticipation of aggressive action against Poland, Hitler renounced the 1934 pact, and within five months he signed a nonaggression pact with Russia, his major intended victim, leaving him free to first ravage Poland.

Hitler cynically regarded pacts as expedient political tools designed to advance his military struggle. The phenomenal run of successes achieved by these tactics came to an end when he failed to get Britain and France to engage in duplicitous diplomacy over Poland as he had successfully done in the case of Austria and Czechoslovakia. This belated French and British intransigency disrupted Hitler's long-standing intention to conquer Russia once Poland had been absorbed. Then reinforced by the vast material resources of Russia, including those in the Ukraine and the Caucasus, he would be positioned to take on France and Britain as a prelude to world conquest. Such an ambition was very real as was seen in the draft of Directive 32 released in army headquarters in June 1941, just prior to Russia's invasion. Once the Russian forces had been "smashed," the directive noted, the Axis powers would rule all of Europe, then the British position in the Mediterranean and western Asia would be assaulted by a "two-pronged attack from Libya through Egypt, from Bulgaria through Turkey and, if necessary, also from Trans-Caucasia through Iran. Gibralter also would be taken."[54]

In February 1941, Hitler had also ordered his military planners to study how to proceed against India through Afghanistan. But after the defeat of Russia, "the ultimate objective of all plans was England." As soon as the Eastern campaign was over, the siege of Britain was to resume in full force: "the lifeline of the Empire through the Mediterranean was to be cut and as soon as a 'collapse' of the British Isles appeared imminent, an end was to be brought about 'through a landing, in England.'"[55]

Hitler's invasion of the low countries and France, however, was a recognition that he would have to reverse his plans by conquering France, at least, and then Britain, too, if necessary, before taking on the Russian giant. In 1940, a part of this plan achieved phenomenal success. In a little more than two weeks the neutral low countries had fallen to mobilized German might, and the British army narrowly escaped total disaster, while the greatly weakened French army was left in a state of shock. On June 5, Hitler ordered what amounted to the *coup de grace* on the French. His Panzer and infantry divisions converged on Paris, more than a million and a half French troops were rendered inactive, and by June 14, the Germans entered Paris. At the same time, German troops encircled the much-vaunted Maginot Line from the rear, and transformed it into a giant military catch basin. The German success emboldened Mussolini to declare war on the Allies, thus aligning his own fate, as well as his fascist state, with the German dictator. On June 25, only three weeks after Germany's assault on France began, the First World War corporal, Hitler, "settled accounts" with his French enemies by humiliatingly bringing them to sign an armistice in the same railway coach in the Compiegne Forest where Germany had been forced to surrender in 1918.

By Nazi standards, although not by those of the French, the Paris peace terms were relatively soft, and deliberately so, since Hitler needed to keep France pacified while he accomplished his other objectives, most importantly the conquest of Russia and the extermination of the Jews. Privately, however, he let it be known that much harsher conditions would be imposed on

France at a later date, and presumably these would be much like the conditions he had in mind if the British had been conquered. The man who had come to power with the incessant complaint about the Treaty of Versailles that had been imposed on Germany would doubtless have outmatched that treaty's severity. As it was, France was divided in two, with the Germans occupying the largest portion, Paris included, while the Vichy government of Marshal Petain was assigned to a small region in the south and southeast of France. Anti-Nazi Germans who had sought refuge in France were to be turned over to the conquerors to be disposed of in their uniquely brutal fashion, and one and a half million of the French military were to be held hostage in prison camps until a permanent peace treaty had been reached—a circumstance that would have been most unlikely had the Germans conquered Britain and Russia. The executions, as well as the exposure until death of thousands of Russian soldiers, gives some indication of what may have been intended for the French prisoners of war. Had Hitler immediately introduced a rule of terror in France, it would have signaled to the British what they could expect if the Germans invaded their land, and this would have reinforced the already strong British resolve to fight the Germans, and ended Hitler's hopes of keeping Britain out of the war. A conspicuous exception to the Nazis' relative restraint was the move to round up Jews for deportation to death camps, and this once again was indicative of Nazi priorities.

In what may also have been an effort to placate the French, Hitler declined to make a triumphal entry into Paris as he had done in Austria, Czechoslovakia, Memel, and Danzig. Instead, after the temporary peace pact was signed at Compiegne, he visited the First World War battlefields in the company of two old comrades from his days as a front line runner. With his architect, Albert

Speer, he also toured Napoleon's Tomb, and other architectural sites, offering criticisms and boasting of his own plans to rebuild his home city of Linz, as well as Berlin, which he planned to call Germania—a name which, to British ears became suggestive of germs and mania. Hitler chose not to rub British and French noses in the defeat as long as there was hope of keeping them quiet while he pursued his campaigns of extermination and conquest in the East.

Much of what Hitler accomplished had been spelled out as early as May 23, 1939, only a month after he significantly renounced the 1934 nonaggression pact with Poland, as well as the 1935 naval agreement with Britain. At a meeting with his top military chiefs, Hitler used the occasion to give his analyses of Germany's political and military future. That his renunciation of the treaty with Poland was a precursor to aggression was made clear. "There is no question of sparing Poland," he bluntly declared, "we (Germany) are left with the decision to attack Poland at the first suitable opportunity." He realized that Czechoslovakia represented his last bloodless conquest. "We cannot," he asserted, "expect a repetition of the Czech affair. There will be war. Our task is to isolate Poland." Such a war with Poland would, Hitler said, "only be successful if the West keeps out of it. If that is not possible, then it is better to fall upon the West and to finish off Poland at the same time."[56] As events unfolded, Hitler was able to quickly conquer Poland before assaulting France, but except for air and naval strikes, and the capture of the British Channel Islands, he chose not to invade mainland Britain. Probably, in anticipation of the Nazi-Soviet pact, Hitler foresaw the possibility that Russia "might disinterest herself in Poland's destruction." He also correctly predicted Britain's resolve, and that the successful occupation of Holland and Belgium, and the defeat of France would provide necessary bases for war against England when, and if, that became necessary. Then *Luftwaffe* attacks, combined with naval operations on British shipping, would create an effective and destructive blockade. Even the upcoming offensive in France was on his mind, as he told his military chiefs that instead of a wheeling motion of his army towards Paris, as in the so-called Schlieffen Plan of the First World War, it would make its principal thrust towards the Channel ports before encircling Paris.

As the spring of 1939 led to the summer, Hitler, on August 22, had more to say to his military chiefs at the Obersalzburg. Primed by the knowledge that a nonaggression pact with the U.S.S.R. was imminent, Hitler again spoke of his intended assault on Poland. "The day after tomorrow (August 25)," he said, "Ribbentrop will conclude the treaty. Now Poland is in the position where I wanted her. A beginning has been made for the destruction of England's hegemony. The way is open for the soldier, now that I have made the political preparations."[57] The continuity between his political and military struggles was made clear.

Hitler did not think then that the Western powers would fight; nevertheless he was prepared for that possibility. In contrast to the speech he would give after the invasion of Poland, in which he accused the Poles of starting the war, Hitler told his militarists: "I shall give propagandist reasons for starting the war...the victor will not be asked afterward whether he told the truth or not. In starting or waging a war, it is not right that matters, but victory...Close your hearts to pity. Act brutally!...Be harsh and remorseless! Be steeled against all signs of compassion...Whoever has pondered over this world order knows that its meaning lies in the success of the best by means of force."[58]

Thus was the tone set for the horrors to come. The *Putsch* mentality that Hitler had suppressed since 1923 was beginning to be exposed again in all of its fiendish horror. The fall of France was followed at the end of 1940 by the takeover of a small part of Britain, namely the Crown fiefdoms that oddly many historians make little or no reference to. These include the Channel Islands of Jersey, Guernsey, Alderney, Sark, and adjacent islets, situated between England and France. Even there, as in other conquered territories, the Nazis followed a pattern which had begun in Germany with Hitler's climb to power. The few Jews in the islands were required to register, and to carry identification as Jews, and Jewish businesses were confiscated and sold to non-Jews. All Jews were sent to concentration camps on the continent, but after a concentration camp was built on Guernsey, some Jews from the continent were brought there to be killed.[59] The round up of the Channel Islands' few Jews, along with Himmler's unsuccessful mission to Finland in 1942 to demand the deportation of a few hundred Jews, were among the many examples of Nazi determination in trying to achieve the Final Solution, and showed that just as anti-Semitic measures had been integrated with Hitler's political struggle, they had also become integrated with his military struggle.

The collapse of France left Hitler standing, like a colossus astride continental Europe, and poised ready to strike again at either Britain or the U.S.S.R.—the two nations which, by their policies, had done the most to advance his initial conquests—the British through appeasement, and the Russians by signing the nonaggression pact. Now Hitler was faced with the crucial question: should he proceed, as he most wanted to do, with the invasion of Russia, or should he first dispose of Britain? Having quickly taken France, an invasion of Britain would certainly seem to have been the most logical of the two choices. Yet, where the invasion of Britain was concerned, a number of factors may have made Hitler pause. As it had demonstrated in Norway, the British navy was a substantial force to be reckoned with, and the anticipated tenacity of the British in defending their island was another important consideration. But there was the further possibility that if Germany attacked Britain, Russia would align itself with Britain to attack from the East. It had already taken advantage of Germany's preoccupation in Poland to invade Lithuania, Latvia, and Estonia, as well as to pressure Rumania into handing over Besserabia and northern Bukovina.

Unless the *Luftwaffe* could achieve air superiority, therefore, an invasion of Britain would likely be very difficult since German troops would have to face not just a superior navy, but a strong air force and a determined populace as well. Besides, unlike Churchill and Roosevelt who both had headed their countries' navies, yet did not exhibit a damaging bias in favor of the navy, Hitler was a landlubber and ex-soldier who was oriented towards a land war, not to the sea. Using his army against a formidable sea power made him less certain of the outcome. An alternative would have been to break British dominance of the seas in the Atlantic and the Mediterranean and in that way to achieve a successful blockade, but this would have taken considerable time—a commodity he could not spare.

While all of these factors were undoubtedly important, it is probable that a much more important consideration was the priority he gave to the conquest of Russia, incorporating, as it did, his intention to exterminate Europe's Jews, as well as to destroy Russia's "Jewish-inspired" Communism. This double-pronged objective constituted a constant theme throughout his career, and had been clearly stated in *Mein Kampf*. As his frequent expressions after Poland's defeat indicated, Hitler was hopeful that Britain would withdraw from the war. Thus, from September 1, 1939, the day the war began, until he launched his attack in the West in May 1940, Hitler had no plans prepared for an invasion of Britain. Nor did he have more than a makeshift plan for such an invasion even after the fall of France, and this adds further support for the belief that Hitler was singularly focused on his major project in the East.

If Russia were to be conquered first, and quickly, then Germany would have benefited greatly from its vast natural resources, particularly Ukrainian grain and Caucasus oil. In the wake of a swift Russian defeat, Britain most certainly would have had to reconsider whether it should stay at war. If so, then Hitler could have reinstated his policy of putting the pressure on Britain to restore lost German colonial territories. Such a policy might then have been the prelude to another series of bloodless conquests in anticipation of eventual territorial gains through bloodshed. "Today, Germany, tomorrow the world"—a favorite Nazi boast, might then have come closer to realization. It is almost certain, however, that had Russia been conquered with anything like the speed of his other campaigns, Hitler would then have invaded Britain. Instead of the expressions of admiration he had made in his speeches, he would have unveiled his real attitude with a program of terror.

Such plans, however, were frustrated by the British, that proud people living on what Shakespeare had described as:

> This fortress built by Nature for herself
> Against infection and the hand of war,
> This happy breed of men, this little world,
> This precious stone set in the silver sea...[60]

Best known as a nation of seafarers, some of whose most illustrious sons had traversed the world's oceans, the British would defend their island in its time of greatest peril, not from the sea, as against the Spanish Armada in Elizabethan times, but in the air against an airmada, in what would go down in history as "the Battle of Britain." In a larger sense it was also "the battle for Western civilization."

This air battle began in June 1940, when the *Luftwaffe* made small-scale bombing raids which were designed primarily to test Britain's air defenses. As the summer wore on, the raids were stepped up with attacks focused on key targets, particularly such major ports as Portsmouth, Southampton, and Belfast (in British Northern Ireland). Major attacks were launched in August and September with massive daylight raids lasting for weeks. British reconnaissance, meanwhile, had observed a build up of barges and other seacraft on France's Channel coast, suggesting that a German invasion might be in the offing. The Royal Air Force targeted these apparent embarkation points to good effect. And although the German daylight raids created devastating damage, the losses to German aircraft were considerable. In one two-week period alone, the *Luftwaffe* lost about 15 per cent of its planes, or more than 1,300. Like valiant sparrows defending their nests from marauding hawks, the Royal Air Force's Spitfire and Hurricane fighters harried many of the larger *Luftwaffe* planes to their doom. The British could remember with satisfaction that it was the maneuverability of the smaller British ships that had contributed also to the defeat of the much larger Spanish Armada ships more than three centuries earlier.

Under Goering, the *Luftwaffe* had developed as a sort of aerial equivalent to the French Maginot Line. The planes were not designed primarily for fighting in the air, but for the destruction of ground targets. Large numbers of planes were believed to be able to fly unhampered to attack their ground targets but, just as Panzer tanks had circumvented the Maginot Line to invade France, so the much more maneuverable and better-armed British planes were able to tackle the German planes from above, below, and from the sides.

By mid-September, the Germans abandoned their daylight raids, but inaugurated nighttime ones instead. Continuous bombings were carried out night after night on various targets ranging from residential and industrial sites, to barracks and schools. But even these raids peaked by the end of 1940. Hitler, it seemed, had abandoned any immediate plans to invade England. Instead, he was plotting what he hoped would be his master stroke against Russia that would bring him access to a majority of Europe's Jews. And, while the British suffered heavy damages, and the loss of 50,000 lives, they could take heart from the increasing supply of vital materials now coming from the U.S., which had begun deliveries after the fall of France.

Hitler's determination to destroy Bolshevik Communism and to exterminate the Jews—the "bacilli" which, as a self-styled Robert Koch, he believed he had discovered—gave rise to a fixation on Russia which was to affect the conduct of his military struggle. This was seen in his decision not to invade England until he had first conquered Russia, and also influenced his attitude towards the Mediterranean, whose importance the British recognized by deploying forces in North Africa, the Suez Canal, and Persian Gulf areas.

By the end of 1940, for example, Admiral Raeder regretfully observed how "The naval staff regards the British fleet as the decisive factor for the outcome of the war; it is now no longer possible to drive it from the Mediterranean as we have so often proposed. Instead, a situation is now developing in Africa which is most dangerous both for

Germany and Europe."[61] And yet, even by April 1941, there was still an opportunity for Hitler to capitalize on German successes in North Africa where General Rommel had converted Italian failure into incredible German success. Had Hitler taken advantage of this situation, which was accompanied by German victories in the Balkans (also brought about by Italian incompetence), then "the British could have effectively been eliminated from the Mediterranean," according to Colonel Walter Warlimont, chief of the German supreme command's operations staff. But, Warlimont said, "The man (Hitler) we had at the head of our forces was simply the standard-bearer of the anti-Bolshevik crusade." The "real background" to Hitler's decision to invade Russia, Warlimont believed, lay in his "permanent, deep-rooted and deadly hatred of Bolshevism." He noted that the period when Hitler was forming the decision to turn on Russia was made about mid-July 1940, about the time when the military had persuaded him to give orders for the British invasion which he later canceled.[62]

In *Mein Kampf*, Hitler had made it clear that Russia would be a target of aggression. "If we speak of soil in Europe today," he wrote, "we can primarily have in mind only Russia and her vassal border states."[63] When Hitler outlined his plans for Russia's invasion to his military chiefs, there is no indication that they challenged the discordance between his frequent and sometimes hysterical denunciations of the loss of German land under the Versailles Treaty, and his intention to conquer much greater expanses of land. The dividing line between Hitler's attempts to correct the "injustices" of the Versailles Treaty and his larger aims of conquest was marked by his entry into Prague in 1939.

Before Hitler could embark on his major venture (the assault on Russia), he was deflected by the failing adventures of his Axis partner, Mussolini. On the other hand,

Italian moves into Egypt on September 12, 1940, had become bogged down—a situation that should have made Mussolini more cautious, but instead made him more eager to emulate the string of successes that the Fuhrer had achieved. Rejecting Hitler's advice, Mussolini, on October 28, sent Albanian-based troops on the march into Greece, but they were soon repulsed by the tenacious Greek forces. Concerned that an Italian collapse in North Africa and Greece would open the way for the British to establish bases that would threaten his pending invasion of Russia, Hitler ordered military help after it appeared that the British had the Italians on the run in North Africa and the Greeks had driven them back into Albania. In order to help the Italians, Hitler had to reach agreements with Bulgaria, Hungary, and Yugoslavia in order to allow his troops access to Greece through their territories. By the end of 1940, Hungary and Rumania gave their consent, followed in February 1941, by Bulgaria. After pressure from Hitler, Yugoslavia's Prince Regent Paul also agreed to allow his country to be used as a conduit for German troops to attack his neighbor. But on March 26, a band of Yugoslavian officers executed a *coup d'état* that brought forth Hitler's fury, particularly since it interrupted his plans for invading Russia, which he had ordered his staff to prepare as early as 1940.

On April 6, an invasion vengefully dubbed "Operation Punishment," was launched against Yugoslavia and Greece by German air and land forces. Hitler's wrath was particularly unleashed on Belgrade, which his bombers virtually leveled, leaving about 17,000 dead. In less than two weeks, the Yugoslav resistance was at an end, and the Greeks surrendered a few days later. A British contingent sent by Churchill to help the Greeks was forced to hastily abandon Greece in what appeared to the British as a traumatic reminder of Dunkirk. Additional salt was added to British wounds with the news that the German Afrika Corps, under Rommel, had rapidly reversed Italian military failure by sweeping the British out of Libya and back to the Egyptian frontier. In May, the Germans also carried out a then uniquely daring paratroop invasion of Crete, but at a cost to the elite parachutists which Hitler felt was much too high to pay.

Puffed up with his additional lightning successes, Hitler, at last, was ready to pursue the objective that had haunted his mind since the days when he committed to *Mein Kampf* his world philosophy. On June 22, 1941, more than four weeks later than he had intended, his now seemingly invincible army bulldozed its way across a one-thousand-mile front into Russia, ostensibly clearing *Lebensraum* for German settlers, but actually providing *Tötungsraum*, or killing space, for the special SS detachments following, and often accompanying, the army. In a proclamation to the German people on the day Russia was invaded, Hitler made no mention of *Lebensraum*, but instead focused on his frequently-uttered theme of a worldwide Jewish conspiracy. Germany had been brought to the hour, he said, "when it is necessary for us to take steps against this plot by the Jewish-Anglo-Saxon warmongers and equally by the Jewish rulers of the Bolshevist center in Moscow."[64] So much for *Lebensraum* that supposedly was the major focus of his war.

Even before the invasion of Russia, Field Marshal von Manstein issued a directive to his troops. Couched in familiar Hitlerian language, it described the upcoming military engagement as a "life and death struggle" against the Bolshevist system. It was a struggle, Manstein asserted, that "is not being carried on against Soviet armed forces alone in the established form laid down by European rules of warfare." Jewry, he reminded, "constitutes the middle man between the enemy in the rear and the still fighting remainder of the Red Army forces and the Red leadership. More strongly than in Europe, it holds all the key positions in the political leadership and administration, controls trades and guilds and further forms the nucleus for all unrest and uprisings." And in language that could have come directly from *Mein Kampf*, Manstein emphasized that the Jewish-Bolshevist system must be exterminated once and for all. "Never again must it encroach upon our European living space." The soldier, he added, "must appreciate the necessity for harsh punishment of Jewry, the spiritual bearer of the Bolshevist terror. This is also necessary in order to nip in the bud all uprisings which are mostly attributable to Jews."[65]

Manstein's directive is important on several accounts. It shows how, whether or not he believed in what he was saying, this high-ranking militarist had come to parrot Hitler's ideas, and indicated that while the army had not been Nazified to the degree that Hitler had wanted, there were significant numbers, and persons of high military rank, who believed that the military struggle was primarily directed against Jewry and Communism, therefore, the "normal" rules of warfare would be dispensed with. Manstein's directive also clearly indicates that living space for German settlements was not the military struggle's prime objective, but rather the extermination "once and for all" of the "Jewish-Bolshevist system," and the "harsh punishment of Jewry, the spiritual bearer of the Bolshevist terror." Manstein's language is clearly the language of the Final Solution, and is additionally significant by its reference to the Jews not as a racial phenomenon, but as a spiritual one. Together with Brauchitsch's terror directive in the event of an invasion of Britain, Manstein's directive reveals a culpability for German atrocities, which

surviving German militarists were unwilling to acknowledge when brought to judgment at Nuremberg.

Manstein and Brauchitsch were among 250 senior officers in the New Reichschancellery in Berlin on March
30, 1941, when Hitler expounded for two-and-a-half
hours on his future plans in the East just as he had talked
to his generals on August 22 and November 23, 1939,
before the Polish and Western campaigns. Noting that
there was still an "ideological gulf" between himself and
the officer corps, Hitler forcefully stressed that the Eastern campaign involved a "struggle between two opposing
ideologies, therefore, Soviet commissars and officials were
to be "treated as criminals whether they belonged to the
armed forces or to the civilian administration." They were
not to be regarded as soldiers nor to be treated as prisoners of war. When captured they were to be handed over
to the field sections of the SS or shot on the spot by the
troops. Thus, there would be no place in the Eastern campaign for soldierly chivalry or what Hitler described as
"out of date notions" of military comradeship, for this
was a "struggle in which not only must the Red army be
beaten in the field but Communism must be exterminated
for all time."[66]

Hitler's speech to his militarists was to form the basis
for the infamous Commissar Order which was drafted
several months later and spelled out in more specific terms
what Hitler had originally generalized. And even though
Warlimont was to self-servingly claim, after the war, that
he had taken it upon himself to dilute the severity of the
order with a resultant lessening of its impact, the facts
show that the Commissar Order greased the path for SS
extermination operations not only against Commissars,
but also and more particularly against Jews. In this, the
army played a significant part, justifying its actions on
the grounds that partisans and commissars were legiti-

mate targets. Indeed, after meeting with Hitler on March 3, 1941, Keitel circulated a memo to the army high command advising that Himmler would act independently and on his own responsibility in carrying out special tasks, i.e., the mass killings. But Hitler wanted even greater army involvement in the killings, and on March 30, he told General Franz Halder, his chief of staff, that: "The troops must strike toward the rear with the same methods they would use in attack. Commissars and GPU men are criminals who must be treated as such. This need not mean that the troops must get out of hand..."[67] In other words he did not want "emotional" killings, but the use of cold, "rational" methods. On the same day Keitel told the generals that they must execute captured political commissars themselves or turn them over to the SS.

Such directives and admonitions to the militarists reflected, on the one hand, Hitler's desire to have the army take part in the exterminations, and, on the other hand, if it could not do so, then to cooperate in handing this task over to the experienced SS killers who could. Ideally, however, Hitler had wanted a totally Nazified army which would conduct the murder operations in full coordination with its military operations. Instead of having the SS operate on the murder front, and the army on the purely military front, he wanted the two fronts integrated. This is really what Hitler meant when, through Keitel, he made known that he wanted the troops to strike in the rear "with the same methods they would use in attack." Because the army was not Nazified, however, it did not fully meet Hitler's requirements. Thus, the real example for the kind of double-edged military-murder operations would be set by the Waffen-SS. The expansion of the SS into the area of military command was an expression of Hitler's dissatisfaction with the army, and a recognition that it would take too long to fully convert it to the tasks of mass murder.

Nevertheless, the military did collaborate, and in some instances were quite enthusiastic when engaged in genocide operations. As with most professions, the militarists exhibited a stoic spirit in which one's emotions are not permitted, indeed can be an obstacle, to the proper performance of professional skills. A doctor overcome with emotion, for example, would be quite incapable of performing an operation for which he had sedulously trained. In civilized societies, such emotional, professional functions are put at the service of positive values. In the case of the German military, the profession itself had become an end and no longer a means to positive ends, consequently the distinction became blurred between just and unjust warfare. As long as the militarists did not allow values to intrude on their professionalism, they approached Hitler's ideal of absolute obedience. "Obeying orders" did, in fact, become the most frequently offered defense by the militarists at the Nuremberg Trials; moral values were rarely presented as a consideration. The militarists were governed by obedience not, as under the Weimar Republic to the Constitution, but to Hitler personally, but such obedience throughout the war was not enough for Hitler who had hoped that the army would become thoroughly Nazified. It was a fruitless hope which haunted him until the end.

It is possible that back in 1934, Hitler had intended the SA to supplant the army, but when it seemed that the army had become increasingly disturbed about the SA as a potential threat to its future, Hitler had to decide whether to side with the SA against the army, or effectively neutralize the SA. He chose the latter course because he had too much at stake, and did not want to risk a struggle with the army which he might well have lost, particularly when Hindenburg was still alive. Even though it was largely Rohm and other SA leaders who were purged, the SA henceforth did not have a significant role because, if it had, it would have renewed the army's fears that the SA was out to supplant it as Germany's "sole bearer of arms." Belatedly, however, Hitler tried to get around this difficulty by expanding the role of the SS which, initially had begun as a personal bodyguard and troubleshooter organization, and Hitler may have earmarked it early on for the major role in the extermination program. This seems evident from the very choice of black uniforms, and the skull and crossbones insignia of the SS Death's Head units, as well as the runic SS symbols which signified, within the SS, Hitler's two-fold mission to first rid Germany of its internal enemies before ridding Europe of the international world of enemies.

The expansion of the war in the East allowed the SS not only to fulfill its primary killing role, but also allowed its Waffen SS units to encroach on the army's job as the "sole bearer of arms." Thus, just as the SA had grown powerful because it had helped Hitler gain political power, the SS grew in importance and became the executor of his most important mission: the extermination of Europe's Jews, and other bearers of the "Jewish poison." And where the SA had been an organization prone to carrying out emotional pogroms, the SS, under Himmler, became cold and conducted a "rational" and meant-to-be final solution to the Jewish problem. And while the army had welcomed the purge of the SA, the expansion of the SS would become a much greater danger than the SA had been.

Even in the very year of the Rohm purge when Hitler vowed that the army would be the "sole bearer of arms," he had already had an armed bodyguard regiment around him under the command of Sepp Dietrich in addition to the *Verfugungstruppen* (political squads), and the SS

Death's Head units of the concentration camps. Hitler was careful, however, not to speed up the formation of Waffen SS combat units so as not to risk a confrontation with the army. At first the Waffen SS's intended military role was concealed by designating it as a special police unit. Under a secret Hitler order of August 17, 1938, however, it was assigned to "special internal political tasks" which came under Himmler as Reichsfuhrer-SS and chief of the German police or—and this was the important point—to be used for "mobile employment under the army in the event of war."[68]

Once the war began, however, the Waffen SS expanded rapidly, and by war's end had nearly a million men. During the campaign in the Lowlands and France, the Waffen SS fought for the first time, and by 1941, six Waffen SS divisions were assigned to the Russian campaign. They drew from Hitler the boast that "I have six divisions of SS composed of men absolutely indifferent in matters of religion. It doesn't prevent them from going to their deaths with serenity in their souls."[69] After 1942, as the Russian campaign ran into difficulties, Hitler increased his rantings against the army's general staff while lavishing praise on the SS troops because they had exhibited what he perceived to be greater ideological zeal. In other words, they were Nazified whereas the army was not.

There can be little doubt that, had Hitler been victorious in the East, the SS, instead of the army, would have emerged as the "sole bearer of arms." After July 1944, for example, the best military draftees were grabbed by the Waffen SS, and by the time the war ended, the Waffen SS had thirty-five divisions compared to nine when the war began. It was also in 1944 that Himmler significantly was made head of what was suggestively dubbed the "Replacement Army," made up of Waffen SS divisions. Facing defeat, Hitler was beginning to reveal his full intentions:

a Nazified army of his own instead of the traditional army, and one in which the tasks of extermination and warfare would be combined within one murderous service instead of divided between professional militarists, on the one hand, and killer SS squads on the other. In 1941 when he was still looking ahead to a successful Eastern campaign, Hitler hinted at what he had in mind for the future. In an edict to Keitel, he wrote: "After the war we shall have many rebellious peoples to rule," and in order to manage them he wanted to "put in control not the army but the combat units of the SS." He, therefore, wanted the SS transformed into a special service branch, "equipped with all arms including air weapons, and under his personal command."[70]

The Nazis had perfected the art of euphemism. Among these were "resettlement," "Final Solution," and other words for extermination, and the cynically cruel inscription "Arbeit macht frei" (work makes free) at the entrance to supposed work camps which were really way stations on the road to death. But the euphemism which outdid all others, and doubtless gave Hitler, and his cognoscenti, particular satisfaction, was *Lebensraum*, for instead of the supposed living space for Germans that it signified, it was really killing and dying space for Jews.

This was clearly seen when the war was over, and Hitler's ambitions for world conquest had ended. Few Germans had settled in his conquered "living space", but millions of Jews and conquered people had met their deaths in mass graves, gas ovens, and on the battlefield. The dead would provide tragic testimony to Hitler's main intention: the extermination of all Jews along with other carriers of what he perceived to be "poisonous" Jewish-inspired political philosophies ranging from parliamentary democracy to Communism. It was the anti-Semitic ideas which had first agitated Hitler's mind as a young man in

Vienna that were now finding a final, and most terrifying expression on, and behind, the battlefield. His mental, political, and military struggles were finally being fused by his demonic will into a "vital scorn for all." He was, it seemed, "a stranger in this breathing world, an erring spirit from another hurled."[71]

As Hitler made clear to his generals, this military struggle would be unlike any other. Nationalism would be engaged in a life or death struggle with international Jewry, of which Russian Communism was the latest and most advanced expression, thus the Geneva Convention covering the rules of warfare would be jettisoned. In any case, Communist Russia was not a signatory to that Convention, therefore, by Hitler's perverse reasoning, this excused Germany from any moral obligation to abide by it even though he and his generals were outraged when German troops were subjected to brutality by the Bolsheviks. And, despite the expedient appendage of the hated term "socialism" to the name of his political party, Hitler would field an army which did not represent the fanatical racist-nationalism that was the party's essence. This is what he had meant when he told his militarists in Berlin that an "ideological gulf" lay between him and them. While he had organized "a party of my own" rather than having joined one of the major "ready-made parties," he did not have an army that he truly could call his own, but a ready-made one which, because he had not personally forged it, as he had his political party, lacked fanatical ideological zeal, and carried too much traditional baggage from an earlier era. His party had been founded on anti-Semitism in order to wage his political struggle against Jewry, but the army was not similarly founded on anti-Semitism. As the war progressed, however, Hitler would try to rectify this by expanding the role of the SS while nazifying the army through the influx of cadres of politically-trained men, and the creation of Waffen SS divisions. And because of the personal oath of obedience he commanded from every individual soldier, sailor and airman, Hitler also issued a series of orders that went a long way towards ensuring that his most brutal methods would be carried out. And while Hitler had risen to power shouting about the injustices of the Versailles Treaty, he would inflict much greater injustices, horrors, and atrocities on the peoples he conquered.

On the front-line, extending about a thousand miles from Odessa on the Black Sea to East Prussia on the Baltic, Hitler's now battle-experienced army, led by its Panzer units, and followed by SS death squads, rushed forward in three groups in the north, the center, and the south, deftly performing pincer movements which cut off hundreds of thousands of Russians who received no advance warning of the German attack. So much for the less than two-year-old Nazi-Soviet non-aggression pact in which the two contracting parties had obligated themselves to refrain from "every act of force, every aggressive action... against one another..."[72]

The first phase of Operation Barbarossa, the code name for the Russian invasion, called for General Ritter von Leeb's Army Group North to make a two-pronged thrust through Lithuania, Latvia, and Estonia toward Leningrad (today, ironically, once again St. Petersburg) with one prong swinging to the north and the other to the south of Lake Peipus. General Feodor von Bock's Army Group Center was to take Minsk and Smolensk in a direct line to Moscow but, at Smolensk, part of Bock's group was to swing north to join Leeb's group in capturing Leningrad, and then to link up with the Finnish army. Once their objectives were attained, the two groups were to throw their joint forces in an assault on Moscow.

221

Rundstedt's Army Group South would be split in two with one segment pushing from the east bank of the Bug River towards Kiev while the second, more southerly segment, would thrust northward out of Bessarabia to rejoin the other segment in capturing Kiev.

The second phase of the overall strategy intended the north and center groups to split again with one branch heading north from Moscow across the Volga towards Archangel while the other branch made its thrust towards Kubyshev about 400 miles north of Stalingrad. Once Kiev was captured, Rundstedt's southern group would make its eastward move to capture Stalingrad.

By September 1, 1941—a little over five weeks after the invasion was launched—it seemed as though the German forces were on their way to achieving their objectives, and to replicating the successful *Blitzkriegen* they had achieved in Poland, the Lowlands, France, Yugoslavia, and Greece. Leeb's Northern Group was pressing on Leningrad in a three-pronged assault while Bock's Center Group had made a rapid advance past Minsk to Smolensk. Runstedt's Army Group South, meanwhile, had sent its northern segment past Slonim and Mogilev above the Pripet Marshes to link with Center Group at Smolensk, the two groups encircling large pockets of Russian soldiers on the way.

Between the Bug River and the Carpathian Mountains in Galicia, the northern branch of Rundstedt's Army Group South forged ahead in thrusts towards Kiev while its southerly segment burst out of Bessarabia by the Black Sea in an encircling movement around Odessa and towards the Crimea. Once past Kiev, the northern branch split again into three segments: one proceeding north to join Army Group Center between the Desna and Dnieper Rivers near Kharkov; another raced towards Dnepropetrovsk on the Dnieper south of Kharkov, while a third branch veered south to help in the advance on the Crimea. These maneuvers had brought the German army well past the 1,000-mile-long Stalin (defense) line extending from Odessa on the Black Sea to the Estonian-Russian border, 100 miles west of Leningrad. For more than half the length of the Stalin Line, the Germans had advanced 100 miles beyond it, but in the Ukraine they had gone more than 400 miles past it. Initially, Bock's Center Group was assigned the major role, and was given the largest force, which included two Panzer groups under tank-tactician General Heinz Guderian, and General H. Hoth, with one Panzer group assigned to each of the other army groups.

A difference of opinion erupted as to how the army groups should be deployed. Some generals favored a traditionalist plan of encirclement involving infantry and tanks swerving their flanks in inward pincer movements at the first tactical opportunity. Guderian, however, favored deep, fast, Schlieffen-like thrusts by the Panzer units which had worked so successfully in the West. In this way, it was thought, the Dnieper could soon be traversed and the way to Moscow exposed. But this time, Hitler came down in favor of the traditionalists even though it was through the advice of Mannheim, another tank specialist, that he had abandoned a traditionalist approach in France in favor of the bold Panzer thrust through the Ardennes.

Although Minsk had fallen on June 30, and Smolensk on July 16, rain and mud, plus Bock's failure to encircle the bulk of Russian troops impeded, until October, the advance on Moscow, still 200 miles away. This gave the Russians time to build their defenses. Nevertheless, Guderian, on the left center, was confident that the Russians could be pursued if they were prevented from preparing a counteroffensive. But instead of aiding the thrust on Moscow, Hitler pulled Bock's Panzer forces away from him. Under Guderian, one Panzer group was dispatched to help Rundstedt's drive in the Ukraine, while Hoth's Panzer group was sent to assist Leeb in the siege of Leningrad.

It was August 21 before Hitler issued a firm directive in which the capture of Moscow was put on the backburner while the new focus was placed on taking the rich industrial and coal-mining Donetz Basin, occupation of the Crimea, and disruption of Russian access to the Caucasian oilfields. Thus, the Moscow assault would have to wait until the Russian armies in the Kiev region were destroyed. Hitler's decision not to press on to Moscow, as he had originally intended, defied General Hans von Seeckt's dictum from the First World War that a blow straight at the heart of an opponent is absolutely necessary because it creates political disorder, and renders the enemy more susceptible to negotiation and surrender.

It was about mid-September before Rundstedt's forces closed around the Kiev area and trapped more than a half million Russians. Another half million were similarly trapped by Army Group North around Vyasma in a battle which lasted from the end of September until the end of October. By then the Russian winter was fast setting in.

All the way back to the days of the Roman Empire it had often been traditional, as well as tactical good sense, for armies to settle down for the winter before resuming their offensives in the spring, and this was the advice of some of the general staff. But Brauchitsch, Halder, and Bock persuaded Hitler to resume the offensive on November 15 which, two weeks after slugging through mud and snow, brought the Germans within twenty miles of Moscow before they were halted. A renewed attack on December 2 only succeeded in winning access to the Moscow suburbs for a small number of troops who were quickly expelled when the Russians, under Marshal

Zhukov, began a massive counteroffensive. The ferocity of the Russian attack brought home to the Germans the full realization that their Russian foes would not favor them with the "cakewalk" they had experienced in the West. Now paying for his lost time in the Balkans, as well as his summer decision to concentrate in the South rather than to forge ahead to Moscow, Hitler gave a "stand fast" order to his troops even though they were neither provisioned nor clothed to withstand the brutal rigors of a sub-zero Russian winter, and least of all under combat conditions.

In the South, Rundstedt's forces succeeded in taking the Donetz Basin and the Crimea, but failed to gain the Caucasus oil which Hitler was so intent on winning, both to greatly supplement his own oil needs as well as to deprive the Russians of theirs. After suffering a setback at Rostov on the Don, Rundstedt suggested a withdrawal to prepare his defenses, but Hitler gave him the same strict "stand fast" order he had issued to the troops at Moscow. This prompted Rundstedt's resignation in the first week of December, which was soon followed by the resignations of Brauchitsch, Bock, and Leeb—the first two on the grounds of illness, and Leeb because of disagreements with Hitler over tactics. Bock would be recalled briefly to the East in 1942, and Rundstedt, in the final days of the war, was brought out of retirement to serve in France.

In 1938, Hitler had used Blomberg's ouster as supreme commander of the armed forces to appoint himself to that post. Now, in the wake of Brauchitsch's resignation, he grabbed the opportunity to appoint himself as successor to the army commander-in-chief. The difference, however, would be that, unlike Brauchitsch, Hitler would not be hamstrung in making decisions. His self-appointment was one more step in Hitler's attempt to nazify the army, and what better way than to have the most fanatical Nazi of all in charge of it. "This little affair of operational command," Hitler belittlingly commented, "is something that anybody can do. The task of the commander-in-chief is to educate the army in the idea of National Socialism, and I know of no generals who can do this in the way I want done. So I have decided to take over command of the army myself."[73] In other words, the long army tradition of professionalism, training in staff colleges, and in the field meant little in comparison with the more difficult tasks of Nazi ideological indoctrination. Henceforth, Hitler would have no intermediaries to deal with in the direct conduct of the war, and at the same time he could end resistance to nazification of the army which he had encountered with a succession of generals starting with Fritsch in 1938. Among his first actions, therefore, and a sign of things to come, was his dismissal, in December, of his brilliant tank-warfare expert, Guderian, because he had disobeyed his "stand fast" order, and withdrew his troops without Hitler's permission.

Guderian, Bock, and Rundstedt had been among those generals who had played a significant part in Hitler's early military successes. Others who had either resigned or were dismissed when they clashed with Hitler included Leeb, Kluge, Manstein, Zeitzler, and Halder. Now, instead of the carefully thought out plans of these and other generals, Hitler, the amateur commander-in-chief (the "Bohemian" corporal as he was disdainfully branded among the general staff) was ready to substitute his judgment for that of the professionals. In this way he felt he could ensure the execution of his ideological intention to exterminate Europe's Jews and all carriers of the Jewish "poison".

Even before the war it had been recognized among the highest army circles that "the army cannot continue its aloofness from the Party. The revolutionizing of the

German nation had proceeded so far that the exclusion of the revolutionary ideas of National Socialism from the army would destroy the fighting quality."[74] For Hitler, this ideological gulf between himself and the officer corps still existed, but now that he was in direct command of the army, it might be further reduced. Even so, in the presence of Halder, he once confided how much he envied Stalin who had violently purged the Red Army command in order to replace it with generals inspired by Communist ideology.[75]

Although Hitler's genocidal intentions against the Jews had been a priority of his political and military struggles, a surprising number of histories of the Second World War make little or no mention of the extermination program which had been so closely integrated with Hitler's military struggle. Yet, in a January 30, 1939, Sportspalast speech, Hitler made it clear that the political and military struggles were closely linked. "The first (political) phase of the struggle is over," he said, "the second (military) phase can start."[76] And, also in a 1940 speech, Hitler said, "I am totally convinced that this (military) struggle does not differ one hair's breadth from the struggle which *I once fought out within myself*, an unambiguous indication that his mental, political, and military struggles were vitally linked.[77] (Italics in the original.)

Before the invasion of Denmark and Norway, Goebbels, on April 5, 1940, also noted that the "same revolution in Europe" would be realized during war as had been carried out "on a smaller scale" in Germany, i.e., removal of the Jews.[78] A similar theme had been struck by Goering on November 12, two years earlier. In the case of war, he said, "a major settling of accounts with the Jews would be the first order of business."[79] His remarks take on even greater significance considering they were made immediately following the *Kristillnacht* pogrom against Germany's Jews which marked the 20th anniversary of Germany's First World War defeat that Hitler regarded as a "stab-in-the-back" by world Jewry and which, in *Mein Kampf* and elsewhere, he promised to revenge by "settling accounts" with the Jews—the same terminology that Goering used.

Lebensraum, therefore, would be the justification for war in the East, and the war would provide the cover for the extermination of the Jews, for as Hitler had told some old comrades in 1932, it was only towards the end of his detention in Landsberg Fortress that he realized "Germany's territorial ambitions must go hand-in-hand with the eradication of the Jews both in Germany and conquered territories."[80] And while *Lebensraum* may have been an eventual byproduct of Hitler's military struggle, extermination of the Jews and Bolshevists had a prior claim on his intentions.

Despite the many statements of Hitler and others linking *Lebensraum*, the war, and the extermination of the Jews, one looks in vain among many histories of the Second World War for any significant mention of what has come to be known as the Jewish Holocaust; in some cases no mention at all. In Liddell Hart's *History of the Second World War*, for example, the word "Jews" seldom appears despite the significant way in which the massive program aimed at their extermination was facilitated by the military operations, and affected Hitler's military judgment. And while Hart's military analyses are a most valuable contribution to the history of the war, the omission of the genocidal program constitutes a serious deficiency in that history, particularly as it relates to the military.

And, in his postwar interviews with German generals, for example, Hart made no inquiries about the role of the army in the exterminations or how it affected the military campaigns or Hitler's decisions. Similarly, A.J.P. Taylor's *The Origins of the Second World War* barely mentions the Jews who figured so prominently in Hitler's mental, political, and military struggles. But Hart and Taylor are but two historians of the Second World War who either ignore Hitler's murderous enterprise, or make short shrift of it even though Hitler's first political utterances, as well as his last, focused on his anti-Semitic mission. Even Churchill's four-volume account of the war has few mentions of the Jews, and the post-war books of German generals also make scant, or no reference, to the Jews or the part that the army played in the extermination program.

And yet the genocidal program, directed principally at Jewry, created considerable difficulties for the military. Most of the transports carrying victims to death camps were heading across territory where the military was moving men and supplies. "The first fifty transports, scheduled for the period November 1-December 4, 1941, were dispatched at the time the German army was making its last offensive before the winter crisis at Moscow.[81] The use of rail transportation for victims drew protests from the army, sometimes to no avail. In discussing Rommel's North African campaign with Hitler at his East Prussian headquarters, General Jodl noted that Rommel had not had supplies for weeks while in the East, army commanders "scream if they're two trains short."[82] There is no record of Hitler's response, if any, but if transportation was in short supply in either North Africa or the East, the blame could be affixed to Hitler, the army's commander-in-chief, whose military hand seemed to be in conflict with his exterminator's hand.

While the military, for example, needed a constant supply of armaments, Hitler personally intervened to order the removal of all Jews from the armaments industry, but one of many indications of the premium he put on the Final Solution even when it hampered military needs. This order was made despite the fact that Hitler had been told by his generals that if the offensive in Russia was to be resumed in 1942, an additional 800,000 men would have to be provided. But Albert Speer, the minister for armaments production, said it was not possible to release such a number from the factories for service in the army.[83] Yet, in the case of the Jews, they were released from war industries and dispatched to their deaths. Thus, in 1942, the year in which the Germans would try to recover the military initiative, and the year when the Final Solution was given its biggest push, was also the year that labor and transport were most needed for the war.

Transportation of victims to killing centers also had its effect on the delivery of supplies to the army which sometimes was held up for weeks at a time waiting for fuel supplies—an incredible irony considering that a campaign was being conducted to gain oil in the Caucasus, but failed in part because troops had insufficient oil supplies. And while the Russians were able to repair railroad tracks as soon as the Germans destroyed them, the lack of labor made it difficult for the Germans to build roads and railways, and this, too, contributed to the setbacks in bringing supplies to the front.

While the German army would make some rebounds, the troika cities of Leningrad, Moscow, and Stalingrad withstood German sieges, and each of these cities, in its own way, reflected the history of Russia as it passed from Czarist times into the modern period of striving industrialism and ideological Communism. Moscow, the center of Czarist as well as Communist Power, provided the vast Russian Empire's heartbeat. By Peter-the-Great's edict, Leningrad had been built on Gulf-of-Finland marshland to provide "a window to the West". Lenin opened this "window" even wider to receive the revolutionary social philosophy of Karl Marx, whose native Germany rejected his international ideas in favor of nationalism. Stalingrad would bear the name of Lenin's successor, who distorted Marxian theory even beyond Lenin's interpretations, and far exceeded his expressions of terror and subjugation although perhaps because he lived longer and had better technology.

Leningrad, Moscow, and Stalingrad, therefore, came to mark the beginning of the end of Hitler's military struggle, and upon the success of this struggle depended the success of his genocidal program. The collapse of the military front meant the collapse of the murder front. From the start of the Eastern campaign on June 22, 1941, until December 6, when the Russians launched their first counter-offensive, activities on this murder front had been carried out with amazing rapidity by the *Einsatzgruppen*. Their target was Russia's five million Jews, most of whom lived in urban areas. When cities fell to the army, therefore, the *Einsatzgruppen* would quickly move in to round up Jews for shooting in ditches or gassing in mobile vans. Thus, cities such as Riga, Kovno, Reval, and Gattschina, captured by Army Group North, would become prime hunting grounds for *Einsatzgruppen A*. Minsk, Smolensk, Rzhev, and Viasma, in Army Group Center's control, would yield other victims to *Einsatzgruppen B*. Kiev, Kharkov, and Poltava were among the cities where *Einsatzgruppen C* found its victims in Army Group South's northern territory, while *Einsatzgruppen D* operated in Army Group South's more southerly regions in such cities as Odessa, Simferpol, and Taganrog.

Einsatzgruppen were divided into units, or *Sonderkommandos* of from 70 to 120 men, and sub-units of from 20 to 30 men. Their ranks were filled by members of the Gestapo, *Sicherheitsdienst* or security police; *Ordnungspolizei* (Order police), *Kriminalpolizei* (Kripo), the Waffen SS, and auxiliary police recruited from foreign territories such as the Baltic States and the Ukraine. Despite postwar efforts by war criminals and some German historians to minimize its role in mass murder, the Waffen SS, in addition to its military combat role, made up about 34 percent of *Einsatzgruppen* members—by far the single largest complement. Ukranian, Baltic States, and other foreign recruits often showed great zeal in killing Jews.

In addition to the *Einsatzgruppen*, killings were carried out under the *Hohere SS-und Polizeifuhrer* (HSSPF), or senior SS and police commander who, in addition to acting as liaison officer with the army and regional authorities, was nominally the commander of all SS and police units in his area. Each regional HSSPF commander came directly under Himmler's orders which originated with Hitler and was assigned command of a regiment made up of *Ordnungspolizei*, Waffen SS, and foreign auxiliaries. The HSSPF's main task was to kill all Jews, commissars, and others who were missed in the *Einsatzgruppen's* first murderous sweeps. By the time the army's offensive came to a halt at the end of 1941, about a half million Jews had been slaughtered, more than half of these by the *Einsatzgruppen*, and the rest by the HSSPF units.

Few things so well illustrate Hitler's main intention in the East than the manner in which the *Einsatzgruppen* killers operated in conjunction with the army. Each of the four killing groups being assigned to follow, and sometimes to accompany, each of the four army groups. The absence of *Lebensraum* groups to prepare for the "resettlement" of Germans, is one more indication that living space was not the main purpose of the army's conquests, but rather the preparation of killing space for the *Einsatzgruppen*. And while frequent references were made by both military leaders and the SS to the "racial struggle" and the necessity of killing the Jews and "Jewish-Bolshevists", there are few mentions of *Lebensraum*. As Goering had said in 1938, in the event of war "a major settling of accounts with the Jews would be the first order of business."[84]

This "settling accounts" with the Jews, initiated immediately after Hitler came to power in 1933, took on increasingly violent forms after the war began, first in the West, and then in the East. In 1942, it would be unleashed in unimaginable horror. The slowing down of Hitler's military bulldozer by the might of Russian arms had the effect of spurring Hitler on to achieve on the murder front what could not be won on the battlefront. This is the real reason behind his "stand fast" order.

Even though, in 1942, the Germans would gain some success in Russia, in Atlantic and Mediterranean naval warfare, and most dramatically in North Africa, the increasing involvement of the U.S., and the renewed Russian and British offensives, would effectively spell the beginning of the end of Hitler's Third Reich. It was also, however, the year in which the Wannsee Conference in the Berlin suburbs resulted in the coordination of policies which almost decimated European Jewry. One major consequence of this conference was that instead of the killers operating in the field in conjunction with army operations, the victims were brought from the far corners of Europe to killing centers at a half dozen Polish sites. This was made necessary by the army's failure to secure enough killing space or to hold it for long enough. Hence, as many victims as possible would have to be rounded up from territories under German control, before those territories would be lost along with potential victims. The loss of territories was due to an army which, in Hitler's mind, had always lacked true National Socialist ardor.

By February 20, 1942, the Russian offensive, begun on December 6, had petered out, and with the advent of March, the spring thaw brought obstructive mud. The Germans alone lost more than a million men; most in combat, but many also to the fierce Russian winter. No longer did Hitler have the resources, either in men or material, to counterattack all along the front. Indeed, the "Master Race" had to frantically seek help from the "lesser breeds" such as the Hungarians and Rumanians, as well as from less than enthusiastic Italians. Even the SS had to lower its standards by recruiting and pressing into service a motley collection of races which previously would not have met "pure race" standards.

Having failed to take Moscow, Hitler concentrated his efforts in the Ukraine and the Caucasus. His plan was for Army Group South's Group B to surge forth in a two-pronged thrust from the Kharkov area with one prong directed towards Stalingrad, and the other through the Caucasus area towards Grozny, and on to the big oil port of Baku on the Caspian Sea. Army Group A would send one branch on the push for Baku, while another branch would aim for Maikop as the first objective on the way to Batumi on the Black Sea.

If successful, Hitler's plans would have barred Russian access to Caucasus oil and the Ukrainian breadbasket. Stalingrad's capture would have provided a beachhead for sending forces northward towards Kazan so as to launch a rear attack on the Russian forces concentrated around Moscow. While the southern offensive was underway, it was also intended for Army Group North to capture Leningrad so that the German and Finnish armies could link as had been originally planned, but unsuccessfully executed, in the first great offensive. While the prime southern offensive, and the secondary offensive in the north were under way, Army Group Center was ordered to adopt a defensive posture.

Hitler's plan posed several problems. By pushing through the Ukraine and the Caucasus and then on to Stalingrad, the German southern army would run the risk of being trapped in a large pocket bounded by the main Russian armies to the north, the Sea of Azov and the Black Sea on the west, the Caspian Sea on the east, and the frontiers with Turkey and Persia (now Iran) on the south. By concentrating his counter-offensive in the southern flank and conducting only a modest attack from his northern flank, Hitler was also risking a strike from the Russian forces against his weakened center which could have exposed to encirclement the northern army, the southern army, or both.

This was the situation confronting the Germans as they began their first counter-offensive on May 8 which took the Crimea's Kerch Peninsula by May 16 leaving only the heavily fortified and southern Crimean port of Sevastapol still in Russian hands until a fierce assault brought it into German hands on July 4. The main German offensive did not begin until the end of May when armored and infantry troops struck east and south from a 400-mile line extending from north of Kursk to Taganrog on the Sea of Azov. By July 22 the front had been widened by more than a hundred miles over the northern half of the sector to more than 200 miles on the southern part of the sector which, from its most southerly point, extended from Taganrog to the outskirts of Stalingrad. By November 18, the front line had been further extended from Taganrog on the Sea of Azov to near Tuapse on the Black Sea, and on the East from the environs of Stalingrad, on the Volga, to the suburbs of Grozny, Ordzhonikidze, and Alagir just about 100 miles from Tiflis and near the strategic Rostov-Tiflis highway, as well as the new railway linking Baku and Astrakahan.

The German gains were important, but achieved at great cost and through difficulties that included the arduous Caucasus terrain, the tenacious Russian soldiers, and the lack of adequate air support. That this German counter-offensive had lasted from May to November was a measure, not only of weakening German strength, but of the increasing capacity of the Russians to wage war. Where it had taken the German Army about a month to conquer Poland and only six weeks to defeat France and chase the British from Europe, it had taken nearly seven months to gain a relatively small part of the largest battlefield in world history.

German gains, however, would not be longlasting. With the approach of winter, the Russian army would be helped by its greatest of all reinforcements: the deadly Russian weather. The early frosts, hardening the roads and making them favorable for travel, enabled the Russians to launch a counterstrike on November 19-20 as a prelude to a major offensive. By the end of December 1942, Russian armies moved from the Caucasus area in a northerly and westerly direction, and threatened to cut off Army Group South. Paulus's Sixth Army was trapped at Stalingrad, and an attempt to break through and relieve it failed. In accordance with Hitler's "stand fast" policy, he refused permission for Paulus to try and break out in retreat. Instead, he promoted Paulus to field marshal partly as a move to strengthen his resolve, but also in the hope that Paulus would not break tradition since no German field marshal had ever surrendered. Hitler's hope was dashed, however, when, on February 2, 1942, a few days after receiving his promotion, Paulus surrendered with his 91,000 men. It was three days after the ninth anniversary of Hitler's ascension to power.

Of an original 285,000 troops including about 50,000 Rumanians, about 145,000 Germans died in the Stalingrad battle and, of 91,000 captured by the Russians, only 5,000 returned to their homeland, many of them having died from typhus and other causes. The Russians lost about 400,000 in the battle. For the Germans it was a disaster comparable to the British and French battle of the Somme in the First World War which lasted from July 1 until November 19, 1916. In that battle, more than a million died, including 650,000 Germans, 420,000 British, and 195,000 French. These lives were lost in the battle for a piece of land thirty miles long and seven miles wide.

The Stalingrad defeat came as a severe trauma to the German army, as well as a humiliation for Hitler who had already publicly announced the capture of the city which, in his eyes, was psychologically important since it bore the name of his tyrannical Russian counterpart. In addition, the Stalingrad surrender came on the heels of the November 8, 1942, landings in North Africa which were meant to support British General Bernard (Monty) Montgomery's efforts to sweep the Germans and Italians from North Africa.

At the beginning of the year, Rommel had launched a counterstroke against British-led forces, pushing the British 250 miles back towards the Egyptian border from their positions in Cyrenaica. By the summer, however, greatly reinforced British forces began to reverse Rommel's successes. And even though a greatly weakened Rommel performed some masterful military strokes, he was ultimately no match for the overwhelming numbers of Montgomery's forces and weaponry, as well as their skillful deployment.

Rommel's efforts to get Hitler to see the reality of his position were fruitless. At Hitler's Eastern front headquarters at Rastenburg in Prussia, Rommel had flown to make a direct appeal to Hitler for additional support. Hitler's reaction was to subject Rommel to one of the explosive rages to which his Eastern front generals had become accustomed and, as he had done with his own Eastern generals such as Paulus, Hitler insisted on a "stand fast" policy in North Africa. In effect, Hitler, the First World War runner, was making mere runners out of the generals; the private first class was asserting priority for his private views over the professional and broader views of his generals.

As he had shown throughout the war, Hitler's fixation on Russia, with its concomitant extermination of the Jews and Communists, had caused him to neglect his other fronts, most notably in the Mediterranean area whose strategic importance had been stressed by both Admiral Raeder and Rommel. Thus, when the Allies made their landings at Casablanca, Oran, and Algiers, their forces, coupled with Montgomery's successes, put the final squeeze on the Germans and Italians. By May 1943, the Axis powers were cleared from North Africa. In addition, some of Rommel's best fighting men were captured and, for the Allies, the way had been cleared for tackling what Churchill dubbed Europe's "soft underbelly".

In July 1943, with North Africa under their control, and now in command of the Mediterranean Sea as well as the skies, the Allies began their attack on the "soft underbelly" by invading Sicily. By August 17, the island was taken, and on September 3—the fourth anniversary of the start of the war—the Allies invaded the Italian mainland. Five days later the Italians capitulated, but German forces in Italy quickly moved to control Italy, and very successfully slowed down Allied progress toward Rome.

Nevertheless, the Germans were clearly on the way to defeat. One indication of this was the meeting in June 1943, at Kirovgrad, between Ribbentrop and Soviet Foreign Minister Molotov, at which the possibility of peace negotiations were discussed. Nothing came of the meeting, however, and for understandable reasons. Hitler, untypically, had maneuvered himself into an unfavorable bargaining position. The Allied successes in North Africa, the conquest of Sicily, the invasion of Italy, the continued Russian advances, the stepped up bombings of Germany by the British and Americans, and the expectation of an Allied second front in the West, did not provide a suitable background for peace talks. Besides, the Russians had been burned once by the Nazi-Soviet pact of 1939, and were unlikely to repeat the experience. About the only plausible explanation for Molotov's meeting with Ribbentrop is that the Russians may have wanted to "set a fire" under their Allies to open a second front by arousing fears that they might once again make a surprise alliance with the Germans.

Hitler's military setbacks had the effect of spurring him into trying to snatch one victory out of his many defeats. The more he lost on the battlefront, the more determined he became to win on the murder front. Thus, under his orders, the mass extermination program, which had been launched under cover of war, was stepped up to achieve the "Final Solution" to the Jewish problem. If Hitler could not defeat the Communist carriers of the "Jewish poison", he at least would try to exterminate as many of Europe's Jews as possible since, in his mind, they were the original carriers. A beginning to that "Final Solution" had been made in Poland when *Einsatzgruppen* rounded up Jews along with Poles, and herded them into concentration camps and ghettoes. And the first mass killings got underway when *Einsatzgruppen* followed the army into Russian-occupied Poland, the Baltic states, and then Russia itself. As Hitler, Goebbels, Goering, Himmler and other cohorts had projected, under cover of war, the Jews would be exterminated.

Hitler's plans for the "Final Solution" were initially predicated upon a successful victory in the East. Hence, on July 16, 1941, weeks after Russia was invaded, he called Goering, Keitel, Rosenberg, Bormann, and Lammers (Reichschancellery head) to his Rastenburg headquarters. There, he told of his plans after his conquest of Russia and other Eastern territories. Actions in the East, he stressed, must be kept secret. "The main thing," he added, "is that we ourselves know what we want...Nobody must be able to recognize that it initiates a final settlement. This need not prevent our taking all necessary measures— shooting, resettling, etc.—and we shall take them."

And Hitler welcomed Russian partisan warfare behind German lines since "it enables us to eradicate everyone who opposes us."[85] In addition to the "final settlement", presumably of the Jewish "problem", Hitler spelled out his program of plunder, terror, and ultimate settlement of Germans in conquered lands. By the end of 1944, however, few Germans were settled in those lands, but about seven million foreigners had been forced to work in German industries and farms, along with two million prisoners of war, including Russians who were compelled to work in war factories.

Coming, as it did, in the middle of his most important military campaign, Hitler's Rastenburg talk shows that the "final settlement" of the Jewish "problem" was prominent in his thoughts. Not only was he fed statistics on which areas had been made *Judenrein* (free of Jews), but he also took an interest in individual executions. Based on his other campaigns in Poland and the West, Hitler had every reason to believe that he could be equally successful in the East. Nevertheless, he knew enough from history and the experience of Napoleon and others, that victory only comes with the enemy's defeat. It was necessary, therefore, to launch the "Final Solution" or mass murder campaign concurrent with his military struggle against the possibility of his army's failure.

Hence, on July 31, 1941, nearly six weeks after Russia was invaded and about two weeks after the Rastenburg meeting, Goering issued a directive calling for the "total solution of the Jewish question within the German sphere of influence in Europe..."[86] Goering, however, was not acting on his own. In matters of the "Final Solution", whether directives were issued by Goering, Himmler, Heydrich, and others, they were issued in fulfillment of Hitler's oral decrees. As SS-Obersturmbannfuhrer Adolph Eichmann testified in Israel: the "Final Solution" for the extermination of the Jews was not provided for under the laws of the Reich, but was a "Fuhrer Order" which, like all such orders, "had the force of law."[87]

Goering's directive was not only an obvious followup to Hitler's Rastenburg meeting, but was a supplement to an anti-Semitic decree he had issued to Heydrich on January 24, 1939, directing him to take steps to "solve the Jewish question by emigration and evacuation in the most favorable way possible, given present conditions." Until 1940, the so-called "emigration and evacuation" policy allowed some Jews to leave Germany and its satellite lands. But, in addition to testing world reaction to receiving Jewish refugees, such emigrations may also have been one way of alleviating the fears of Europe's Jews as to their ultimate fate. "Evacuations" was the euphemistic term for moving Jews into concentration camps as part of a first phase or temporary measure ("given present conditions") pending their final fate. After the fall of France and the defeat of Poland, emigration was abandoned as plans were prepared for the invasion of Russia which was designed to clear the way for the systematic extermination of European Jewry.

"Present conditions" in 1939, therefore, were not yet suited for the "Final Solution". This would have to come with war in the East.

Plans to coordinate the "Final Solution" were soon prepared by Heydrich who, acting in accordance with Goering's directive, had originally scheduled a conference for December 9, 1941 at 56 Am-Grossen-Wannsee to coordinate the exterminations. But the Japanese attack on Pearl Harbor two days earlier caused a postponement until January 20, 1942. The Russian counteroffensive, launched from Moscow in December, gave a sense of urgency to the planned extermination of the Jews. It would have been obvious to Hitler and his genocidal cohorts that continued Russian advances would spell an end to mobile *Einsatzgruppen* killings. Instead of following a victorious German army, these murder squads would find themselves accompanying the army in retreat. It was necessary, therefore, to put an even more urgent emphasis on the mass killings. The Jewish victims would have to be rounded up from throughout Europe and hurried to the gas ovens. And since trains would be transporting victims to the death camps in Poland, it was necessary that the German army "stand fast" no matter what the odds and even in violation of professional military tactics, so that the "Final Solution" would become as near final as possible.

By issuing his "stand fast" orders to his army, Hitler would make sure that, from beginning to end, the military struggle would serve his overriding purpose: the destruction of European Jewry. As Eichmann was to tell authorities in Israel, there had been a time when no project could be undertaken unless it was "war-important". But, as the war gained momentum, the term "war-important" was complemented by another term, "war-crucial," and when a choice had to be made, "it was the war-crucial projects that were given priority." Eichmann acknowledged that the "Final

Solution" to the Jewish "question" came under the heading of "war crucial". Thus, applications for transports to carry victims would be granted initially by the Ministry of Transportation if they were regarded as "war-important," but later transports would only be authorized if they were declared to be "war-crucial."[88]

At the first Wannsee conference on January 20, 1942 (there would be two others in March and October), Heydrich invited fourteen officials whose departments would be involved in the "Final Solution". Among these was Eichmann who, as head of the Bureau for Jewish Affairs at the Reich Security Headquarters, was to make certain that the Jews, rounded up from one end of Europe to the other, would be transported by train to the death camps. In Eichmann's record of the conference, he recounted that it was opened by Heydrich with the announcement that he had been appointed "special deputy charged with the preparation of the final solution."[89]

Heydrich estimated that "in the course of this Final Solution of the European Jewish problem, approximately eleven million Jews (would be) involved." Then, he proceeded to provide estimates of the number of Jews in each country ranging not only from Russia and Poland to France and Germany, but to Ireland, England and Switzerland as well—an indication that the latter three countries were targeted for the extermination of Jews even though those countries were not part of Hitler's supposed *Lebensraum* objective. In the case of the neutral Republic of Ireland, which had maintained friendly relations with Germany, it was once again evident that the extermination of Jews was Hitler's priority. And once the Jews from all designated countries were brought East, they would be separated in accordance with age, sex, and fitness for labor. Some of those selected for labor, Heydrich assumed would die in due course from their labor while others would die because "if left to live, they would constitute germ cells of a new Jewish development."[90]

Hitler's Rastenburg meeting on the "Final Solution" was not only followed up by Goering's directive to Heydrich, and Heydrich's Wannsee conference. Soon after the meeting, Himmler met with Rudolph Hoess, a convicted murderer who had found his way into the Nazi movement through the *Freikorps*. Himmler had news for Hoess. Hitler had given the order for the "Final Solution" of the "Jewish problem" and Himmler had selected a large site in Upper Silesia which would be used to carry it out. The details, Himmler said, would be supplied to Hoess by Eichmann. The SS, he added, "must carry out this order. If it is not carried out now, then the Jews will later on destroy the German people."[91]

At a subsequent meeting between Hoess and Eichmann, the details were discussed for the construction of Auschwitz, the largest of the six killing centers which would go infamously down in history as synonymous with the Jewish Holocaust. A feature of this center, and doubtless welcomed by Eichmann, was the existence of a railroad line that could bring trains loaded with victims right to the gates of their impending hell. At Auschwitz, Hoess perfected the killing process by disarmingly disguising the gas chambers as showers, providing orchestral music, and landscaping the building with plants and flowers. Two other innovations were the introduction of Zyklon B (prussic acid)—a much quicker method of killing than the carbon monoxide used at the other five Polish killing centers—and larger furnaces in the crematoria. And, in one of those cruel ironies that history often throws up, the German name for poison gas is "Giftgas". By late November 1944, Auschwitz fires consumed their last victim who was but one of nearly two million destroyed in this most notorious of the Hitler-inspired "satanic mills". The total of six million Jewish dead in all killing operations fell short of Heydrich's goal of eleven million.

As early as the winter of 1941, when the German army was blocked by the Russians at Moscow, it was evident that the Germans faced defeat. And, it is significant that, at this point, Hitler ordered the coordinated effort to achieve the Final Solution. Despite some brilliant German counterstrokes, the Russians kept advancing. And just as the Germans had been halted at Moscow in 1941 and surrounded at Stalingrad in 1943, Leningrad, which had been under German siege since the fall of 1941, was finally relieved in January 1944. Thus, the Russian troika cities of Moscow, Stalingrad, and Leningrad had held off the once thought invincible army of Hitler's Third Reich.

All along the front, from the Baltic to the Black Sea, the Russian armies kept advancing and, early in the year (1944) they were closing in on the frontiers of Rumania and Poland. Ironically, both German and Russian soldiers showed that it is not only under democracies that soldiers can fight valiantly, but under dictatorships as well. From his Wolf's Lair headquarters in East Prussia, Hitler became very much a lone wolf, confining himself to his headquarters and, apart from his noonday Fuhrer's conferences, he engaged in the most quotidian of activities: a walk with his dog, or chats with his household staff. The conqueror, who had triumphantly entered Prague, Vienna, and Paris, was given to brooding when events over which he had no control began to unfold with increasing rapidity.

On June 4, 1944, Rome fell to the Allies only two days before they opened the long-awaited second front with the invasion of France. Backed by the prodigious output of American industry, an Armada such as the world had never seen of more than 4,000 ships landed

Allied forces on the beaches between Caen and the Cherbourg Peninsula. Mighty barrages from naval guns coupled with virtually unimpeded bombings and strafings from the air prepared the way for the successful establishment of beachheads.

Even though the Germans had long been expecting an invasion, they were caught off guard because the weather forecast for June 6 was unfavorable for sea landings. Another surprise was the Allied decision not to land directly at port cities, but to bring innovative prefabricated concrete "Mulberry" docks along with them. The consensus among Hitler's generals was that the invasion would be launched in the Calais area—the shortest point between England and France—but Hitler, who had initially taken a typically maverick view that the attack would come in the Cherbourg area—later supported the Calais thesis. Naturally, he blamed his generals for not expecting the Cherbourg attack as he already had a penchant for doing in the East, despite the fact that he had insisted on personal command of his armies, and had severely restricted his generals' options for independent action.

On June 23, Hitler's difficulties were greatly compounded when the Russians launched a great new offensive which cost the Germans twenty-five divisions out of about fifty on the central front. On the northern sectors, the Russians advanced on the Baltic states and south of the Pripet Marshes. In the midst of this dreaded two-front war, Hitler's growing alienation from the general staff literally exploded on July 20 in the form of a bomb attempt on his life at his headquarters. It issued from a conspiracy among a group of higher army officers and commanders, but the man who volunteered to plant the device was Colonel Count von Stauffenberg, a highly respected officer who had lost a hand and an eye in Rommel's North African campaign. Had they been successful, the conspirators planned to form a provisional government with Field Marshal von Witzleben as commander-in-chief of the army, and General Ludwig Beck as regent. The government would then contact the Allies and sue for a peace that they hoped would benefit Germany. While other plots against Hitler had been discussed, this was the first to be carried to a nearly successful conclusion.

However the assassination attempt is viewed, one cannot escape the thought that it was not only much too belated, but was also marred by the self-serving motives of some of the conspirators who, no doubt, hoped to redeem the greatly-tarnished image of the military by virtue of its long-standing support of Hitler, and its omissive complicity as well as active collaboration in the genocidal horrors. It is also of interest that the army officers, who were so efficient in warfare, were unable to successfully rid their country of a single leader. But for a fluke, however, it might have been otherwise. Stauffenberg had planted the bomb in his briefcase under the headquarters conference table, but after he left the room, the case was shoved to the other side of the table's supports and away from Hitler. This, coupled with the fact that the conference had been switched to a wood-frame building instead of the thick concrete bunker where Hitler's conferences were usually held, caused the blast to be diffused outward instead of being compressed inward.

The great hatred that Hitler nurtured for years against the general staff was subsequently expressed against the conspirators and all who were even suspected of being involved. In all, about 5,000 persons were subjected to a bloodbath, but the main conspirators were humiliatingly condemned by kangaroo courts. Upon Hitler's orders, they were painfully hanged by piano wire and their bodies were spiked on hooks like cattle in an abattoir. And just as

Germany's Jews had been forced to pay for the damages wrought by the Nazis on *Kristillnacht* in 1938, Hitler billed the widows of the dead men for the costs of their executions and burials. They also had to pay the postage for the bills. Hitler took particularly sadistic pleasure in a private viewing of the films showing the conspirators in their death agonies. Some of the "luckier" ones were beheaded or committed suicide. Rommel, the great hero of the North African campaign, was believed to be implicated in the plot, and was given the choice of a "trial" that meant certain execution, or suicide. To spare his family and himself from a period of long-drawn-out suffering, he chose suicide—a decision which, for political reasons, was welcomed by the Nazis who did not want to add to their troubles by trying a highly popular war hero.

By August 1944, a month after the assassination attempt on Hitler, these troubles were mounting. As word had seeped throughout Europe about the real purpose of the deportations of Jews, there were signs of rebellion among the designated victims. The most significant such event had occurred in the spring of 1943 when Jews organized armed resistance in the Warsaw ghetto. Although the ghetto was devastated and most of its inmates were wiped out, the resisters had put up a valiant fight, killing more than 100 Germans and wounding another 1,000. In another sign of defiance on September 6, 1944, Greek, French, and Hungarian Jews dynamited two of Auschwitz's crematoria. By then, the Allies were sweeping through France on their way to the Reich itself. Paris had been liberated on August 23. On both the Western and Eastern fronts, the once seemingly invincible German army was in a state of collapse. From spring until the end of December the Russians pressed relentlessly forward. Rescuing the part of their homeland which had fallen into German hands in 1941, they cut through the Baltic States, Rumania, Bulgaria, Hungary, Czechoslovakia, and Poland—a virtual re-tracing of the German army's path after the fateful invasion it launched on June 22, 1941.

But even before the Russians had advanced thus far, former German partners, Bulgaria and Rumania, saw which way the wind now lay and switched their allegiance to the Allies. This had the effect of soon ending the extermination of the Jews in those countries. But, in Hungary—the only European country involved in the war which had lost none of its Jews to the killing centers— the Germans forestalled Hungary's defection.

On March 15, 1944, Hitler resorted to tactics he had used during his period of bloodless conquests. Learning that Hungary was considering withdrawing its troops from the Eastern front, Hitler met at Klessheim Castle near Salzburg with Hungary's regent, Miklos Horthy, ostensibly to discuss the troop withdrawals. Instead, Horthy was subjected to treatment similar to that which Austrian Chancellor Schuschnigg had experienced in 1938 and Czechoslovakia's President Emil Hacha in 1939. As with the other two heads of state, Horthy bowed to Hitler's demands which were accompanied by a Hitlerian tirade. Horthy agreed to the establishment of a fascist government headed by the Nyilas, or "Arrow Cross" movement which zealously helped the Nazis add hundreds of thousands of Jews to the "Final Solution" machinery.

The case of Hungary offers a particularly conspicuous example of how Hitler's top priority was the annihilation of European Jewry. When Hitler met with Horthy, the Russians were on an unstoppable advance and would soon be crossing the borders into Hungary. There was little real military advantage that Hitler could have gained from his meeting and despite the ostensible reason for the meeting, the discussion of Hungarian troop withdrawals, it became clear that Hitler had come to discuss how best to get at Hungary's Jews.

As Horthy would later inform his country's Crown Council, Hitler had accused him of not carrying out the extermination of Hungary's Jews. Hitler was no doubt particularly angered at Horthy because a year had elapsed since they had previously met at Klessheim Castle when the main topic of discussion was also the Jews. As Paul Schmidt, the German interpreter at that meeting, would record, Horthy wanted to know what he should do with Hungary's Jews, and Hitler had responded that "where the Jews were left to themselves, as for instance in Poland, the most terrible misery and decay prevailed. They are just pure parasites. In Poland this state of affairs has been fundamentally cleared up. If the Jews there did not want to work, they were shot. If they could not work, they had to succumb. They had to be treated like tuberculosis bacilli, with which a healthy body may become infected. This was not cruel, if one remembers that even innocent creatures of nature, such as hares and deer, have to be killed, so that no harm is caused by them. Why should the beasts who wanted to bring us Bolshevism be spared more? Nations that did not rid themselves of Jews perished..."[92]

At the meeting with Horthy in 1943, Hitler was accompanied by Ribbentrop, whose foreign office, throughout the war, did its utmost to make sure that collaborator countries would initiate anti-Semitic legislation patterned on the Nuremberg Laws as a preliminary to Jewish annihilation. That Hitler, while facing certain defeat, would meet with Hungary's regent twice within two of the most crucial periods of his military struggle to discuss the extermination of the Jews, shows clearly what was uppermost in his mind, and which he felt could not be left to his paladins. In light of Horthy's procrastination, it seems that Hitler must have believed that he was the only one who could get Horthy to facilitate Jewish extermination. Hitler's eagerness to annihilate Hungary's 700,000 Jews is further evidenced by his order which brought two Panzer divisions from Poland to relieve Budapest—an action which outraged his foremost tank expert, Guderian, who was not even consulted. There could clearly be only one reason for such an order: Hitler wanted Budapest under army control in order to ensure the roundup and deportation of the Jews before the Russians arrived to frustrate that effort. Thus did Budapest reflect the strategy that Hitler had pursued throughout his military struggle of using the army to facilitate the annihilation of Europe's Jews.

Because Hungary was the last country, within Germany's sphere of influence, which had not yielded up its Jews, it took on a singular significance. This was evident not only from Hitler's personal interest, as revealed in his talks with Horthy and the assignment of the Panzer divisions to Budapest, but also by Eichmann's marshaling of the most experienced and dedicated extermination experts for the special, and urgent, operations in Hungary. Under Eichmann, this group, the *Sondereinsatzkommando Eichmann*, worked feverishly to ensure that the "Final Solution" would belatedly succeed in Hungary. During 45 days of operations beginning on May 15, 1944, Eichmann and his team engineered the annihilation of nearly 400,000 Jews. The Arrow Cross extremists would account for the murder of about 80,000 more, many of them shot, tortured, and dumped into the Danube.

Tragically, Eichmann's zeal to transport to their deaths as many Jews as possible came at a time when his boss, Himmler, was entertaining thoughts of capitulation and was preparing to order the dismantling of Auschwitz and his death-dealing organization. Relentlessly, however, Eichmann pursued his task for as long as he could. His last brutal action was to force thousands of Jews, many of them elderly, to march 120 miles from Budapest to Strasshof "reception" center near Vienna. Many died on the seven-day march during a killer-cold November 1944, while others perished when they were sent to concentration camps. Although the Eichmann-ordered march was the last big deportation and signaled the end of the active killing process, many thousands of concentration camp inmates would die of starvation, disease, and brutalities until the camps were liberated. And while many Germans disclaimed all knowledge of the concentration and extermination camp deaths as though they would not have condoned them if they had known about them, yet there is much postwar evidence to suggest otherwise. Besides there was no great postwar enthusiasm for bringing the perpetrators to trial for their crimes, and even resentment that the Allies did so. Whatever imperfections the Nuremberg Trials had, it must be noted that they offered a great deal more civilized justice than the brand of "justice" the Nazis dealt out not only to their foreign captives, but also to many of their own people, including the piano-wire hanging victims of the July 1944 bomb plotters.

By mid-December 1944, before the death camps were exposed and when it appeared that the Allies were unstoppable, the Germans launched a totally unexpected counteroffensive in the Ardennes—in the very same area, and with much the same tactic they used in their devastating attack in the West in 1940. This time, however, their forces were hastily collected. "I started this war with the most wonderful army in Europe", Hitler would comment, "today I've got a muck heap."[93] In addition to SS and regular Panzer units, they included a motley crew of relatively untrained infantry. The momentary success of the Ardennes offensive was due in large part to German alertness in taking advantage of a weakness in a small segment of the Allied front. But, after the initial shock of the German thrust, the Allies quickly recovered, and vigorously resumed their offensive which was aided by almost complete domination of the air. Goering's *Luftwaffe*, which had failed Hitler in the Battle of Britain, as well as in Russia, was again of little help in stemming the Allied advance.

By year's end the German threat had been effectively removed. In retrospect, Hitler's Ardennes offensive resembled the last nervous twitch of a wild beast shot by a hunter. Had he achieved another Dunkirk, it is likely that he would have been able to strengthen his forces in the East and to achieve some successes that would have permitted continued annihilation of the Jews. The tremendous economic and technological resources at the disposal of the Allies, however, would have made Hitler's recovery brief indeed, particularly since America was only months away from exploding the first atomic bombs. The massive and continuous Allied bombings of such German cities as Hamburg and Cologne, makes it safe to assume that had the atomic bombs been ready while the war with Germany was still in progress, Germany would, if necessary, have been targeted. Unfortunately, the Allied bombing raids on German civilians, together with the atomic bombings in Japan, have subsequently given license to unrepentant Germans, neo-Nazis, and revisionist historians who try to equate Nazi atrocities with Allied military operations. Such arguments also overlook the self-implicating fact that for twelve years, the great majority of Germans zealously subscribed to the organic Hitlerian concept in which all actions were conducted by, and for, one people, one Reich, one Fuhrer.

The final year of the war opened with continued Allied advances in the West coupled with the launching on January 12, 1945, of Russia's big offensive in the East. On April 12, Roosevelt died of a stroke and this raised Hitler's unrealistic hopes that the Allied coalition would collapse. In an order issued on April 15, which once more reflected Hitler's habit of projecting onto others his own evil characteristics, he told his forces: "Now that fate has removed from the earth the greatest war criminal of all time (Roosevelt), the turning point of this war will be decided."[94]

On April 22, two days after his 56th birthday, Hitler's fantasies received the shock of reality in the form of the hated Bolshevists who were, by then, advancing on the Reichschancellery itself. Hitler suddenly decided that he would stay in his Berlin bunker not, as it turned out to "stand and fight", as Goebbels presented it to the German people, but to commit what amounted to a honeymoon suicide in his bunker with Eva Braun, his mistress of longstanding.

Ironically, when concrete bunkers were being built on the German-occupied British Channel Islands, Hitler had stressed that they should be used only as protection from artillery fire. In all other circumstances, he asserted, the German soldiers on the islands must stay outside and fight since "whoever disappears into a bunker is lost."[95] Applied to Hitler, this admonition proved to be prophetic. On April 30, 1945, the day after their wedding, Hitler and Eva Braun retired to their sitting room where they ended their lives; she with poison, he reportedly with a pistol shot to his head. That shot stilled forever the genocidal, hate-filled, solipsistic mind of a man of whom there is no record that he ever engaged in any substantial physical activity. Yet, millions of others, with ant-like concentration, carried out his horrendous and bloody program.

Only the day before, Hitler had acted briefly as though a last-minute miracle would occur. General Walter Wenck had been charged with scraping together a raggle-taggle army of Hitler Youth, elderly men, and some regulars to organize the relief of Berlin. In an order of the same day, Hitler asked his *Wehrmacht* headquarters: "Where is Wenck's advance guard...When will he arrive?...".[96] But, by then, Hitler was like the unsaddled Richard III crying out at Bosworth Field: "My horse! My horse! My kingdom for a horse!"

On May 2, German troops in Italy capitulated, and on May 7, Jodl, who had obsequiously served Hitler throughout the war, now signed the document of unconditional surrender of all German forces. In the Far East, the Japanese, whose rapid conquests throughout the Pacific had provided successful parallels to those of the Nazis in Europe, had experienced a similar ignominious rolling back of their short-lived and ill-gotten empire. On August 6, they became the first victims of the unlocking of the primal knowledge of atomic energy. The U.S. Air Force dropped the first atomic bomb on the people of Hiroshima. Three days later, Nagasaki and its populace became the victims of a second atomic bomb. Seeking to take advantage of the inevitable victory over Japan that the atomic bombings signified, the Russians declared war on Japan. It was too late, however, for them to win much in the way of territorial concessions. By September 2, the Japanese sat with American military leaders to sign the "instrument of surrender". Thus did the most horrifying and all-encompassing war in human history come to its end. With about forty million dead, one could observe that never had the pens of peace postscripted such horrors.

Soon historians would move in to survey the wreckage that, for good and ill, politicians and militarists had created. The names of Roosevelt, Churchill, Eisenhower,

Montgomery, and others would appear on the scrolls of the good while the names of Hitler, Himmler, Goering, Goebbels, Eichmann, Hoess, and many others, would resound through history like answers to a roll-call in hell. History would also record that one of the most frequently used words by these Germans, who had directed horrors like none other in history, was "decency".

But, the one name to emerge from the savagery to dominate all others was that of Hitler, the man who even before his suicide, vented the hatred that was at the core of his being. The German people he had so often exalted as "the master race" were now held in contempt. When Speer challenged Hitler's order for the destruction of all military, industrial, transportation and communication installations along with all stores, Hitler now felt that there was "no necessity to take into consideration the basis which the people will need to continue a most primitive existence". In any case, "those who will remain after the battle are only the inferior ones, for the good ones have been killed".[97]

Hitler's hatred also found more immediate targets. Upon his orders, Eva Braun's brother-in-law, General Hermann Fegelein, was taken out and shot in the Chancellery garden after being hauled back to the Führer's bunker from which he had earlier defected. Goering and Himmler, the two men who, with Hitler, had constituted Nazidom's unholy trinity, were expelled from the party and stripped of all offices.

Goering had sent a telegram to Hitler asking whether, if Hitler was planning to remain in Berlin, he (Goering) should assume the Reich leadership in accordance with Hitler's succession decree of June 29, 1941. The telegram really represented a very practical inquiry, but under the Iago-like promptings of Martin Bormann, Hitler interpreted it, and another telegram which Goering had sent to Ribbentrop, as a treasonable attempt to assume power. Hitler's break with Himmler came when Hitler received a report that Himmler had been trying to initiate peace negotiations through Sweden's Count Bernadotte. His reaction reportedly was terrible, calling Himmler's action "the worst treachery he had ever known". The German flyer Hannah Reitsch would later relate how Hitler "raged like a madman. His color rose to a heated red, and his face was almost unrecognizable."[98] Such a reaction reflected Hitler's anger at the man who, above all others, was responsible for carrying out his most important project—the extermination of European Jewry.

That this had been his overriding intention there could be little doubt. It was the sight of the Jews in their caftans in Vienna which had helped stimulate his mental struggle; in his correspondence from the front in the First World War, it was the Jews he had blamed for the "stab-in-the-back" which brought Germany's defeat; it was the Jews who were the focus of his *Reichswehr* report after that war had ended; it was hatred of the Jews which would be the foundation of his political party and the stimulus for his political struggle; it was the Jews who would become the focus of his military struggle, and now that his own death was near, it was the Jews who would gain prominent mention in his political testament. "It is untrue", his testament recorded, "that I, or anybody else in Germany, wanted war in 1939. It was wanted and provoked exclusively by those international politicians who either came of Jewish stock, or worked for Jewish interests." Hitler's testament does not explain how, if Jewish interests had started the war, those same interests had been powerless to save millions of Jews from extermination.

The army, which Hitler had exalted on his road to power, now also was berated because it had not been sufficiently

Nazified. "In future", he wrote, "may it be a point of honor with German army officers, as it already is with our navy, that the surrender of territory and towns is impossible, and that, above all else, commanders must set a shining example of faithful devotion to duty until death." Conspicuously absent from praise was Goering's *Luftwaffe* which, because of its dedicated Nazism, Hitler had held in such high esteem that it blinded him to its military failings. Similarly, Hitler's fanatical anti-Semitism had blinded him to the highly professional merits of the army's general staff which, before Hitler's oppressive meddling, had handed him his most stunning successes, most notably in the invasions of France and Poland.

Now, as a reward for being truly Nazified, the navy, which had played third fiddle to Goering's *Luftwaffe* and the army, would gain a new elevated status with the appointment of Admiral Donitz as Reich president, supreme commander of the armed forces, minister of war, and commander-in-chief of the navy. In what would become a dying-swan cabinet, Goebbels was appointed Reich chancellor, Bormann, party chancellor, and Seyss-Inquart, foreign minister. Speer, Hitler's architect and armaments minister, who had told the Führer that the war was lost and had blocked his leader's scorched-earth policy, was brushed aside for his much-belated truth-telling, and replaced by his deputy, Sauer. Hitler's testament also admonished this new Nazi administration to "above all uphold the racial laws to the limit, and to resist mercilessly the poisoner of all nations, international Jewry."[99] In his personal will Hitler let it be known why, at the verge of his self-inflicted death, he had decided to marry Eva Braun, and he gave directions for the disposal of his property, including his art collection. His Gotterdammerung wedding was performed by a justice of the peace who had been hastily brought to the bunker. His name was Wagner.

CHAPTER THREE: BIBLIOGRAPHY

1 Shirer 300.

2 Adolf Hitler, *My New Order* (New York: Reynal & Hitchcock, 1941) 309-333.

3 Hitler, *My New Order*, 333-334.

4 Hermann Rauschning, *The Revolution of Nihilism* (New York: Garden City Publishing Co., Inc., 1942) 236.

5 Hans Kohn, *The Twentieth Century* (New York: The Macmillan Co., 1949) 209.

6 Hitler, *Mein Kampf* 168.

7 *Mein Kampf* 339.

8 *Mein Kampf* 169.

9 *Mein Kampf* 561.

10 *Mein Kampf* 359.

11 *Mein Kampf* 328.

12 *Mein Kampf* 334-338.

13 *Mein Kampf* 169.

14 Alexander Mitscherlich and Fred Mielke, *Doctors of Infamy* (New York: Henry Schuman, Inc., 1949) 91.

15 Hans Adolph Jacoben, *Der Zweite Weltkrieg* (Frankfurt am Main, 1965) 180.

16 Maser, *Hitler's Letters and Notes* 243-250.

17 Walter Warlimont, *Inside Hitler's Headquarters* (New York: Praeger Publishers, Inc., 1964) 42.

18 Pieter Geyl, *Encounters in History* (Cleveland: Meridian Books, 1961) 265.

19 Neumann, *Behemoth* 125-126.

20 *Mein Kampf* 682.

21 Telford Taylor, *Sword and Swastika* (New York: Quadrangle Books, 1969) 142-143.

22 Nuremberg Document 3569.

23 Roper, *Hitler's Secret Conversations* 106.

24 Heiden, *Der Fuehrer* 296.

25 Taylor, *Sword and Swastika* 129.

26 Shirer, *Rise and Fall* 318.

27 *Mein Kampf* 169.

28 Taylor, *Sword and Swastika* 129.

29 Warlimont, *Inside Hitler's Headquarters* 239.

30 Warlimont, 329.

31 Pierre Galante and Eugene Silianoff, *Voices from the Bunker* (New York: Putnam's Sons, 1989) 19.

32 *Mein Kampf* 13.

33 *Mein Kampf* 13.

34 Gordon Brook-Shepherd, *The Anschluss* (New York: J.B. Lipincott & Co., 1963) 45.

35 Hitler, *My New Order* 467.

36 *My New Order* 582.

37 Shirer, *Rise and Fall* 531.

38 Memoranda of Chvalkovsky's talks with Hitler and Ribbentrop on January 21, 1939. Documents on German Foreign Policy IV, 190-202.

39 *My New Order* 584-585.

40 Shirer, *Rise and Fall* 454.

41 *Rise and Fall* 485.

42 *Rise and Fall* 454.

43 *Rise and Fall* 489.

44 *My New Order* 969.

45 Rauschning, *The Voice of Destruction* (New York: Garden City Publishing Co., 1944) 140-141.

46 *Voice of Destruction* xii.

47 Winston Churchill, Vol. 1 *The Second World War* 9th Edition, (Boston: Houghton Mifflin, 1954) 425.

48 *My New Order* 702.

49 *My New Order* 758.

50 *My New Order* 766.

51 B.H. Liddell Hart, *The German Generals Talk* (New York: Morrow Quill Paperbacks, 1979) 135.

52 Shirer, *Rise and Fall* 485.

53 *Rise and Fall* 784.

54 Warlimont, *Inside Hitler's Headquarters* 132.

55 *Inside Hitler's Headquarters* 134.

56 Shirer, *Rise and Fall* 485.

57 *Rise and Fall* 531.

58 *Rise and Fall* 532.

59 Charles Cruikshank, *The German Occupation of the Channel Islands* (Guernsey: The Guernsey Press Co., Ltd., 1975) 214-219.

60 *The Complete Works of William Shakespeare*, ed. William Aldis Wright (Garden City: Garden City Books, 1936) 360.

61 Warlimont, *Inside Hitler's Headquarters* 128.

62 *Inside Hitler's Headquarters* 130.

63 *Mein Kampf* 654.

64 Hitler, *My New Order* 986.

65 Nuremberg Document PS-4064, Order by Field Marshal Erich von Manstein, Nov. 20, 1941.

66 Warlimont, *Inside Hitler's Headquarters* 161.

67 Case XII, No. 3140; extract from Halder's diary.

68 Hans Bucheim, *Anatomy of the SS State* 262.

69 Gerald Reitlinger, *The SS Alibi of a Nation* (Englewood Cliffs: Prentice Hall, Inc., 1981) 147.

70 Reitlinger, 151.

71 Andre Maurois, *Byron "The Corsair"* (New York: D. Appleton Co., 1930) 253.

72 Hitler, *My New Order* 967.

73 Franz Halder, *Hitler als Feldherr* (Munich, 1949) 45.

74 Rauschning, *The Revolution of Nihilism* 147.

75 Hart, *The German Generals Talk* 198.

76 Hitler, *My New Order* 777.

77 Domarus Reden 1603.

78 Karl Dietrich Bracher, *The German Dictatorship* (New York: Praeger, 1970) 408.

79 *The German Dictatorship* 368.

80 Maser, *Hitler's Letters and Notes* 243-250.

81 Raul Hilberg, *The Destruction of the European Jews* (New York: Quadrangle Books, 1961) 298.

82 Warlimont, *Inside Hitler's Headquarters* 199.

83 Liddell Hart, *History of the Second World War* (New York: G.P. Putnam's Sons, 1970) 243.

84 Bracher, *The German Dictatorship* 368.

85 Shirer, *The Rise and Fall* 941.

86 Dawidowicz, *The War Against the Jews* 130.

87 *Eichmann Interrogated* tr. Ralph Manheim, ed. Jochen von Lang in collaboration with Claus Sibyll, (New York: Vintage Books, 1984) 124.

88 *Eichmann Interrogated* 166.

89 *Eichmann Interrogated* 89.

90 Shirer, *The Rise and Fall* 966.

91 Hilberg, *The Destruction of the European Jews* 564.

92 Klessheim conference summary April 17, 1943 by Dr. Paul Schmidt, foreign office interpreter Nora Levin 607-608 D-736 "D" for documents processed by British prosecutors.

93 Warlimont, *Inside Hitler's Headquarters* 495.

94 Warlimont, 513.

95 Cruikshank, *The German Occupation of the Channel Islands* 516.

96 Warlimont, 516.

97 Shirer, *The Rise and Fall* 1104.

98 H.R. Trevor Roper, *The Last Days of Hitler* (New York: The Macmillan Co., 1947) 169.

99 Roper, *The Last Days* 177-179.

CHAPTER 4

THE NEO-PAGAN REVENGE: AN HISTORICAL REFLECTION

Hitler's three struggles—mental, political, and military—were linked by one overriding intention: to rid the world of Jews, and all Jewish influences, including Christianity that he saw as "a rebellion against the natural law; a protest against nature... the systematic cultivation of human failure."[1] And since Christianity had destroyed pagan culture, Hitler would launch a neo-pagan revenge against Jewry and Christianity. Because of its millions of adherents, however, he could not directly assault Christianity until he had consolidated his power within Germany and throughout Europe. His initial target, therefore, was not Christianity, but the Jews and communism. But this did not prevent him from pressuring both the Protestant and Catholic churches in ways that he thought would lead them to render allegiance first to the Führer and then to God.

Why, then, were the Jews and the communists singled out as enemies, with the Jews assigned priority status for destruction? And why was it that the long Western tradition of anti-Semitism assumed such virulent aspects in the 19th Century and threatened to undermine Western civilization in the 20th? The answer to these questions lies within the history of both Christianity and Judaism, and can be simply stated this way: in trying to provide a matrix under which the pagan cultures of Greece and Rome could be brought together, Christianity, a Judaic offshoot, became unduly influenced by Greek philosophy and Roman pragmatism, and failed in its mission of unifying the world. With the aid of Greek philosophy, the Church had developed an orthodoxy of doctrine and dogma and, at the same time, patterned its hierarchical and authoritarian structure on the Roman Empire.

There was some justification for this since Christianity had to disseminate an essentially Jewish religious message into the Greco-Roman world so as to topple the pagan gods. But, in so doing, the Church suppressed the prophetic and moral spirit of Judaism that had launched Christianity in the first place, and tended toward an otherworldly, spiritual view that bore resemblance to the platonic ideal world of which the real world was but an inferior and shadowy form. Consequently, over a very long period of time, but gaining fervor after the Reformation, and later with the Enlightenment, Christianity came under increasing attack because of the discrepancy between its professions of spirituality and its practice in what was perceived to be hypocrisy. This was the basis for Marx's criticism that religion was "the opium of the masses." And there was much truth in this since the direction of human attention to another world tended to divert attention from the ills of this one.

Hitler, however, was more perceptive. He saw what Marx did not, that even though Christianity did not practice what it preached, its teachings had found their way into the secular realm, contributing to the development of social democracy, communism, internationalism, egalitarianism, and much more. Where Marx saw Christianity as a failure, Hitler saw it as succeeding all too well and particularly with the advent of communism which he viewed as the latest development and final bolshevization of the world that Christianity had inaugurated.

In the essentials Hitler, of course, was right. Egalitarianism was the offspring of Christian thought and its dissemination, in mundane form, was often due to the zeal of lapsed Christians and Jews whose moral impulses turned from thoughts of another world to correction of injustices and wrongs in this one. This displacement into politics of the Christian form of the Jewish spirit followed the parable of the mustard seed, and took a very long time to develop, but gained momentum in the 18th Century following the American and French revolutions, and the advent of liberal democratic and socialist ideologies. The latter were filled with the kind of messianic hope that had first been nurtured by Judaism, but were universally disseminated by Christianity.

In the next century, however, one socialist doctrine surfaced to dominate all others. Authored by Marx and his collaborator, Friedrich Engels, and published in 1848 as the *Manifesto of the Communist Party*, it sent shudders around the world among old regimes while raising hopes among believers in an ultimate universal comity. "The Communists," the manifesto declared, "disdain to conceal their views and aims. They openly declare that their ends can be attained only by the forcible overthrow of all existing conditions." And, in fearful language, it added: "Let the ruling classes tremble at a communist revolution. The proletarians have nothing to lose but their chains! They have a world to win. Working men of all countries, unite!"[2]

Communism became history's first secular "religion" that was openly atheistic. It was addressed not to any one country, but to all the world which was divided into two classes: the minority who ruled and the majority they ruled. Communism could be achieved only through forcible world revolution by which the ruling classes would be overthrown. In 1917, almost seventy years after the publication of the Communist Manifesto, Lenin put it to the test in Russia by overthrowing the ruling class and proclaiming the dictatorship of the proletariat. The reality turned out to be quite different. The Union of Socialist Soviet Republics, as the new Communist empire was designated, became a dictatorship *over* the proletariat, and lasted for barely seventy-five years, during which atrocities and genocide were perpetrated on a scale unmatched in history even by zealots in God-inspired religions. And Lenin's cry of "all power to the soviets" gave way to all power to the Party. Consequently, while expressing moral outrage at the injustices of the capitalist system, the world's first professedly atheistic "faith" unleashed its own oppressions and made the same error as Christianity, by failing to practice what it preached; succumbing to the will to power, and claiming an infallibility of doctrine that could not be supported by reality.

Before it collapsed, Soviet communism provoked reactions that, for the first time, brought to consciousness aspects of history that previously had been veiled or only vaguely sensed. One of the most important consequences of these reactions was that the long-standing and perplexing riddle of anti-Semitism had become amenable to an answer. And linked to this answer was a host of other questions involving politics, religion, and history itself.

The strongest reaction to Soviet communism would be led by Hitler, for whom all of these questions had long held an obsessive fascination, particularly as they applied to the Jews.

It was Hitler's belief that these people, with their many spiritual descendants such as Christianity, social democracy, and communism, had effectively diverted history from its natural course under the aegis of Greco-Roman civilization. Not Jesus, whom Hitler conveniently, arbitrarily, and erroneously decided was an Aryan, but St. Paul, the Jew, was the instigator who spread Jesus's message of the equality of all people under "the single God" as a way of ruining the Roman Empire. In Hitler's eyes, Rome was Bolshevized, and this "Bolshevism" produced the same results in Rome as later in Russia. "Just when Christianity was tottering, the Jews restored it to pride of place; Christianity in its Bolshevistic form." Christianity, therefore, was the prototype of Bolshevism—the former being the work of Saul (St. Paul), and the latter initiated by Marx. Paul's organization of the Christian "prototype Bolshevism," Hitler believed, marked the end of a long reign "of the clear Greco-Latin genius."[3]

In these, and other statements, however vulgarly expressed and filled with inaccuracies, Hitler, nevertheless, focused on central historical themes that have been acknowledged by both Jewish and Christian scholars, namely that Judaism's great and revolutionary contributions to the world have been a monotheistic religion, the refinement of the moral conscience, and the recognition that history involves humankind in purposeful action as agents of God. These represent a significant part of the Jewish heritage which Christianity set out to disseminate throughout the world and implant in minds imprinted with diametrically opposed outlooks. Such concepts as equality, human rights, the belief in freedom and personal dignity, derived from the Judeo-Christian heritage, have now been accepted throughout large parts of the world. But where these are now eagerly sought, as part of world progress, Hitler viewed them as the worst of horrors, and the Jews who unleashed them were a "poison," which he considered it his mission to eradicate. The end of his military struggle, he declared, would "see the final ruin of the Jew," who could "take credit for corrupting the Greco-Roman world."[4] With military victory, Christianity would fare no better. "I shall then consider that my life's final task will be to solve the religious problem… "[5]

Hitler's fierce reaction toward the Jews whom he saw as the originators of Christianity, as well as the secular "religion" of communism, provides the key to the 20th Century's violent eruption of anti-Semitism on such a scale and, as a final solution to the historical "Jewish problem." As long as the Jews were confined largely to a ghetto existence and were barred from full rights in gentile society, and as long as the Jewish spirit was primarily given theoretical and ritual expression within Christianity, anti-Semitism was sporadic, and largely inchoate. But once this spirit found practical expression in democratic politics, but most importantly in international communism, anti-Semitism became fully conscious. In Nazism particularly, but also in other manifestations of fascism, it revealed itself as a reaction of the Greco-Roman elements in the Western consciousness against its Jewish component.

While the signs of this development had been evident throughout Christianity, they became much more obvious in the 18th Century with the spread of rational thought. In addition, this was the century in which Jews, in increasing numbers, were being emancipated and energetically making the most of their freedom. They availed themselves of university education, and entered professions and businesses that were formerly barred to them, and in which they excelled disproportionately to their numbers in the gentile world.

The coinciding, therefore, of greater Jewish visibility and the increasing awareness of the historical role of the Jews contributed to the exacerbation of anti-Semitism. Fed by the revival of classical learning during the Renaissance, and without the cohesive influence of religion, Enlightenment thought contributed to the dislocation between God and humanity to the point at which, with Nietzsche, God would be declared dead.

But, before Hitler came on the scene, Nietzsche had spelled out a philosophy that clearly provided Hitler with the core of his own world view. For example, Nietzsche asserted that the Jews "with awe-inspiring consistency dared to invert the aristocratic value-equation... saying 'the wretched alone are the good; the poor, impotent, lowly alone are the good' while the 'powerful and noble are on the contrary the evil... '" And, in an emphatic allusion to Christianity, Nietzsche adds, "One knows *who* inherited this Jewish revaluation... " With the Jews, he asserted, "there begins *the slave revolt in morality*: that revolt which has a history of two thousand years behind it and which we no longer see because it has been victorious."[6] (Original italics.)

Nietzsche's pronouncements were among a number of developments which showed that the long-developing neo-pagan counterattack against religion had come fully into the open. The separation of the spiritual and temporal powers, of church and state, was also an early acknowledgement that the kingdom of God was not of this world—an idea that one aspect of Enlightenment thought would reinforce with the view that without God, humans could stand alone and perfect themselves and society. It was only a matter of time, therefore, before politics would promote the progress and welfare of humanity without acknowledging the religious ancestry of its ideology. Having given birth to ideology, the-ology was disowned by its own child, a fact best demonstrated by the moral fervor of the French Revolution with its symbolic dethronement of God and the installation of a statue of the "goddess" reason in Notre Dame Cathe-dral. Considering that much of human history, including the Revolution, was dominated by males, the choice of a female statue seems ironic, unless it can be seen as intended to make amends for the primacy which, since Adam, had been assigned to man, and has been followed by an intermi-nable line of father gods, father tyrants, father monarchs, fatherlands, and father churches. But where the Reforma-tion had merely sought to reform the Christian Church, Enlightenment thinkers wanted the reformation of the world. And, as part of that reformation, the Church was viewed as dispensable. That was made clear in Voltaire's incessant cry: *"Ecrasez l'infame"* (Crush the infamy), meaning the infamy of religion. These, and other factors, would inaugurate the secular usurpation of religion's vocation.

As with all historical developments, it is not possible to pinpoint when the pagan counterattack began; the seeds of history are often planted long before they pierce the soil and blossom. Indeed, there is much to suggest that a pagan resistance to Christianity has accompanied Chris-tianity since its inception, and gained strength with the reassertion of pagan thought patterns during and after the Renaissance. But, if one were to select a significant point in the pagan counterattack against Christianity, the 14th Century Italian Boccaccio would loom significantly. His *Decameron*,—a tale about seven women and three men who flee from a plague-ridden city—exhibits a thinly-dis-guised disgust with Christian clerics. In his *Fiammetta*, the seminal source of the modern novel, there is no men-tion of Christianity or God; the whole story is set in a Greco-Roman mold. Fiammetta yields her virginity to her lover with no qualms of Christian conscience. Instead, she is encouraged by a vision of Venus in a flimsy dress, intended to abet her passion. Despite his conversion in 1361, Boccaccio remained, for the rest of his life, devoted to the classical world, and his writings rejected Christianity for paganism. In the *Decameron*, Christianity is acknowledged; in *Fiammetta*, it is not even mentioned. Long after Boccaccio, it can be seen that just as Christianity toppled the ancient pagan gods without destroying paganism, the neo-pagan modern world has gone a long way toward toppling the Christian god which was Hitler's conscious intention. And just as paganism, in the forms of art, literature, architecture, philosophy, politics, and even sports, was displaced into Christian civilization, now Christianity has been displaced into the secular world.

Politics is at the center of this displacement, and for this reason it has been at the eye of the hurricane of action, reaction, interaction, reform, and revolution. As most everyone knows, politics in the Western world originated with Greece and Rome, but throughout the centuries it has undergone many changes that have resulted from pressures to improve the human condition through such guarantees as liberty, equality, and manifold civil and human rights. If these had been proposed for universal application, in ancient Greece or Rome, they would have brought certain death to the proposers, as indeed was the case for the early Christians who first voiced such ideas. Since antiquity, however, these ideas have grown like mustard seeds within the Western world, and have gained universal currency. For the most part, their advancement, under such general political categories as liberalism, democracy, and socialism, has been incremental, reluctant, expedient, or all three. At bottom, the history of the Western world is the history of the resistance of power structures, however democratic in appearance, to the penetration of liberal ideas that came out of Judaism and Judeo-Christianity. Democracy is really conservatism's concession to liberalism.

At its best, it is progressive-conservative or to use a medical metaphor, it is the dispensation of medicine instead of the surgery that social conditions sometimes warrant. At its worst, it is virulently reactionary. The truth is that liberal ideas in the West have been accepted slowly, and in small doses, often in order to save old regimes, and because the rise of science, technology, and industrialization meant mass production requiring mass markets which, in turn, meant mass worker-buyers with more pay and more say. Thus was inaugurated the age of limited, or incremental, democracy which began in some enlightened European nations, but gained impetus in America with its vast resources, initial small population, and rapid industrialization. Starting in the 18th Century, however, and stimulated by the Industrial and the French Revolutions, the largely gratuitous and expedient democratic, or medicinal, approach to social problems, was dealt a series of shocks in the form of socialist ideologies calling for radical social surgery instead of medicine—the most radical being Marxist communism.

Soviet communism, therefore, drew universally strong reaction from religion in both its organized institutional form and in its secular political guise. From so-called Christian nations, as well as from the Vatican, communism was denounced because of its avowed atheism. Yet, just as important from the religious standpoint, was the perceived threat of this new competitor "faith" that promised to usher in the millennium that had long been religion's hope. And while capitalist democracies would join with the religious in attacking "Godless communism," there was plenty of evidence that atheism was not the real concern, but rather the threat that communism posed to the world's economic order that was

largely under the control of the major capitalist democracies which had gained a long headstart in economic
expansion and worldwide investments. These democracies were increasingly revealing a different kind of
atheism—one in which God is invoked, but not really
believed in. The symbolic evidence of this could be seen
in London, New York, and other major cities where the
architectural focus was not, as it had been of old when
cathedral spires aspired heavenward, but on towering
financial structures aspiring toward profits. Indeed, the
often-used term "democratic capitalism" seemed a contradiction in terms, particularly since representative
democracy stopped at the corporate door.

The most violent reaction to communism, however,
came from Germany and not because communism was
atheistic, but primarily because of its international and
professedly egalitarian character. Among the reasons for
this was that Germany, in comparison with France, Holland, Britain, Spain, Portugal, and the U.S., had been
relatively retarded in its expansionist development. And
this was due to a number of historical reasons, the most
important being the Thirty Years War, the Napoleonic
invasion, and Germany's First World War defeat. With
the latter two experiences, in particular, internationalism, as represented in the French revolutionary cry of
"Liberty, Equality, Fraternity," appeared as a threat to
Germany's strongly-held sense of identity that became
paranoid with the threat of yet another internationalism,
in the form of communism, which already had captured
the loyalty of large numbers of the German working class.
The post-Versailles clash between German nationalists
and communists provided a microcosm of macroscopic
socio-political trends that included the extremes of the
left (Marxism), the right (fascism), and intermediary social democracy. In order to gain power, Nazism (the most

extreme of the fascist movements) had to conceal its wolf-
ish aims in the sheep's clothing of democratic
electioneering while appealing to the masses with the bait
of both nationalism and socialism. But once in power,
Nazism found itself in mortal combat with the strange
alliance between the most extreme form of socialism, on
the one hand, and the halfway house of social democracies, on the other.

Western history, therefore, has provided the inspiration for world revolution, and it is one of its many
paradoxes, that while much of the rest of the world
showed little signs of dynamic social progress, it was
the infusion of Oriental thought, in its Judaic and Judeo-
Christian forms, that acted as the catalyst for Western
progress, however bloody, tragic, and turbulent it has
often been, and which now has been exported universally. The reasons for this are many, but the central fact
is that Western political and social ideas have been imbibed by revolutionary leaders and their followers in
India, Africa, and Asia, some of whom graduated from
prestigious Western universities. Consequently, it could
be asked, from where, except in Western civilization,
did the impetus originate for parliamentary democracy,
the acceleration of science and technology, the rule of
law, capitalism, socialism, communism, and the concepts
of human and civil rights? Even if not always for the
best, all of these, and more, are transforming the world,
and all but science and technology, which Hitler welcomed as instruments of power, he sought to eradicate
because he saw them as transcending nationalism based
solely on soil and blood. Hence, it is important to exam-
ine why Hitler drew from the Greco-Roman elements in
his psyche in order to assert his identity, and to best
fulfill his intention.

It is known that Hitler's childhood had left him with an emotional warp. He was a hater, and haters not only need a focus for their hatred but, unless they are antisocial or sociopaths, they must identify with those influences or organizations which provide avenues for the expression of hatred and dominance. Thus, he hated the expressions of love, equality, freedom, and mercy he had been taught in the Roman Catholic Church, but admired its Roman aspect of discipline, dogma, authority, and organization. Many times during his political and military struggles, he had read Schopenhauer's writings, with their emphasis on "the world as will and idea," and he drew much inspiration from Nietzsche's prophecy of the advent of the Superman, and his announcement of the death of God. Indeed, although Nietzsche's philosophy was centered on a vital individualism, and was neither anti-Semitic nor chauvinistic; it provided the framework for a great deal of Hitler's world view. Hitler's speeches, conversations, and writings, are riddled with Nietzscheanisms in which Judeo-Christianity is seen to be responsible for the transvaluation of values, and the inauguration of ideas of human equality.

Hitler picked up on Nietzsche's view of the masses as little more than cattle, and the need to replace pity with ruthlessness. He also shared Nietzsche's view that the Jews had initiated a "slave revolt" against the Greco-Roman civilization. This "unspeakably disastrous initiative," Nietzsche said, amounted to a Jewish "declaration of war"[7]—a phrase which Hitler often used in accusing world Jewry of starting the Second World War. Hitler also slavishly followed Nietzsche in blaming Paul of Tarsus for the spread of Christianity. Without Paul, said Nietzsche, "there would be no Christianity; we would hardly have heard of a little Jewish sect whose master died on the cross."[8] Hitler went one up on Nietzsche by seeing Christianity as a prototype

Bolshevism. "The religion fabricated by Paul of Tarsus," said Hitler, "and which was later called Christianity, is nothing but the Communism of today."[9] Thus, like Nietzsche and many other German and Austrian writers and thinkers, Hitler turned his back on Judeo-Christianity, and his face toward Greece and Rome.

Hitler admired the Greek city-state of Sparta with its iron rule of the many by the few, and for the same reason, he saw much to commend in the rule of millions in India by a "handful" of Britons. As previously noted, Karl May's yarns about the killing of American Indians would come to mind in the conquest of Eastern Europe and Russia where, Hitler noted, "There's only one duty, and that is to look upon the natives as Redskins."[10] He thought America was moving in the right direction when its immigration quotas gave preference to the white race, and he approved of the American South when it held blacks in slavery.

It will be remembered that, as a youth, Hitler had stood on the mountainside in Linz, still under the spell of Wagner's *Rienzi*, and how he later would say: "It was then that it all began"[11]—a reference to the sense of destiny the opera had instilled in him. This experience shows how impressionable the young Hitler was, and is of the utmost importance when seen in relationship to Western civilization's cultural-psychological legacy. In one way and another with the advancement of printing, radio, television, movies, and much more, this legacy has become a universal inheritance of religious, historical, political, social, and scientific ideas that have been transmitted from the past to the present, and are shaping the world's future.

Hitler's fascination with *Rienzi* was derived from his admiration for pre-Christian Rome. The career of Cola di Rienzi, the medieval tribune, upon which the opera was based, followed in its essential details, Hitler's own political story. The Rome of Rienzi's time had lost much of its grandeur; it was no longer the "eternal Rome" of the imperial caesars, but had become a relatively unimportant city when the Papacy moved its seat of authority from Rome to Avignon and was governed mostly by the French. Rienzi had marshaled support for a revival of the old Republic. He called forth the ghosts of Rome's past, and had focused a renewed patriotism on ancient symbols of power and glory. Central to his purpose was to rid Rome of all foreign, or feudal-Christian influences, so as to restore its ancient purity in preparation for cleansing all Italian soil. His short-lived political venture failed, but it helped trigger a literary revival of the Latin past, and became merged with an already revived interest in the study of ancient Greece.

This focus on the buried past, or revival of classical letters, became known as the Renaissance which did so much to reinfuse the Western mind with classical modes of thought. It was a *reinfusion* since the classical world had long been incorporated into Christianity. But the Renaissance had the effect of directing attention to classical politics, art, and thought in ways that were less directly monitored by the Church. In addition, the spread of classical translations and later, the advent of mechanical printing presses, as well as the establishment of Greek and Latin curriculae in schools and universities, ensured a much wider penetration of the Western mind by classical scholarship. The Renaissance contributed to such developments as Judeo-Christian humanism, the Enlightenment, positivism, dogmatic rationalism, anti-theism, atheism, anti-Christianism, and what has been called the "drama of atheist humanism."[12] It also helped spawn a variety of ideological distortions in which the powers of reason were placed at the service of the irrational, of which Nazism was the nonpareil exemplar.

If Rienzi's Rome had lost much of its ancient grandeur, then Germany, after the First World War, found itself no longer the "new Athens" that had surprised the world with the profundity of its classical scholarship, but instead was subjected to the stranglehold of the American, British, and French war victors who imposed crushing reparations that had contributed to a harrowing economic depression. This, at least, was how Hitler and many Germans had come to view their country's plight. In addition, Hitler saw, in all of Germany's ills, the hand of world Jewry which he believed had contributed to Germany's defeat, and whose influence had infiltrated Germany itself. Like Rienzi, he wanted to purge Germany of all foreign influences, and restore it to a purity based on an imaginary, mythical German past, but more particularly on his version of Greco-Roman civilization. Christianity, he often remarked, had undermined Greco-Roman civilization, and ushered in a period of darkness that lasted for nearly two thousand years. Again, as with Rienzi, Hitler focused his people's attention on patriotic symbols, architecture, and art forms that drew their inspiration from pseudo-mythology and Greco-Roman civilization. Like the Roman legions of yore, Hitler's legions marched with eagle banners held high, and hailed their leader with stiff-arm salutes in the manner that Roman emperors had been accustomed to.

Hitler was not the first, and will probably not be the last dictator to emulate the Roman emperors, and to seek the *Renovatio Romani imperii*—the renewal of the Roman Empire. His Axis partner, Mussolini, saw himself as a restorer of the Roman Empire. He strutted Caesar-like during his brief time on the world stage, and razed buildings in Rome in order to create an unobstructed view of ancient Roman ruins. Napoleon, too, was fascinated with the world of Roman caesars and borrowed, for his coronation, a wreathed crown, and eagle-emblazoned chain from ancient Rome. "Don't make any mistake," he is reported to have said, "I am a Roman emperor, in the best line of the caesars."[13] The persistence into the 20th Century of Roman imperial models was theatrically demonstrated at the coronation of the Central African Republic's self-styled emperor Bokassa who showed that even copycats like Napoleon can be copied. For his coronation, Bokassa wore an elaborate robe that was custom-made in France as a replica of the one Napoleon wore for his coronation. Bokassa also was enthroned on an ornate, gold throne shaped like the imperial Roman eagle. As Arnold Toynbee noted: "Every passing year of our own history that makes Greek and Roman history chronologically more remote, brings it closer to us psychologically. If there is any key to the riddle of our destiny, that key lies here... "[14]

Or, as Lord Acton wrote: "A speech of Antigone, a single sentence of Socrates, a few lines inscribed on a rock in India... the footsteps of a silent yet prophetic people who dwelt by the Dead Sea... come nearer to our lives than the ancestral wisdom of barbarians... "[15] And, when describing what George Eliot was about in *Romola*, Felicia Bonaparte noted: "As in memory we carry with us the whole of our lives, so in imagination we bring into our own consciousness the life of mankind and possess it as concretely as if we had lived it ourselves."[16]

While many cultures have contributed to Western civilization, the major influences have come from the Jewish, Greek, and Roman cultures. Where once these three collided as cultures, they now inhabit the Western mentality, not in harmonious fusion, but in a state of confusion that often erupts into political and military hostilities. In each individual, for example, and with varying degrees of intensity, the tendency is to express, or assert, an identity that reflects the dominance of one or another of these three cultural-psychological types. The person who is predominantly contemplative, idealistic, or artistic will exhibit the mark of the Greek while the person of pragmatic disposition, who is not greatly attracted to idealism and art, will show a Roman aspect, perhaps in politics, business, law, or some other practical pursuit. The person in whom the Jewish and Judeo-Christian identification is strongest will tend to make strong moral judgments such as are displayed in a passion for justice and revolutionary politics. In the assertion of an identity, the ego will attempt to submerge those elements that hamper its identification, and extol those which aid it, and much the same thing happens where national egos or identities are involved. As Theodore Mommsen, Germany's eminent classical historian, wrote: It was during the time of Cato that Romans were opposed to Greek literature very much as, in the time of the Caesars, they were opposed to Christianity. The nobility, Mommsen wrote, "and above all the government, saw in poetry, as in Christianity, an absolutely hostile power; Plautus and Ennius were ranked with the rabble by the Roman aristocracy for reasons nearly the same as those for which the Apostles and bishops were put to death by the Roman government."[17] In its turn, the Roman Catholic Church, inspired by Rome rather than Christ, proscribed literary and scientific works, and burned heretics, only to be outmatched later by the Nazis who not only burned books and banned art, but sought to burn an entire people.

Although the tensions between these dominant cultures were exhibited when they first came into contact, it was not until the 19th and 20th Centuries, that these tensions became highly aggravated, and were reflected most tragically in anti-Semitism, but also in the writings of Nietzsche and others, as well as in the field of art, literature, music, and politics. Most people go through life unaware of the cultural influences on their consciousness, and their dominant cultural-psychological traits are not always readily discernible. However, as William Barrett noted, "Habit and routine are great veils over our existence." But once the social fabric is rent, "one is suddenly thrust outside, away from the habits and norms once automatically accepted," and it is there "on the outside that one's questioning begins."[18]

Hence, in times of personal or national crisis, identity becomes more evident, particularly in the alignment, or identification, with a specific political party and, as in time of war, with one's country. In some individuals this need to identify can emerge in unpredictable ways. Thus, in order to subdue the Jewish element in his mind, Hitler recruited his Roman constituent. It was precisely when he was a young man in cosmopolitan Vienna that he turned his attention to the Jews, and this coincided with the Viennese academy's rejection of his artistic, or Greek-like aspirations. As he himself related, he switched from art to politics, thus giving greater expression to the Roman constituent in his mentality. Even so, his practical, or Roman spirit, took on artistic colorations. His people became material to be shaped in accordance with his political aims. As William Irwin Thompson noted in his insightful study of the Irish uprising in 1916: "The Irish revolutionaries lived as if they were in a work of art," and when, during a revolution, "history is made momentarily into a work of art, human beings become the material that must be ordered, or twisted into shape."[19]

Indeed, the Irish Republic (initially the Irish Free State) and Germany offer interesting parallels, and show how the past, even when refracted through the prism of the present, can become a potent, though expedient, element in nationalism. These two countries were fiercely nationalistic, and the primary obstructer of their national aims was Britain. In both countries, a romantic revival of folk culture and pseudo mythology was employed to reinforce a national identity. German romantics, such as Herder, the Grimm brothers, Arnim, and Brentano, extolled the virtues of spontaneous folk art at the expense of classical culture. The myths, epics, and folksongs collected by the romanticists were supposedly communal works that grew out of the organic community. But later scholarship suggests that folk culture, including songs, titles, and period clothing, quite often were really adaptations, by the lower classes, of cultural styles that had originated among the aristocracy. Although higher art has sometimes drawn inspiration from folk culture, the reverse is often the case.

In the modern era, folk culture is no longer a vital force, but is trotted out on sentimental and ceremonial occasions, and often for the benefit of tourists. And, in contrast to Ireland, folk mythology in Germany constituted a relatively minor ingredient in the Nazi program which owed much more to the distorted classicism promoted by Hitler, who publicly subscribed to mythology, but privately acknowledged that "nothing would be more foolish than to reestablish the worship of Wotan. Our old mythology had ceased to be viable when Christianity implanted itself."[20] And Hegel took issue with revivals of mythology such as culminated in Wagner's *Ring of the Nibelungen*. "The history of Christ, Jerusalem, Bethlehem, the Roman law, even the Trojan War, hold much more of the present for us than the adventure of the Nibelungs which, for the national consciousness, are past history— a past completely swept away. To insist on making something national—a popular bible—out of such materials is utterly stale and inane."[21]

In contrast to the Germans, the Irish had little to do with classical models, but relied almost solely on Celtic mythology to bolster their nationalist cause even to the extent of reviving the Gaelic language. As it turned out, however, once the Irish gained a large measure of independence, Gaelic, except for the remote part of Ireland, where a relative few still spoke the language, would become something of an anachronism that was used for family and place names, street signs, and the passing of civil service exams. To this day, the real *lingua franca* of the majority of Irish remains English, and there is little Celtic mythology reflected in Ireland's Constitution or its parliament (the Dail). Both owe more to the Enlightenment thought of American and British constitutional and parliamentary innovators than to the inhabitants of a remote and mythical Ireland. Indeed, the Roman Catholic Church has had a greater influence on the Irish Constitution than anything from the Celtic past—an indication that, in modern times, the Roman influence can arrive, if not by conquest, at least through the Church door.

As it turned out, however, the Celtic revival was inspired by the Scottish historian James Macpherson whose *Poems of Ossian* were the supposed primal compositions of the Celts. But, as with German folklore, later scholarship questioned, even discredited, the authenticity of Macpherson's tales. Celtic and German mythology, nevertheless, did play their part, however transient, in stirring nationalistic feelings so that Yeats, the foremost of the Celtic twilighters, would give oxymoronic expression to the Irish uprising's "terrible beauty" that was born from the Celtic literary revival; not nearly so terrible, as it turned out, as the Nazi revolution which received its impetus from a polluted osmosis of literature's *Stürm und Drang* movement and had nothing beautiful about it at all.

The Irish and German experiences provide particularly significant examples of how excessive nationalist movements can focus on the past as a means of asserting a national identity in the face of what are perceived to be barriers to that identity. Hitler realized better than anyone else, however, that even though myth can be useful as nationalist window dressing, it was Roman organization, pragmatism, and ruthlessness that had conquered the ancient world, leaving a legacy for others to emulate, as had been the case with the Holy Roman, and British Empires. Hitler knew that while myth, even when manufactured, may help as midwife to revolution, it requires much more to organize and build a modern revolutionary state.

Nazism found mythology additionally useful, however, as an anti-intellectual fender against rational criticism of its ideology. Hence, the myth of the Volk served as an emotional parallel to the military's Siegfried Line that was designed to keep out invaders. Yet, perhaps the most damaging evidence of the fallacious assertion that the Volk grew organically out of soil and blood, was the necessity for the Nazi regime to introduce highly rational organization and police control over the entire nation so as to stifle any expression, Volkist or otherwise, that conflicted with the ideas of the Nazi leadership—a leadership that did not grow organically from the Volk, but from garbled notions that Hitler had purloined from the confusion of Western ideas crowding his mind, and from which he fashioned an identity for himself and his people.

In recent years, "identity" has become a much used word in numerous scholarly journals and books dealing with such topics as religion, psychology, philosophy, and politics. It is even ubiquitously evident in the popular press. Yet, the concept of identity often is applied in a rather imprecise way. Since Hitler was involved in a particularly intense quest for individual, as well as national identity, it is possible that his life and thought may offer some clues as to what identity really means.

Like all humans, Hitler had an awareness of self that enables one to awaken each day with the feeling of being the same person as the day before. If one did not have that awareness, one would have to begin each day anew as though one were a quite different person. Each day, in effect, would bring a new life; a new identity. This self-awareness is so much taken for granted that it is rarely questioned. But, in addition to this inchoate awareness of a permanent self, the conscious aspect of humans appears to have the need to assert an identity that is most representative of the inexplicable who or what it is that awakens each day from the unconscious state of sleep. This conscious assertion of identity is known as ego, as distinct from the existent being one is constantly aware of. Hence, it has become common knowledge that an essential of the human condition is self-awareness or self-consciousness—a kind of duality of being—in which there is a conscious self that is aware of another self, and yet the two somehow are intimately connected.

This duality, or what has been described as a conflict, between the "real soul and the pretender soul,"[22] or split between the head and the heart, thoughts and feelings, reason and emotion, permeates a great deal of modern Western literature, philosophy, and politics, and is reflected, with varying degrees of intensity, in such apparent antinomies as classicism versus romanticism in literature, art, and philosophy; conservatism and liberalism, capitalism and socialism, nationalism and internationalism, as well as the split of the Roman Empire and Christianity into their Roman and Greek aspects, and the modern ideological split between East and West that gave rise to the Cold War. These, and other manifestations of duality, have also expanded the range and depth of human experience. Indeed, it is this provocative interaction that is the uniquely dynamic mark of Western history and presents such a contrast to the history of all other civilizations. Reflecting, as they do, the three prime human elements of thought, practice, and morality, the triadic interplay of Greek, Roman, and Jew, offers a corrective to excesses by any one influence.

Thus, while the ancient world of the Greeks and the Romans gave way to the Christian world, then to the modern, the basic outlook of these three cultures still inhabits the Western mind and is reflected in Western institutions, religion, politics, art, and thought. The modern world is an outgrowth of these distinctive cultures which first clashed in physical combat, but now act in opposition within our psyches and in politics sometimes, as Nazism showed, to devastating effect, but also at times provoking acute ego-introspection. "Antiquity and the Middle Ages," said Lord Acton, "are the two civilizations that have preceded us, and the two elements of which ours is composed. All political as well as religious questions reduce themselves practically to this. This is the great dualism that runs through our society."[23]

Acton's observations about Western civilization's unique, if turbulent, mixture of cultures have been echoed by other writers. And, in passing, it should be noted that "pure race" theorists, and those who accuse Western historians of Eurocentrism, might well ponder why more homogeneous civilizations such as the Chinese, Japanese, and the Indian, did not develop a great capacity for either social change or outreach to other cultures until they were impacted by Western ideas and technology which were the dynamic progeny of the Greek, Roman, and Jewish cultural-psychological mixture.

For Matthew Arnold, the principal conflict between these three centered on Hebraism and Hellenism. The uppermost idea with Hellenism, he noted, was "to see things as they really are; the uppermost idea with Hebraism was conduct and obedience." The Greek quarrel with the body and its desires was, "that they hinder right thinking, the Hebrew quarrel with them is, that they hinder right acting." The Greeks, said Arnold, were invested with "sweetness and light," in which difficulties were kept out of view, and the "beauty and rationalness of the ideal have all their thoughts." With Hebraism, however, "there are difficulties in 'knowing thyself,'" as Socrates urged, because humans have sin seated on their shoulders like a "hideous hunchback." Between Hellenism and Hebraism, Arnold says, "moves our world. At one time it feels more powerfully the attraction of one of them, at another time of the other; and it ought to be, though it never is, evenly and happily balanced between them."[24]

William Barrett, the American philosopher, saw Hebraism as "containing no eternal realm of essences, which Greek philosophy was to fabricate, through Plato, as affording the intellectual deliverance from the evil of time." Such a realm of eternal essences, Barrett adds, "is possible only for a detached intellect, one who, in Plato's phrase, becomes a spectator of all time and all existence,'" and by contrast, the ideal man of Hebraism "is the man of faith."[25] Hebraism focuses on the concrete, particular, individual man, and does not "raise its eyes to the universal and abstract." The Greeks, however, were the first thinkers in history, discovering the universal, the abstract and timeless essences, forms, and ideas. "The intoxication of this discovery (which marked nothing less than the earliest emergence and differentiation of the rational function) led Plato to hold that man lives only insofar as he lives in the eternal."[26]

In his study of the Enlightenment, Peter Gay notes that the world was viewed as divided between ascetic superstitious enemies of the flesh, and those who affirmed life, the body, knowledge, and generosity; between mythmakers and realists, priests and philosophers. Gay sees this division as centered on Hebrews and Hellenes and reflected in history as a conflict between two irreconcilable patterns of life, thought and feeling, giving each era a dominant style, with "either reason or superstition in control" This conflict between Hebrews and Hellenes was "at once the source of disaster and of progress."[27]

While Arnold and Gay have focused on the Hebraic and Hellenic elements in Western culture, their studies take little note of the Roman influence. And even if it is implied in their writings, neither Arnold, Barrett nor Gay have explicitly recognized that cultures such as Hebraism and Hellenism can have no influence within Western civilization unless they are kept alive in the mind. Among modern thinkers who have recognized that this must necessarily be so, was British philosopher, John Macmurray. In contrast to Arnold, Barrett and Gay, Macmurray saw the major conflicts in the Western world as having their origin in the confused mixture of Greek, Roman, and Jewish elements within the Western mentality.

Macmurray noted, for example, that the tendency in Western civilization has been for the Roman influence to dominate the other two, for even though Greek culture and the Judeo-Christian religion were accepted within the Roman Empire, it was only as "tributaries and servants of imperialism." The Romans found Greek art useful as adornments to their lifestyle. Much, one might add, like some wealthy Americans and Japanese who, if they but understood the despairing meaning of some of the modern art they have bought, might hang themselves rather than their expensive paintings. An idealized Christianity, Macmurray noted, served as a "dope" for the masses, distracting them from thoughts of revolt. The modern world, Macmurray believed, remains in the Roman mold, and is essentially imperialist. Industrial management and the maintenance of power for the defense of law and property is the modern world's governing ideal as it was for the Romans, and art and religion have been harnessed and subordinated to that ideal. Even in the extremes of fascism and communism, Macmurray noted, "We are Romans at heart," though art and religion can be used "so long as they play the part of menials to our ideal of social efficiency."[28]

For their part, and under the influence of Stoic philosophy, the ancient Romans kept reason and emotion strictly compartmentalized. Emotion was subordinated to a practical rationalism in which law, rules, plans, and policies were elevated to the highest level of statecraft. And these were implanted in the hierarchical order from the emperor down. Duty and obedience were the greatest of virtues, and public duty (*res publica*) had priority over private needs. In addition to such obvious Roman survivals in our time, as the U.S. Senate and the Capitol, neo-imperialism, or even the highly popular Caesar's Palace in Las Vegas, the appreciation of Roman sentiments of public duty were almost universally and uncritically acclaimed in President John F. Kennedy's inaugural address when he said: "Ask not what your country can do for you, but what you can do for your country."

The transmittal to our time of the Roman sense of duty to state and leader owes more to one man, Cicero (106-43 B.C.E.), the stoic Roman lawyer, than to anyone else. His influence was immense on such early Christians as Saints Ambrose, Jerome, and Augustine. Ambrose's *On the Duties of Ministers* owes its debt to Cicero's *On Duties*. As related by Plutarch, Cicero's life and his writings became an important influence on the revival of classical thought during the Renaissance. Martin Luther believed

Cicero's treatises were superior to Aristotle's; Queen Elizabeth I had read most of Cicero's works by the time she was sixteen. Others who were influenced by him include John Locke, Edmund Burke, William Pitt the Younger, Joseph Addison, Edward Gibbon, Samuel Johnson, Jonathan Swift, and innumerable Western statesmen, including the American founding fathers. Cicero's linguistic style, even if considerably tarnished, continues to echo feebly in legislative chambers around the world, along with his principles of duty and statecraft. In Cicero's view, the state represented the highest good, therefore, the highest duty is to the state, higher even than a son's love or duty to his father. If, for example, the son discovers that his father is stealing from the temples or digging an underground passage to the Treasury, it is the son's duty to put his country's safety before his father's and report him to the authorities. Euthanasia was also on Cicero's mind when he asserted that "the means of subsistence may, if necessary, be transferred from the feeble, useless person to the wise, honest, brave man, whose death would be a grave loss to society."[29] Such an abstract view of humanity found tragic expression in Nazi Germany, and has been injected into current debates on medical ethics.

The cold rationality of some Ciceronian concepts is thrown into sharp relief when one reads St. Augustine's *Confessions* written more than four centuries after Cicero. Where Cicero upholds a sense of public duty, Augustine responds to something more emotional and personal. Both men were trained in the law, yet Augustine's writing is like the eruptions of hot volcanic lava; Cicero's is like cooled lava rock. One cannot imagine, for example, that Cicero, the silver-tongued orator and seeker after praise and dominance, would say, as does Augustine to his God, that he had decided to withdraw "the service of my tongue from the marts of lip-labor" so that the young, not students in God's law, but in the "lying dotages and law skirmishes, should no longer buy at my mouth for their madness."[30]

Augustine willingly gives up his lawyer's "lip-labor" to serve God while Cicero continues to express himself for the good of the state. This contrast between the man of faith and the man of rational self-control is shown also by two important incidents in their lives. When Cicero's beloved daughter, Tullia, dies, he writes to his friend, Atticus, describing how he has isolated himself and does not talk to a soul: "I fight against tears as much as I can, but as yet I am not equal to the struggle."[31] This is the only instance in his letters where one can see Cicero's emotions getting the better of him, and it is particularly revealing insofar as that even when alone with his grief, he feels constrained by his sense of public conduct to struggle with his emotions. There is no such struggle when Augustine accepts God. "I cast myself down I know not how, under a certain fig tree," he confesses, "giving full vent to my tears, and the floods of mine eyes gushed out an acceptable sacrifice to Thee."[32] Cicero, the Stoic, sees emotion, even as an expression of personal grief, as something to be struggled against; Augustine, the Christian convert, sees it as something to surrender to.

Life for Cicero invariably meant "public" life, hence he is never really happy away from it, and surely the same can be said of many Western democratic legislators who, unlike Augustine, enjoy their "lip-labor." Cicero's letters, as Edith Hamilton noted, were written at one of the momentous periods of history, yet they were nearly always dull. They were, she said, about daily life and full of trivialities, whereas his public orations dealt with "elevations, power, distinction." Cicero might be writing from his lodgings on the Acropolis, or from Delos, the marvelous isle, or from strange cities and lonely mountain camps in the unknown east, but as far as his letters are concerned, "he might as well be in his house on the Palatine."[33] Cicero could not adequately express his most private feelings. Only when he is writing or speaking on the large topics of public and national life does his language soar.

The large events, such as wars and conquests, have the effect of obscuring the quieter, less noticeable ways in which cultural ideas are cross-fertilized; the way in which ideas from one culture are planted in the minds of people from a totally different culture, and then slowly germinate. In sometimes dramatic descriptions, history records how the Romans conquered the Greeks and a large part of the ancient world, but history acknowledges that there is a special sense in which the Greeks conquered their conquerors through the more subtle infusion of Greek ideas. This is why the lives of Cicero and Augustine, two of antiquity's most influential figures, provide striking examples of how the amazing process through which Christianity, an entirely new and quite alien way of looking at the world and human significance, first entered the cultural and mental life of the Greco-Roman world and set it on a path of revolutionary transformation.

Although St. Paul makes a number of references to the difficulties encountered in spreading the Judeo-Christian message—a "stumbling block to the Jews" and "foolishness to the Greeks"[34]—it is in the mental outlook of Cicero and Augustine that one can clearly see the transition taking place from the antique world to the Christian, just as centuries later with Machiavelli and others, one can see the reassertion of pagan attitudes. Unlike Augustine, Cicero had no exposure to Christianity, and remained in the classical mold until his death. His mind had incorporated the thought of Socrates, Plato, and Aristotle into his rhetorical skills as a lawyer and statesman. But Augustine, who also was trained in Greek thought and legal rhetoric, was brought to the Oriental faith of Judeo-Christianity precisely because of the lack of feeling he experienced while reading Cicero's *Hortensius*, a book exhorting readers to study philosophy. Augustine could admire Cicero's speech and writings, but "not so his heart." In a way that was not intended, Cicero's book altered Augustine's affections, and turned his prayers, as he described it, "to Thyself O Lord; and made me have other purposes and desires."[35]

Augustine's conversion experience, however, clearly shows the difficulties and struggles involved when the Greco-Roman mind becomes a resistant host to Judeo-Christian beliefs, for it would be ten years after reading Cicero's philosophical book before he fully committed himself to Christianity, and would become one of its greatest champions just as, many centuries later, Hitler's mental struggle would make him Christianity's worst enemy. The contrast between Augustine, the new Christian man of the heart, and Cicero, the pagan man of the head, foreshadows the split between reason and emotion that would plague Western humanity for centuries to come.

Rome's emphasis on rationality could be traced to its tradition of *Mos maiorum* (customs of the fathers). And yet, when one examines history's many masculine-dominated societies, one sometimes sees the quietly subversive influence of women—the resistance of women in the fatherlands; the revolt of the heart over the excesses of the head. It was Augustine's mother, Monica, who first became converted to the Christian faith, just as Constantine's mother, Helena, had encouraged her son to accept the new faith which he would make the official religion of the Roman empire. If Judaism and Christianity can be said to be the seedbed for a world revolution of human rights, then these two women, along with Mary, the mother of Jesus, were clearly in the vanguard.

Augustine's conversion is one of many during the early days of Christianity. It differs from St. Paul's because it was a prolonged experience in which Augustine had to wrestle with the habits and psychological outlook of a lifetime. In addition, he was a Greco-Roman pagan of North African origin, taking upon himself a new psychological outlook. On the other hand, Paul was a Hellenized Jew as well as a Roman citizen, and had served the Roman authorities in persecuting the first Christians. As a Jew, who was knowledgeable about the Greek and Roman worlds as well as the Jewish religion, he was well-equipped to mediate the Christian message to the polyglot, yet predominantly triadic (Greek, Roman, and Jewish) Mediterranean culture. His dramatic and apparently instant conversion on the road to Damascus, however, contrasts sharply with Augustine's slow growth into the Christian faith. And, unlike the Jewish apostles who formed the nucleus of the early church, and who came from working class backgrounds, Paul was the first of a long line of Christian converts who were well-educated, came from higher social strata, and were among the leaders of the Christian movement. And while many from the ranks of the poor would become Christians, they did so, in the main, because of the caliber of these leaders, and sometimes because they had little choice when the emperor, kings, and princes became converts and mandated Christianity as the only acceptable faith. In some cases, the Jews were granted dispensation to adhere to their faith, but this could, and often did, change, depending upon circumstances. This does not mean to say that Christianity did not have strong appeal to the masses. It did, and one of its most attractive features, particularly among the poor, was the infusion of a sense of hope and dignity in an oftentimes despairing and fatalistic world.

When one speaks of the Greek, Roman, and Jewish spirits coming together in uneasy residence within the Western mentality, this might be viewed as an oversimplification. It can be argued, and rightly, that within the Greek, Roman, and Jewish cultures, there was a great deal more diversity than any of these labels would suggest. Certainly not all Greeks were profound thinkers and artists; not all Romans shared a pragmatic and stoic disposition, nor were all Jews inspired by prophetic utterances or guided by their conscience. In addition, the Greeks were not the only people to develop a high level of art and thought; the Romans were not alone in establishing a system of laws and practical organization; nor were the Jews singular in expressing a profound religious sense. The Greeks, however, refined thought in a way that had never been done before by focusing the mind on the most important of human questions, and trying to systematize their answers in a cohesive philosophical framework. And what the Greeks attempted in the realm of thought, the Romans, with a different disposition, refined the concepts of law and administration to new heights of practical genius. For their part, the Jews had made revolutionary breakthroughs in religion. There was only one God for all humankind, not many Gods, and he had a special mission for Israel. Belief in many gods leads humans to believe they are members of separate and special human families. One God promotes the belief that all humans belong to one family, thus placing a barrier against any kind of separatism; of race, religion, sex, or class.

The consequences of this were momentous, resulting in a new view of human relationships. In addition, the idea of a working partnership in which Israel would help to achieve God's goals inaugurated true history in that, for the first time, humans could view their actions as purposive instead of being determined, and history as intentional-prospective instead of retrospective-reactive. Instead of looking to the past, history's focus would be on the future. The secular maturation of such a view gave rise, in the modern era, to political, civil, and human rights movements such as had never been known before in all of history, and would indeed have been treated by all authority in ancient times as treason or madness. Judaism must also be credited with the idea of history not as an indefinitely recurring or endless cycle, but as a linear development—a cosmic drama with a beginning and an end—a past, present, and future. "Without its messianism," Fredrick Lohr believed, "Europe would revert to the static, backward-looking mentality of those civilizations that preceded it and which, whatever their merits, have no claim to be called historical except that they once existed."[36] In other words, all pre-Christian civilizations lacked the mark of true history that is inaugurated when humans develop an intention that is focused on a long-range goal. A parallel development arising from Jewish monotheism was the refinement of the moral conscience whose importance can clearly be seen when contrasted with the Greek refinement of thought. The Greek tendency to see humans as primarily thinking animals gave rise to a quest for the ideal, while the Jews saw humans as fully engaged thinking, feeling, and working creatures with an acute moral awareness that made them judge the rightness or wrongness of their actions in the sight of God. For the most part, however, Jewish morality was primarily a collective morality accentuated by the angry admonishments of the prophets when the people of Israel transgressed from the path of righteousness. Such constant reminders of wrongdoing sharpened the conscience, kept the Jews focused on what they perceived to be their historical mission, and prevented them from falling into the psychological dualism that had caused the

Greeks to abstract from the world or the Romans to become so involved in this world that another world held little attraction for them.

Within Christianity, the Jewish conscience became more sharply focused on the individual and thus presented a potential threat to all authorities insofar as each individual could claim the right to challenge state authority when it was felt to be against conscience. Thus, conscience can be seen as the avenue to self-rule, self-realization, and freedom. That is why, to take liberty with Lord Acton's renowned phrase: all power tends to curb conscience, and absolute power curbs it absolutely. Dictators, particularly, recognize that where there are too many individuals acting in accordance with conscience, there will be fewer to follow the leader. Thus, it is that those who escape from the responsibility of conscience, are the surest guarantors of tyranny. Hitler clearly recognized this, and the source of conscience, when he described conscience as "a Jewish invention; a dirty and degrading self-mortification of a chimera"[37] which he vowed to stamp out.

Even though Greco-Roman civilization ended when it was superseded by Christian civilization, Greek and Roman thought patterns have survived in Western mentalities, and institutions to this day. And, with the Renaissance revival of classical learning, Greek and Roman mental attitudes, even if modified by Christianity, reached an even larger public than in the original Greek and Roman civilizations. Instead of the writings of a few Greeks and Romans reaching a quite limited and aristocratic audience, they were disseminated from monasteries, schools, and universities throughout the vast reaches of what had been the Roman Empire and, with the Age of Discovery, to the new lands developed by the Portuguese, the Spanish, the French, the British, and the Dutch. And, along with the spread of classical learning, went the Bible.

Thus was the odd mixture of Greek, Roman, and Jewish cultural-psychological elements set to become a universal influence, at first within a religious context but, by the 20th Century, mostly through secular national and international political ideologies such as Marxism, fascism, and democracy.

The mixture of Christian and Greco-Roman cultures had the effect of bringing about what Carlyle called "natural supernaturalism," by which he meant the interpenetration of the two. Even Proudhon, a confessed humanitarian atheist, could admit "We are full of Divinity... our monuments, our traditions, our laws, our ideas, our languages, and our sciences—all are infected with this indelible superstition, outside of which we are not able either to speak or act, and without which we simply do not think."[38]

Proudhon's characterization of religion as a superstition was frequent among Enlightenment thinkers. By contrast, many of today's thinkers and historians regard religion as a vestigial and useless appendage that will atrophy much as the tail supposedly did from the end of the human spinal column at some unknown point in evolutionary development. Others dismiss religion because it is not amenable to scientific investigation in the way that the anatomy, or chemicals, are. Notwithstanding such attitudes, it has to be conceded that, considering the impact (for good and ill) that religion has had on history, it would be very unscientific to ignore it, particularly when science alone cannot comprehend it, and religious themes continue to haunt the secular world. And while applied science has changed the world, it has not *moved* the world. Religion and politics *have* because they are the repositories of feeling from whence comes all human motivation. "The broad masses consist neither of professors nor of diplomats," said Hitler, and he might have added scientists. "The scantiness of the abstract knowledge they (the masses) possess directs their sentiments more to the world of feeling. That is where their positive or negative attitudes lie... Faith is harder to shake than knowledge... "[39]

Hitler's designation of his party as National Socialist was a clear recognition of the two forces (international socialism and nationalism) that provide the major focus of modern history. This has become particularly evident in recent years with the breakup of the Soviet Empire and the resurgence of nationalism. And yet the formation of the Commonwealth of Independent States by most of the former soviets provides clear recognition of the need to balance national interests with wider regional concerns. The modern pattern for such a balance had been set by the British Commonwealth of Nations and, more recently, the European Union that particularly provides startling and heartening evidence of how once bitter antagonisms can be buried in imaginative solutions which can recognize the need to conserve national identities as a way of providing diversity within larger unities. Just as the United States has demonstrated that people of many colors and creeds can be embraced, if uneasily at times, within one nation, the European Union has shown that national identities do not have to be erased as the world makes it way piecemeal and tentatively toward one community of nations.

As the experience of Nazism demonstrated, however, extreme nationalism can become an irrational monster when it fears all tendencies toward internationalism just as Soviet Communism aroused justified concerns that it was bent on forging a universal empire based on what was touted as an infallible ideology. The will to national identity of the Nazis represented a chauvinistic extreme; the Soviet Communists: a chiliastic one. As the world appears to be realizing, any new ordering of the world will require a balance of national and international interests. The will-to-identify as a nation must be balanced with the will-to-humanity. The desire for repose in unique customs and traditions has to be balanced with a desire for beneficial and universal change.

To Hitler, however, the will-to-humanity was utterly unacceptable. His importance to an understanding of history, therefore, is that by warring against world Jewry and all that he believed Judaism had inspired, he unveiled the spiritual motivating forces of history. Although patterned on distorted Greco-Roman forms, his struggles were set in motion by a nationalist will-to-identify—something that would have appeared absurd to Greeks and Romans who felt confident they were already Greeks and Romans without having to become such. For the ancient Greek, Greekness was not a matter of becoming, but of being, something accepted as existent; one simply was Greek by birth or not at all. "Know thyself" was the highest Greek oracular pronouncement, not the Nietzschean admonition to "Will a self." In the early days of the Republic, the organic concept of identity was also the mark of the Romans, but, as Rome expanded into an empire, so, too, did the Roman concept of identity; it became a legal, not an organic concept, opening Roman citizenship to different peoples throughout the empire.

A will-to-identify; a willful decision to become something or someone other than they already were, was totally foreign to Greeks and Romans. Nor could they have understood the modern idea of political movements inspired by ideas of changing the existing social, economic, and political order, and bringing about something entirely new. The Greeks were particularly conservative in this regard, which is one reason they sentenced Socrates to death for what were believed to be his corrupting new ideas. Even in art, the Greeks varied but little from what they perceived to be ideal forms. While the materials of a building might change from wood to stone, the form remained conservative. Although revolts and wars were common to Greece and Rome, as they had been in all civilizations, revolutions of the Nazi, Communist, or social democratic kind would have been unthinkable. And the suggestion that history had an inner meaning, that it was moving toward some ultimate goal, would have sounded irrational.

The idea of an historical goal that has given rise to political movements in modern times derives its messianic content from Judeo-Christianity. And, in their different ways, Marx and Hitler, both atheists, expressed this messianism most clearly. In his desire for a world revolution that would usher in a secularized, communist dispensation, Marx echoed biblical prophecies of the millennium. Hitler's motives were quite different. He was, in effect, trying to put a stop to history; to social, political, and international movement. He wanted to achieve a racial petrifaction of Germany yet, by so doing, he had to expand his nationalism into internationalism; his political party had to become a political movement. But if he was right in his belief that all internationalism and historical movement had its origin in Judaism and Christianity, then the inspiration for his own movement was subconsciously derived from the Jewish spirit he believed was a poison and sought to stamp out.

If, as Hitler strenuously maintained, all is biology, then movement of any kind beyond what is biologically determined would be impossible. It was not biology that had enabled him to formulate an intention to engage in politics, gain power in Germany, and attempt to exterminate European Jewry, communism and, if he had had his way, Christianity was well, but that uniquely human capacity to wed will, idea, and subject in unified action.

As Hitler's mental, political, and military struggles showed, he steadfastly maintained his long-rang intention. He demonstrated that this intention could sometimes (as with the Nazi-Soviet Pact) be served by resorting to short-range intentions that appeared to depart from his main one. It was this realization that led to the phenomenal success of his political struggle. He hated democracy, yet, as a short-range intention, he used democracy to gain power in order to destroy democracy. He preferred a thoroughly politicized army, yet effectively diminished the one he had (the Stormtroops) in the hope that, in time, he could politicize the regular army or replace it with the SS. His order for the Final Solution, as well as his "stand fast" order to his troops, was meant to fulfill his intention, but, instead, hastened its end.

The intentional nature of Hitler's aims raises some interesting questions that will not be pursued here. If, for example, under his assumed identity as a German, it was possible to maintain for more than thirty years an intention to roll back history, is it possible that an historical intention can persist throughout the centuries? Is history, perhaps, like a relay race in which ideas are carried part of the way by different "runners," each of whom has the finish line in mind? Certainly, the introduction of the Judaic and Christian sense of moral purpose, and the idea of history as a bearer of meaning has contributed to the will-to-humanity that has been reflected in different ways by the larger groupings of countries, particularly in modern times, that cannot be explained by economic and political necessities alone.

But, as with many human intentions, the will-to-humanity is fraught with dangers. There is the danger that in pursuing the intention to achieve an idea of "humanity," the reality, diversity, and complexity of real humans will be made to conform to that idea. As Nazi Germany showed in an extreme and irrational way, the major ingredient in nationalism is a fear of losing a national identity that incorporates customs and traditions built up over a long period of time. The nationality, or national quality, of a people, like the personality or quality of a person, is a justifiable source of pride. Unfortunately, however, and particularly in times of national stress, nationality can be converted by reckless demagogues into rabid nationalism. A revealing aspect of such nationalism is that either the restraints of religion are cast off, or religion is made to serve national interests. In this way, the state subverts religion and its tyrant leader becomes deified. Misguidedly trying to save their nationality—the qualities they valued as a people—the Germans invested their hope of salvation in Hitler, consequently their national and personal qualities were greatly debased.

As Hitler, Stalin, and other tyrants have demonstrated, the vacuum created by God's absence is readily filled by evil men committing monstrous deeds. If there is no authority higher than what humans create, then there is no higher than human appeal. Thus, today's wrongs can become tomorrow's "right;" today's error, tomorrow's "truth," and what human leaders can give, they can take away.

The "sacred balance" between gods and humans that was so important to the Greeks, and was reflected in their thought and art, also influenced the Christian attempt to achieve a balance between Greek, Roman, and Jewish cultures within the shared belief in one God and one humanity. It was this universal outlook that inspired Thomas Aquinas's great philosophical synthesis of God, nature, and humanity. A great deal of the universalist outlook in politics, science, and art can be traced to Aquinas's *Summa Theologica*, including comparative studies in biology, language, religion, and much else. Such a universal perspective helped trigger a Western outreach to the rest of the world that has been accelerated in our time. It has also, however, contributed to illegitimate offspring in the totalitarian ideologies such as Nazism and Communism.

It has been the marriage of the kind of comprehensive rationality associated with Plato, Aristotle, and Aquinas, with Roman pragmatism, that is responsible for the vast changes wrought in the physical and social conditions of the world that are now so apparent. Less visible, but perhaps more important, has been the moral impulse, from Judaic and Christian religious teachings, that has influenced change in a manner best designed to liberate the human spirit.

Despite the errors and compromises that churches and synagogues have sometimes made with the world's recurring Caesarisms, therefore, they are still the best witnesses to human significance; the sometimes flickering candle in the darkest times. Nazism and Soviet Communism attempted to snuff the light of belief, and almost succeeded. The danger now facing much of the world is that with the displacement of religious ideas into the secular world, politics may be viewed as religion's replacement instead of a temporary, and often inept, helpmate. In the conceivable future, the world might well be reconstructed to the material and social benefit of all humankind, but at the expense of spirit.

Nazi Germany provided history's most dramatic example of how an economically depressed nation was rapidly transformed into an economically sound and militarily powerful nation, but the Faustian bargain was a demand on the German soul. It was precisely the moral conscience in Western civilization that Hitler saw as the greatest stumbling block to inaugurating his "New World Order," and he clearly recognized the origin of this conscience in Judeo-Christianity, therefore, the Jews would

be targeted first as the carriers of this "poison" (conscience), and Christianity would have similarly been
wiped out if his mad scheme had been successful.

In the wake of the Holocaust, it would seem time to
banish simplistic explanations for anti-Semitism. Certainly economic conditions and other factors can
contribute to anti-Semitism. What is perilous, as well as
culpable, is to see them as the main reason for this ideology of hate whose persistence alone demands explanations
beyond the vulgar anti-Semitic offerings that the Jews were
scapegoats, or that they were "Christ-killers," or that they
are part of a worldwide conspiracy, or that they control
the Western world's prime institutions. The real reason
for anti-Semitism is that, because of its Jewish religious
basis, the Western world has not fully admitted the historical importance of the Jews or the validity of
Judeo-Christianity, and the commitments it requires from
each person no matter what the economic, social, or political circumstances.

It is not really the inaccurate charge that a few Jews of
long ago were "Christ-killers" which sticks in the Western craw, but that the Jews were the Christ-donors. It is
the Jew that was introduced into the Western mentality
through Christianity that so disturbed Hitler because it
gave rise to demands for justice, equality, and human
rights. The Jews in their caftans in Vienna were the visible, corporate reminders of this psychological reality,
triggering Hitler to embark on his neo-pagan revenge that
would rid the world of Jews, Christianity, and anything
or anyone who could be seen to reflect the "chimera" of
the Jewish moral conscience.

In trying to eradicate Judeo-Christianity *and* the Jews,
Hitler provided the most significant clue to history that
so far has been disgorged, for the Jews represent the corporate Israel without which the mystical Israel

(Christianity) would be stripped of historical symbolism. And while millions of other humans fell victim to the Nazis, it was *only* the Jews who were selected for the "Final Solution" because, in a negative way, Hitler recognized their significance as the authors of intentional history. Such significance, or meaning, is at the heart of both Jewish ritual and Christian liturgy, and if it should be concluded otherwise, then rabbis may just as well turn their backs on the Torah, and priests, and other clergy dispense with their cassocks and collars. In so doing, they would affirm Nietzsche's assertion that "God is dead," and hand Hitler a posthumous victory.

CHAPTER FOUR: BIBLIOGRAPHY

1 Roper, *Hitler's Secret Conversations* 76.

2 *The Portable Karl Marx* ed. Eugene Kamenka, (New York: Penguin Books, 1983) 241.

3 *Hitler's Secret Conversations* 158.

4 *Secret Conversations* 136.

5 *Secret Conversations* 158.

6 Nietzsche, *On the Genealogy of Morals*, ed. Walter Kaufman (New York: Vintage Books, 1969) 34.

7 *Genealogy* 34.

8 Nietzsche, *A Nietzsche Reader*, tr. R.J. Holingsdale (New York: Penguin Classics, 1977) 174.

9 Roper, *Secret Conversations* 664.

10 Waite, *The Psychopathic God* 11.

11 Payne, *The Life and Death of Hitler* 53.

12 The title and theme of Henri de Lubac's book (New York: Meridian Books, 1953).

13 Emil Ludwig, *Napoleon* (New York: Cardinal Pocket Edition, 1965) 525.

14 Arnold Toynbee, *Greek Civilization and Character* (New York: Mentor Books, 1953) xii.

15 Lord Acton, *Lectures on Modern History* (London: The Fontana Library, 1966) 19.

16 Felicia Bonaparte, *The Triptych and the Cross* (New York: New York University, 1979) 111.

17 Theodore Mommsen, *History of Rome* Vol. 2 New York: Charles Scribner's Sons, 1888) 563.

18 Williams Barrett, *Irrational Man* (New York: Doubleday, Anchor Books, 1962) 135.

19 William Irwin Thompson, *The Imagination of an Insurrection* (New York: Harper & Row Publishers, 1972) v.

20 Roper, *Secret Conversations* 85.

21 Kohn, *The Mind of Germany* 115.

22 Saul Bellow in conversation with the author at the California Institute of Technology on February 10, 1980.

23 Lord Acton as cited by Peter Gay in *The Enlightenment* (New York: W.W. Norton & Co., Inc., 1979) 425.

24 Matthew Arnold, *Culture and Anarchy*, ed. J. Dover Wilson (Cambridge: Cambridge University Press, 1978) 130-131.

25 Barrett, *Irrational Man* 76-77.

26 Gay, *The Enlightenment* 33.

27 John Macmurray, *Freedom in the Modern World* (London: Faber and Faber, Ltd., 1935) 75-76.

28 *Cicero Selected Works* (New York: Penguin Books, Ltd., 1965) 169-194.

29 *The Confessions of St. Augustine*, tr. Edward B. Pusey (New York: Collier Books, 1972) 133-134.

30 Edith Hamilton, *The Roman Way* (New York: W.W. Norton & Co., 1968) 69.

31 *The Confessions of St. Augustine* 39.

32 Hamilton, *The Roman Way* 64-65.

33 I Corinthians 1:23, *The New Testament* in the King James version of the Bible (New York: The World Publishing Co., 1948).

34 *The Confessions of St. Augustine* 39.

35 Fredrick Lohr, *Greek, Roman and Jew* (London: London Forum Publications, 1952) 35.

36 Roper, *Secret Conversations* 129.

37 Pierre Proudhon, *Systeme des Contradictions Economiques*, ed. Roger Picard, 2 vols., 1923, 1, 53, 55-56.

38 *Mein Kampf* 337.